THE SIEGE OF JERUSALEM

The Siege of Jerusalem
Crusade and Conquest in 1099

Conor Kostick

continuum

Continuum International Publishing Group

The Tower Building   80 Maiden Lane
11 York Road   Suite 704
London SE1 7NX   New York, NY 10038

www.continuumbooks.com

First published 2009

British Library Cataloguing-in-Publication Data
A catalogue record for this book is available from the British Library.

ISBN 9781847252319

Typeset by Newgen Imaging Systems Pvt Ltd, Chennai, India
Printed and bound by the MPG Books Group, Bodmin, UK

To my old friend,
Nathan Reynard

Contents

List of Figures   viii

Preface   ix

Acknowledgements   xiii

Chapter 1 In the Beginning   1

Chapter 2 Endurance   25

Chapter 3 Factions and Schisms   51

Chapter 4 Thirst   66

Chapter 5 Siege Warfare   79

Chapter 6 Preparing for the Assault   92

Chapter 7 The Storming of Jerusalem   104

Chapter 8 Friday, 15 July 1099   115

Chapter 9 The Aftermath   132

Chapter 10 Legacy   155

Appendix   174

Abbreviations   185

Notes   187

Bibliography   195

Index   205

List of Figures

Figure 1 The route taken by the First Crusade

Figure 2 The environs of Jerusalem

Figure 3 The topography of Jerusalem

Figure 4 The layout of Jerusalem at the time of the Crusade

Figure 5 Water sources in the vicinity of Jerusalem

Figure 6 The view from the Pool of Siloam to the walls of Jerusalem, from W. H. Bartlett, *Walks About the City and Environs of Jerusalem* (London, 1845), p. 69

Figure 7 Siege equipment 1: a basic mangonel, used on both sides

Figure 8 Siege equipment 2: a hybrid trebuchet, used by the crusaders

Figure 9 Siege equipment 3: a ram from the front

Figure 10 Siege equipment 4: a ram from the back

Figure 11 Siege equipment 4: a siege tower from the front

Figure 12 Siege equipment 5: a siege tower from the back

Figure 13 Siege equipment 6: a crow, used by the Provençal army

Figure 14 The assault on Jerusalem stage 1

Figure 15 The assault on Jerusalem stage 2

Figure 16 The assault on Jerusalem stage 3

Preface

Tuesday, 7 June 1099. A crowd of gaunt people was gathered on a hill watching the brightening eastern sky. About a mile away the walls and buildings of a city became more distinct in the dawn light. Everyone had stumbled through the darkness of the previous night to reach this point. Just as the skylarks, finches, swallows and swifts greeted the new day with their distinctive songs, so too the crowd now began to mutter in a range of voices: prayers whispered in all the languages and dialects of Christendom.

As the light grew stronger, the crowd became more distinct. Here, an archer, with an unstrung bow over his shoulder. There, a leather-clad spearman, leaning on his weapon as a stave. And among those ready for war could be seen a surprising number of unarmed people, including priests, nuns, women and children of all ages. All of them, man or woman, soldier or cleric, looked hungry, but although their bodies lacked all measure of surplus fat, they were not emaciated. Rather, they had the cords of tough muscle only obtained through years of hard labour. And these people had laboured.

Nearby, mounted, and accompanying those on foot with a certain complacency, were a group of 70 knights, formed up in a disciplined row. Their chainmail armour and burnished helms shone, tinged with the pink of the dawn. It was the raid of these knights ahead of the army the previous day, and their return with the news that the city was close, which had caused the ragged crowds to stumble all night across a rocky terrain in the hope of seeing the physical manifestation of their dreams. Proud of their responsibility for those beneath them, the knights were alert, scanning the brightening sky in all directions for dust clouds in the morning air, for a sign, in other words, of their enemies. Ahead of the row of knights was a small cluster of warriors, whose banners and spears focused on the two leaders of the troop: Tancred and Gaston of Béarn.

Only 26 years old, Tancred was nevertheless the hero and talisman of the present company. Others, especially the Provençal army miles further back to the rear, hated the Italian Norman for his arrogance and his treacherous policy towards them. But even his worst enemies would admit that there was no braver warrior in the entire Christian army and no sight more liable to lift the heart than that of Tancred's small band of knights charging ferociously in to battle behind their red banner. A little older, a lot darker, the Pyrenean nobleman Gaston of Béarn sat next to the Norman champion. The relationship between the two was of equals. More than that, it was of men whose common interest united them across all barriers of language and past allegiances. For Gaston and Tancred occupied the same political position inside the Christian army. They were both leaders of a small band of knights, but with nothing of the following or authority of the truly great princes. Or at least, not yet. Win a reputation for bravery, win more followers and, above all, win booty to reward those knights who took the chance of serving with them, and who knew what lay ahead? This land was full of rich cities and the fortunes of war were fickle. Tancred's own grandfather, Robert Guiscard, had, through conquest more than through diplomacy, risen from being the sixth son of a poor Norman noble to becoming an Italian Duke, solemnly recognized as such by the papacy.

On the previous day, both Tancred and Gaston – independently – had ridden right up to the walls of the city. Both had relied on the reputation of the great Christian army half a day behind them to intimidate the local Muslim forces. Gaston had been the quicker and the bolder; his 30 knights had galloped through the outlying farms around the city gathering up beasts and valuables. But when the commander of the garrison of the city realized how small this Christian force was, he ordered a troop of swift light cavalry to chase Gaston and his men. The chase led several miles to a cliff face, where the Pyrenean knights reluctantly abandoned their booty. But no sooner had the Muslim cavalry turned back towards the city with the animals and baggage than Tancred and his 40 knights arrived, curious to see what the dust clouds in the valley below them signified. The Normans rode down the hillside to greet their co-religionists. A hasty conference led to quick agreement. Both Tancred and Gaston were seeking fame and fortune, which was all the more likely to come their way as a united body. And so it proved in this encounter. The 70 Christian knights were sufficiently intimidating to scatter the Muslim troop and drive them all the way back to the gates of the city.

These knights had learned hard lessons on the journey. There was to be no stopping to gather up the scattered loot or wandering beasts. The Muslim light cavalryman was expert at riding and firing a bow at the same time. Given a chance to reorganize themselves, this force of the city's garrison could harass the Christians from afar, killing precious mounts, without ever coming within reach of a lance. Only after the city gates had slammed shut did the Christian knights wheel about to go searching for the booty that they now shared between them. That night the main body of the Christian army acclaimed the deeds of these two young lords, whose mutual satisfaction in the day's events proved to be a firm foundation for future co-operation.

When the tale of this adventure had circulated around the camp fires of the Christian army, what caught the imagination of the crowd was the fact that the city they had fought to reach over the course of three years was so close that a rider could reach it in a few hours. At first individuals, then entire bands, gathered their meagre belongings and set off under the stars. After all, in their excitement, they would hardly have managed to sleep. What did it matter that such a chaotic enthusiastic night time march was contrary to all military discipline? By now their enemies feared them and were unlikely to be preparing ambushes. In any case, surely this close to their goal, God would protect them.

The vanguard of the sprawling Christian army had rushed forward in the darkness. But the majority waited until dawn. Even so, it was impossible to maintain discipline. The knights understood the danger of the army acting like an ill-organized rabble but their desire to get ahead of those on foot before the route was completely congested only added to the confusion. An uncharacteristic flow of horses, foot soldiers and carts, like a swollen river, carried the Christian forces in a turbulent rush towards the city.

Bringing up the rear, with the stragglers, was the elderly count of Toulouse, Raymond, the fourth of that name. Fifty-one years old, grey bearded and with a scar that ran across the side of his face and over a missing eye, the count was walking barefooted and in a rather ill temper. Only his entourage of Provençal priests and clerics were taking seriously the words of a lowly visionary, Peter Bartholomew, who had died in a trial by fire to prove that the count was especially chosen by God to lead the Christian army. Peter Bartholomew had warned the crusaders that their approach to the Holy City must be barefoot and with hearts full of contrition or they would lose God's favour, but in the excitement of their proximity to the city the crowds had forgotten all about this prophecy. Even the bulk of Raymond's own knights and followers had rushed on with the others. The count himself patiently placed his bare feet on the path and walked through the dust created by the thousands ahead of him. If his fellow Christians failed to observe this act of humility, at least the all-seeing eyes of God observed it.

Ahead on the ridge, the crowd was swelling and spreading. Despite deep political rivalries between the Saxons, the Normans, the Provençals and the many other regional contingents, a sense of shared achievement came over them all as they watched the buildings of the nearby city become distinct under the brightening sky. They were filled with the realization that at last they had reached their goal, a place that had seemed almost mythical. The word now taken up joyously, shouted out through their tears, was comprehensible across all their respective languages: 'Jerusalem'.

Acknowledgements

I would like to thank Nathan Reynard, to whom the book is dedicated, for his encouragement and very helpful comments on an earlier draft. The book has benefited from a grant by the Grace Lawless Lee Fund of Trinity College Dublin (TCD) for the commissioning of high quality maps and diagrams to accompany the text. I am very grateful for this assistance and to Russell Liley and everyone at Freeline Graphics for converting my crude drawings into the vivid images that the book now contains. My depiction of the crusaders' siege equipment was greatly enhanced by the work of my TCD colleague Colm Flynn, who kindly made available to me the results of his research on the artillery of the siege. The diagrams of the final assault on the city incorporate a photograph of the model of Jerusalem made by Stefan Illes and this appears courtesy of the Tower of David Museum, Jerusalem.

Chapter 1

In the Beginning

On 18 November 1095 a council of some 300 clerics from all over Europe convened at Clermont in southern France for the most important assembly of their generation. The city had been a notable political centre for hundreds of years, ever since – at the end of the first century BC – Agrippa had ordered the construction of major road east to west across France, from Lyon to Saintes. The fact that Clermont lay on such a major route helped make it the choice of venue for the pope, Urban II, to host a major synod at which he intended to establish papal authority in the country. Urban also had a special message to deliver on the last day of the council, for which announcement prominent secular lords and indeed more humble folk were encouraged to journey to the city. As the council deliberated over matters such as church reform and the scandalous affection of Philip I of France for Bertrade of Montfort, wife of Fulk IV of Anjou, the numbers arriving at the city in anticipation of the pope's important declaration grew larger. So, on the 27 November, with its business done, once it had been realized that no building could contain the numbers wishing to attend, the assembly adjourned to a field outside the city where the papal throne had been set up.

Against the striking background of the Puy-de-Dôme, a dormant volcano, the pope delivered his message to the crowd, still and attentive, straining to hear every word. The time had come, Urban shouted, to assist their fellow Christians in the East, whose suffering at the hands of the Saracens was growing daily. The time had come, also, when Christians should cease warfare against one another. Rather, they should direct their military prowess against the enemies of God. Let the followers of Christ form an invincible army and wage war against the Saracens. For those guilty of sin, there was no better way to earn a remission of their penance than to join this Christian army in its march to the East.

'God wills it! God wills it!' roared the crowd in reply as they surged forward. The clergy and princes nearest the pope prostrated themselves and begged for absolution. It was a thrilling moment for those present, in which passion and excitement overwhelmed any reservations. Cold calculation and logistical considerations were irrelevant. The pope had given those present a dream. The land in which flowed milk and honey was to be theirs. Knights could earn salvation and the favour of God without having to give up the horse and lance. It was a divine mission, a pilgrimage, a war, all combined in a movement that would see God's people marching just as though they were the Children of Israel being delivered from Egypt.

The unexpected enthusiasm and cries of the crowd meant that some of the behind-the-scenes planning was lost. It was possible, at least, to see from his gestures that the pope was appointing Adhémar, the statesmanlike bishop of Le Puy, to a special role. But the subsequent speech of the envoys of Count Raymond of Toulouse was hardly noticed except by those nearest the pope. The roars of approval and enthusiasm meant a rather confused and chaotic end to the council, which broke up without appreciating the message Count Raymond had crafted for them. The elderly veteran of decades of political manoeuvring in Provence was willing to assign Toulouse over to his eldest son, Bertrand, and lead a substantial force east in the service of the pope. Naturally, being respectful of church authority, the count did not insist on being sole leader. Rather – as his envoys put it – together Raymond and Adhémar would be another Aaron and Moses, the divinely inspired leaders of the Children of Israel.[1]

This was all very well, and accorded with the perspective for the journey that had been outlined earlier, at Nîmes, when a meeting had taken place between Raymond and Urban. But their discussion had envisaged a more modest and restrained assembly held within the cathedral, where the tall vaulting provided fine acoustics for carefully worded speeches. Within moments of the Pope's actual announcement, however, it was evident that the reality of the enterprise was going to be of much greater scope than Urban, Raymond and Adhémar had anticipated. And as the crowds dispersed from Clermont, the storm showed no signs of abating.

The world was astir. All Christendom soon became agitated by the appeal to join an armed penitential expedition to Jerusalem. The pope had stamped his foot and not one, but several enormous armies now unexpectedly sprang into being, each with their own leadership and with none of them showing the slightest appreciation of the idea that Count Raymond was another Aaron.

The message that left Clermont and began to spread rapidly around Europe ignored all but the core ideas expressed by Urban: that there was to be an expedition to Jerusalem by a Christian army greater than any that had ever been seen and those who joined it would earn a heavenly reward. Attempting to keep the popular enthusiasm for the mission from distorting his conception of it, the pope sent several letters explaining the purpose and the armed pilgrimage and restricting which categories of persons should participate. The spiritual reward that he offered participants was remission of their sins. He also set the start date for the departure of the crusade, 15 August 1096.

Urban, however, had set in motion social forces far beyond those he could control and his letters had only limited effect. For the most part the details of his message were lost. Every social class of person thought that they were eligible to participate in the journey. Everyone, including educated clerics, believed that to join was to merit more than forgiveness for their sins: to join this fight for God was to be guaranteed of a place in heaven. And many thousands of people, impatient to start, intended to do so in the spring, rather than after the autumn harvest.

It did not help the pope that a number of self-appointed preachers began to travel through Europe gathering recruits for the journey with their own version of the crusading message. There were the women who found a cross, fallen from heaven, who very many people prepared to follow to the east. Another woman made an extraordinary impression when she claimed to be the mistress of a goose that was divinely inspired. Word of this saintly bird spread through castles and towns and while there were those who scoffed at such superstition, when she reached Cambrai, a huge city then theoretically part of the empire of the German king, Henry IV (today at the north-eastern edge of France), a large assembly filled the church, to witness the woman and her goose as they arrived at the city and walked together up to the altar.[2] But among all the popular preachers of the journey to Jerusalem, there was one whose activities made him the dominant figure, to such an extent that for many it was he, rather than the pope, who was the authoritative voice of God in this matter.

Peter the Hermit was a small, middle-aged, man with a tremendous turn of phrase and corresponding powers of persuasion. Riding a donkey, he dressed in the humble garb of a hermit. His critics pointed out that despite this show of modesty, Peter did not forgo meat and wine, as a true hermit should. But his critics were few. As Peter travelled from town to town, he displayed a letter, which, it was popularly believed, God himself had given to the hermit. In fact, Peter's letter was from the Patriarch of Jerusalem appealing for assistance from the Christian west. Having been in the Holy City as a pilgrim, Peter had witnessed for himself how the followers of Christ were being exploited, how the holy places of the city were refused to all those who did not have gold, and how many devout Christians died outside the walls with their desire to worship in Holy Sepulchre unfulfilled.[3]

Great multitudes came to hear Peter. Some, believing themselves in the presence of a living saint, strove to obtain relics from the hermit, even prizing the silver hairs from the tail of Peter's donkey. Peter spoke to all social orders and all responded to him. The rich gave generously and with their wealth Peter was very generous on behalf of the poor. He was particularly concerned with the most unfortunate women of the cities of France. Peter's generation, more than any other, had seen the church wage a vigorous campaign to end clerical marriage, even to the extent of mobilizing crowds to drive from the churches those clergy who refused to renounce their wives. In addition to the numbers of cast-off and impoverished women who, for one reason or another, had lost their male guardians, the towns of Peter's day were filled with women who as a result of the campaign against the sin of Nicholiatism had fallen from a respectable and secure state to a precarious existence. To them and all marginal women, Peter offered dowries so that they could regain through marriage their lost security.

In the course of his constant travels and urgent exhortations, Peter recruited an enormous army of men and women, some 40,000 strong, for the march to Jerusalem. But it was noticeable that there were only around 500 knights amongst this force. The vast majority of Peter's army were foot soldiers and poorly equipped farmers.[4] Nevertheless, it was an extraordinary achievement for a hitherto unknown hermit to raise the largest army in Christendom. That success itself testified to many that divine will was being made manifest through the small but passionate preacher. For the participants themselves, their lowly status was a badge of pride: divine approval was more likely to come to the humble than the proud.

The appeal of Peter's preaching was assisted by the fact that life for the poor was extremely harsh in 1094 and 1095, the two years preceding his Pied Piper speaking tour. In those years famine and plague had ravaged northern Europe. Famine had reduced the poor to living on the roots of wild plants, and even the rich were threatened by the shortage of crops. The 'plague' described by the chroniclers was in fact an outbreak of ergot poisoning in the rye crop. This sickness caused limbs to wither and blacken, as though burnt by an invisible fire. In abandoned churches the rotting trunks of the unfortunate victims of the mould were piled up in stacks. How much more attractive was the prospect of moving to the Promised Land? Hundreds of farmers seized the opportunity provided by Peter's expedition, loaded up their carts with all their household belongings and together with their wives and children set out with the hermit. These farmers were not just intending to fight as part of a Christian army: they were emigrating. The value of land and farms collapsed as a rush of people strove to turn their fixed property into coin for the journey.[5]

At Peter's right hand was one of the few nobles to join this popular march, the Burgundian knight, Walter Sanzavohir. Walter left Cologne for the long journey through central Europe to Byzantium shortly after Easter, 12 April 1096, with just eight knights but thousands of men and women on foot. Some eight days later, Peter followed him with a war chest full of gold from the donations of the wealthy towards the cause. As they passed through Germany, incredulous peasants scoffed to learn that this rabble intended to march all the way to Jerusalem. But soon these cynics in turn became inflamed by the excitement. Perhaps, after all, they were living in an age where God's handiwork was more manifest than at any time since the days of Christ. Were there not signs in the heavens? The celestial portents alone testified that this was the time to abandon the routine but grim struggle for a living and exchange it for a blessed journey to the Promised Land. New armed bands formed from those who had formerly been labelled 'Epicureans' for their refusal to undergo the hardships of the march. Gottschalk, for example, was a German priest who had been inspired to assist in preaching the journey to Jerusalem after attending a sermon by Peter the Hermit. With his own effective speaking skills, Gottschalk drew together a sizeable army of pilgrims in the Rhineland, this time including very many knights.[6]

Right at the outset of the crusade the darker side of this popular enthusiasm for the divine mission was evident. Among the contingents that formed up in the wake of the passage of Walter and Peter through Lotharingia, Francia and Bavaria were those who turned the passions aroused by the hermit into warfare against the local Jewish population. The Jewish community of Cologne were surprised by a sudden attack on 29 May 1096 and after a great massacre, their property was shared among a crusading army. At Mainz a powerful local noble, Count Emicho, together with his fellow knights Clarembald of Vendeuil and Thomas of Marle, had been awaiting the arrival of the pilgrims to lead a similar onslaught against the Jewish population of the locality. Forewarned by the experience of their co-religionists in Speyer and Worms, the Jewish community of Mainz sought protection from Bishop Ruthard and paid an incredible sum of coin for it. But Ruthard was unable to prevent Emicho and his army breaking into the episcopal palace where most of the Jewish community had gathered and slaughtering them all, men, women and children.[7] Is it any wonder that when news of these massacres reached the Near East, the Jewish population of Jerusalem chose to fight side by side with the Muslim population of the city against the crusading army. After all, outside the city walls were Clarembald, Thomas and other knights who had already led Christian pilgrim armies against unarmed Jews.

The idea of taking the cross and marching to capture Jerusalem appealed just as much to those at the top of the social spectrum as to those at the bottom. Although no king found the crusading message persuasive, very many senior lords – for a variety of reasons – welcomed the idea and took the cross. Of these, the most exalted in status, if not in the number of his followers, was Hugh of Vermandois, known as Hugh the Great, brother of the now excommunicate King Philip I of France. Almost as prominent in the higher reaches of the European nobility was Robert Curthose, the eldest son of Duke William I of Normandy, the conqueror of England. The adventure of the crusade appealed to this dissolute lord, who abandoned his hunting and depredations in Normandy in anticipation of pursuing the same interests in the Near East. A more pious crusader and equally prominent noble was another Robert, the second count of that name from Flanders. Robert had been regent of Flanders between 1085 and 1091 when his father, Robert I of Flanders had been on pilgrimage. These two men of the same name, but of very different character, co-operated to bring a sizeable army from northern Europe. Their acceptance of the cross had come as a surprise to the pope, who now found he had to grant the northerners their own papal legate, Arnulf of Choques, an outspoken teacher from the cathedral school at Caen who joined the expedition as chaplain to Robert of Normandy.

Not be to outdone, when Stephen, the elderly and wealthy Count of Blois, took the cross he too had the pope give legatine powers to his chaplain, Alexander. Thus as the news from Clermont had spread north, the unanticipated response to the idea of a penitential expedition to Jerusalem had required Urban to revise his initial conception of the leadership of the undertaking. Instead of one Christian army, at the head of which was the experienced Count Raymond and the Bishop of Le Puy, there were now three armies marshalling their forces with papal approval. Not to mention that Peter and several popular armies were already underway, albeit with a rather more tenuous relationship to the papacy. And the mobilization of Christendom for Holy War was not finished, for two more powerful armies formed up in support of the expedition. One was drawn from the people of Lotharingia, the other composed of Normans from southern Italy.

Three brothers of Boulogne (located in modern day north-eastern France beside the English Channel), took the cross: Eustace, the elder, destined to inherit the family lordship of the city; Godfrey, who was adopted as heir to his maternal uncle's position as Duke of Lower Lotharingia; and Baldwin, the youngest, who had left a career in the church to enjoy the lifestyle he preferred, that of a knight. The decision of such important nobles to journey to Jerusalem encouraged many other prominent figures from Lower Lotharingia and nearby regions to attach themselves to this contingent. Not all were vassals of Godfrey, but as duke of the region from which many of them came, Godfrey carried the greatest authority in the Lotharingian army, more so, indeed, than his elder brother. In accordance with papal direction, the German contingent set out in August 1096, finding themselves travelling in the wake of the political chaos generated by the fact that on the route ahead of them had gone the various contingents of the People's Crusade.

Last to form up were those whose general was Bohemond, leader of a south Italian Norman army. The Normans were recent arrivals in southern Italian politics, but had defeated the local nobility, the papacy and the Byzantine Empire, to become the ruling elite of the region. When Robert Guiscard, the lowly sixth son of a minor Norman family, went to Italy he did so as a mercenary, but by the time of his death in 1085, he was the Duke of Apulia, recognized as such by the papacy.

In 1096, news of the crusade reached Amalfi at a time that Bohemond, eldest son of Robert Guiscard, was fighting for the city in alliance with his uncle, Roger I of Sicily, against his half-brother, Roger Borsa. Suddenly, an entirely new horizon opened to Bohemond. He took aside his young nephew Tancred and tried to persuade the talented warrior that their fortunes would be better served in the east than squabbling over their family inheritance in Italy. Tancred was sceptical until he was promised the role of second-in-command and that he would have the same freedom of action as would a duke under a king. The agreement was struck. Norman adventurers in search of fortune knew the value of uniting together against the world and when they did so thrones tumbled. Bohemond announced to his army his intention of supporting the papal initiative. Demonstratively, he cut up his most valuable cloak to make crosses. Not only did his own men rush to follow, but also – and this was the first fruit of Bohemond's adoption of the crusade – so did hundreds of knights who had been vassals of his ally. Lamenting the loss of his army, Roger was forced to abandon the siege of Amalfi and return to Sicily.[8]

Did any of those who took the cross really understand what lay ahead of them on the route to Jerusalem: three years of marching; gruelling sieges; ferocious battles; several periods of famine and months of pestilence? No other medieval army made such a journey to reach its goal. No other medieval army set itself such an extraordinary goal. The journey from Paris to Jerusalem is over 2,000 miles and while the initial stages were through the territories of fellow Christians, over 1,000 miles of the journey were travelled through land controlled by their enemies. There were something like 100,000 people who set off in 1096 to conquer Jerusalem for Christ. When, in 1099, the Christian army began the siege of the city, they numbered about 20,000. Fewer than one in five who took the cross reached their goal. Many had turned back at various difficult points along the journey, but just as many had died. Fields and ditches along the trail of their marches were marked by hundreds of graves.

If the hardships and battles that lay ahead were unknown, the same cannot be said of the geography of their journey. The pilgrim route for European Christians to Jerusalem was long established, with popular tracts in circulation that specified the exact distances to be travelled each day and the halting places. Older still were the network of Roman roads that for over 1,000 years had linked the peoples of the Mediterranean. The crusaders took a variety of different Roman roads in 1096. These all led, however, not to Rome, but to Constantinople, one of the world's most fabulous cities and claimant to the inheritance of the Roman Empire.

From the perspective of the Greeks, the west had lapsed into barbarism, while from behind their impressive double-ringed walls, the rulers of the Byzantine Empire had preserved the only culture that deserved to be considered civilized. Constantinople in 1096 was a city of relics and statues. It was a city of enormous wealth, of busy commerce, of intense enthusiasm for public games, but above all it was a city whose elite were locked into a vicious but subtle striving for position within a bureaucratic hierarchy whose intricacies were completely lost to the outsider. Where to sit for a public function? Which dyes could be used to colour the clothes you were allowed to wear? How should the person at your side be addressed? These were all supremely important matters to the Byzantine noble and it is no wonder that as the western lords arrived, dressed as they pleased, speaking to their hosts in curt indelicate phrases, eating in great mouthfuls, and showing more interest in their horses than the artistic work on display around them that the Byzantine elite collectively raised their eyebrows in a horror that was not entirely pretence.

The fact that the first armies to arrive at Constantinople were the popular ones inspired by Peter the Hermit did little to warm the Greeks towards the crusading project. If Pope Urban's initial plans had come to fruition in a more modest way, the representative of the Latin Church would have been the extremely tactful Bishop Adhémar of Le Puy and at his side the dignified and cultured count Raymond of Toulouse. As the papal legate was to show during the expedition, by emphasizing the common cause of all Christians it was possible to create very smooth working relationships between Latin and Greek clergy, especially in the lands regained from their pagan enemies. Instead, in the middle of July 1096, the Byzantines received Walther Sanzavoir and his army. The crowds of crusaders were at first suitably impressed by the size and wealth of the city. They settled in their camp and, in limited numbers, took tours of the city to visit the saints. But as the days passed, their boldness grew: soon bands of crusaders were stealing into the city and prising lead from the church roofs to sell back to the Greeks. They even began to raid wealthy houses, leaving the properties burning once all valuables had been seized.[9]

At the head of the Byzantine hierarchy was the emperor, who in 1096 was the former general and astute politician, Alexius Comnenus. Alexius, 48 at the time that the crusaders arrived at his capital, had come to power in 1081 in the by now traditional Byzantine manner: military coup. Naturally, the Greek emperor wanted to ship this turbulent barbarian army across the Bosphorus and away from the environs of his capital, but Walter insisted upon waiting for his comrade, Peter the Hermit, who, it was thought, was not far behind. Indeed, Peter arrived at Constantinople on 1 August, but his army was in a very different condition to that of his companion. At the town of Nish (now Niš, in southeastern Serbia) on the fringes of the Byzantine Empire, on or around 4 July 1096, a dispute had arisen between Nicetas, governor of Bulgaria, and Peter's forces. A body of 1,000 headstrong and imprudent crusaders attempted to storm the city. In response to this attack Nicetas unleashed his full force, scattering the crusaders, who eventually reformed with the loss of about a quarter of their number and the war chest of silver and gold. It was a chastened and much reduced force of Latin troops that arrived at Constantinople with Peter.[10]

An even more shattering blow, however, had struck the troops further to the rear led by Gottschalk. Coloman, the king of Hungary, had at first been tolerant of his fellow Christians' desire to march through the kingdom in order to fight for Jerusalem. The reckless behaviour of the crowds, however, their frequent attacks on the property of his people and the danger as more and more armies were rumoured to be on their way, led to the Hungarian population becoming uneasy and, indeed, downright hostile. A dispute in the market at the fortress of Mosony (now Mosonmagyaróvár) had led to the Bavarians and Swabians driving a stake through the genitals of young Hungarian. As word of this incident spread, Coloman came under pressure from his warriors, who insisted upon taking up arms against the insults of the intruders. But when the Hungarian army came to the Benedictine abbey of St Martin at Pannonhalma, they found the crusaders drawn up in solid formation, ready to fight for their lives. Realizing that there was going to be no easy victory against an unprepared rabble, Coloman and his officials entered negotiations with Gottschalk. Agreement was reached that if the crusaders handed over their weapons to the Hungarians for safekeeping, they would be permitted markets and safe travel though the kingdom; their weapons would be returned at the border. Grateful for the opportunity of avoiding a battle, Gottschalk and his more responsible officers persuaded the German army to accept the king's proposal. They piled up their weapons in good faith. Once the crusaders were safely disarmed, Coloman and his troops then attacked without mercy. The ensuing massacre was the first great disaster to fall upon people who had taken up the cross. Only a handful of Gottschalk's people escaped, returning to Swabia with a tale of terrible betrayal.[11]

While this contingent of the People's Crusade was being annihilated, Peter met with Alexius: the small, roughly dressed, hermit with the sophisticated emperor bedecked in gold and purple. The meeting was relatively successful. Alexius was pleased with the humility shown by the leader of the Latins, while Peter was grateful on behalf of his people that the Byzantines had donated a massive hoard of coins to replace that which had been lost at Nish. It was by mutual agreement that Peter's army was shipped across to Asia Minor five days later, to take up station in the fortified camp of Civitot on the thin strip of costal land still controlled by the Byzantines.

There, the limits of having a hermit as a military leader became evident. Following the advice of the emperor and his own assessment of the situation, Peter wished to hold the popular army in check until the nobles of Europe arrived, with their experienced leaders and large bodies of armoured knights. Wait six months? When they had a divine mission and already greater numbers than any army in memory? Why, they were capable of great deeds. Two months of idleness saw what little discipline Peter's army had break down, as rival contingents formed and outdid one another in undertaking daring raids against the Muslims, travelling as far as Nicea in search of booty. The hermit had no reliable chain of command, no loyal officer corps, to reign in these provocative expeditions and insist upon a policy of patiently awaiting the princes.

As yet, the enormous agitation that had bestirred Christian Europe mattered very little in the Near East. A series of reports stating that armies of Franks were marching east had been circulated in the major Turkish and Arab ruled cities and, over time, as the truth of them was confirmed, a sense of trepidation would grow among the Muslim and Jewish populations. But in the summer of 1096, the attention of the ruling Seljuk dynasts was on their own political rivalries. In particular, Qilij Arslān I, the young sultan of Rūm, the first Muslim-ruled region in the crusaders' path, had only come to power in 1092. His priority since then had been the restoration of a sultanate that had lost ten years earlier with the death of his father. In the three years preceding the arrival of the crusaders Qilij Arslān had spent more time on horseback than in his palace, riding back and forth with his troops across Anatolia enforcing submission to his rule on the cities and tribes of the region.

The Turkish leaders of the region were able to call upon a variety of soldiers to serve them, but every ruler also had a permanent standing force of cavalry, their *askar*. These were technically of very low social status, slaves or freedmen, but in practice the elite household guard. As the popular proverb put it regarding those who lived off the labour of others, life was easy for 'the horse of the *askar*, with fodder, pasturage and little to do.'[12] These lightly armed troops were expert with the bow, the favoured weapon of the Muslim world. They could fire at a gallop; indeed they could turn and fire over their shoulder at a chasing opponent. Qilij Arslān, like his fellow rulers, had an *askar* recruited personally and closely devoted to him as well as garrisons stationed across his realm who could be mobilized rapidly to create the core of his full army.

Nicea, on the north-western edge of the sultan's empire, was considered an impregnable strongpoint. It had natural defences in the form of a large lake against the western wall, new fortifications and towers along the city walls, and it was far from his enemies. The only possible assailants were the Byzantines, who had always shown a preference for signing peace treaties over making war. So confident was Qilij Arslān in the defences and location of his capital that while he and his warriors rode up to 500 miles to the east, his family and treasure were left at Nicea. It was a shock, then, to have messengers catch up with him with the news that the rumoured Christian barbarians had arrived and their foragers were pillaging the lands all the way up to his capital.

Qilij Arslān responded quickly, collecting up all his available forces, raising levies and hiring mercenaries. His first target was a small fortress about three miles north east from Nicea that the Christians had captured and were now using as a base from which to conduct their raids. Inside the castle was a force of some 3,000 Swabians who, having been become envious at the sight of booty brought back from a raid of the French and Italians, had marched out from Peter's camp and successfully assaulted the stronghold. The first attempt by the troops of Qilij Arslān to retake the fortress by storm failed, the Swabians inside fought bravely. They could be driven back from the walls by an immeasurable hail of arrows, but every time the Turkish army attempted to ascend the walls the Swabians charged out to beat them off with sword, battleaxe and spear.

Thwarted in attempts to storm the fort, the Turkish forces changed their approach; utilising their advantage in missile fire to keep the top of the walls clear while wood was brought all the way up to the gate of the castle and piled high against it. The conflagration that then started led not only to the destruction of the entrance but many buildings inside. Leaping from the walls, the defenders tried to save themselves. But very few escaped. About 200 young men, the most suited to the slave market, were kept as prisoners, the rest of the garrison were slain. Unsure as to the full strength of his enemies, Qilij Arslān did not follow up this victory with an immediate attack on the fort of Civitot, where the bulk of the crusaders were camped, but sent spies ahead, while taking the precautionary measure of withdrawing the bulk of his forces to Nicea.[13]

The sight of the clouds of smoke to their west and the arrival of scouts with news about the events at the fortress precipitated a crisis back at the main camp. Peter the Hermit had been detained in Constantinople for several days, on a mission to obtain more supplies from the emperor. This left Walter Sanzavoir as the most authoritative figure in the camp, but by no means its general. Walter's advice was to wait for Peter and not to rush recklessly to avenge those who, it was suddenly appreciated, were no longer dismissed as foolish Germans, but remembered as comrades and martyrs. This council quietened the majority, who settled down to a defence of the camp. The lull lasted eight days, during which time Qilij Arslān took the measure of the crowds that faced him. They were large in number, but the vast majority were foot soldiers and that was no threat to light cavalry with a near infinite supply of arrows.

On Tuesday 20 October 1096, Qilij Arslān sent an advance party of 100 well-armed riders to see if he could draw out the Christian army from its defences. Coming across small numbers of pilgrims, in one or twos, fives or tens, this advance party scattered the bands of foragers and beheaded those whom they captured. These skirmishes had the desired effect. For the rest of that afternoon and into the night a great tumult broke out in Peter's army. Walter and several other knights continued to insist that no action be taken until Peter returned and they could benefit from his talismanic presence as well as his counsel.

Among the foot soldiers were a more professional and seasoned force than most in the camp. Only 200 strong, those who marched with Godfrey Burel as their commander and standard-bearer nevertheless were famous within Peter's army for having been first to dare the ladders at the Hungarian fortress of Zemun. That castle had been stormed by Peter's army when they observed that weapons and goods belonging to captured stragglers from Walter's army were being boastfully displayed on the walls. The assault on Zemun had made Godfrey's name and although he was a foot soldier, not a knight, he was considered of such importance that when Peter had been obliged to hand over two prominent figures as hostages for safe passage through Bulgaria, Godfrey was one of them. And it was Godfrey who now insisted on a policy of immediate action.[14]

There was in Peter's army a sense of pride that they were humble folk and equally a feeling of resentment that God's mission should be delayed for the sake of princes. Godfrey Burel cleverly appealed to this sentiment by accusing Walter and the other knights of being cowards and of little use in war despite their distinguished lineage. The more these knights forbade the army to march, the more bitter became Godfrey's taunts. Such accusations before the thousands of onlookers were too insufferable to be borne, it was better to die in battle than live with the label of coward. In a deadly rage, Walter and his fellow knights announced that they would lead the army out, to their mutual ruin, if such was necessary to prove their worth.

The following morning, at the first sign that the sky was brightening in the east, trumpets sounded throughout the crusader camp. Twenty-five thousand men on foot and 500 knights on horse formed themselves up into six divisions and marched out with enormous clamour and pride in their strength. Only the sick, those without arms, and the countless numbers of women with the army, remained at the camp. The crusaders set forth in complete ignorance of the fact that Qilij Arslān with his main army had come up during the previous day and was camped barely three miles away.

The sultan was, at first, taken aback by this unexpected sortie by the army from the fort at Civitot. Fortunately for Qilij Arslān, the lack of mounted scouts on the Christian side meant that he could hastily withdraw from the mountainous and forested terrain near the camp to a plain more suitable for his cavalry to manoeuvre around the Christian foot soldiers. As the Christian army came out of the woods and reached the open fields their boastful clamour ceased. Formed up across the plain was the huge Turkish army. Not be to deterred, the crusaders encouraged each other with shouts invoking God, before the first two divisions, the knights of the Christian army, set out to close with the enemy. Qilij Arslān waited, allowing a gap to open between the Christian riders and their foot soldiers, and then signalled that his troops should fire. The arrows poured down, not on the front ranks of the fast moving cavalry, but on their second division and the foremost of the foot soldiers, many of whom, as intended, now shrank back from the lethal clouds of darts. A disastrous split had opened up in the Christian ranks. The foot soldiers at the rear halted and formed up in the relative safety of the trees, at the head of the path back to the camp. Those at the front hurried to keep up with the knights.

The more heavily armoured western knight, if he could get within reach of his Muslim opponent, had the advantage in close combat. With their front ranks undisrupted, Walter and his companions on horseback crashed among the Turkish riders and in moments had cut down hundreds of Turkish troops. But as they scattered, the Muslim archers directed their arrows into the horses of the Christian knights. Too few to maintain the momentum of their initial success, Walter and his illustrious companions were soon fighting on foot. At close range, layers of chain mail armour were no protection against contemporary light bows, let alone the sophisticated wood, horn and sinew composite bows favoured at the time by the Turkish cavalry. Staggering, with one arrow after another smacking through his armour and deep into his flesh, Walter continued to slash out at the enemies nearest him, before expiring with seven arrows penetrating his chest. Did he die with bitter satisfaction at having given the ultimate proof of his courage?

Ironically, as the dismounted crusader knights were killed, bravely fighting to the last, Godfrey Burel ran. It was the sight of their hero slipping through the woods back towards the camp that unnerved the rearguard. Thinking only of their own survival, they broke in panic. But the Turks were quickly upon them and, as is so often the case in war, the real massacre began with the rout rather than the battle itself. For three miles the Turkish army, rejoicing at their victory, chased the fleeing crusader troops all the way back to the camp and right into it, not allowing the Christians a moment to regroup.[15]

The slaughter was immense, but not total. Once again beardless and attractive young men were spared for the slave market, as were young girls and the more appealing nuns. The only other survivors were some 3,000 soldiers who instead of making for the camp had run to a ruined fortress on the beach, where they desperately piled stones into the breaches. Many of these men were killed by the heavy fall of arrows that now rained down upon the ruins, but some survived until the departure of the Turkish army the following day, when news came that the Byzantine Emperor was on the way to assist the remnants of Peter's army.

Qilij Arslān returned to his capital, with immense booty and a triumph that looked set to make him famous. Those who had feared the consequences of a massive Christian army coming to the Muslim world had cause to celebrate; the young sultan of Rūm had destroyed the threat with ease. There was no harm in being seen as a champion of Islam against the Christians, but what this victory really meant for Qilij Arslān was that he could now concentrate his forces 500 miles to the east, where the Danishmend ruler, Malik Ghazi Gumushtekin 'the wise', was becoming a decisive rival. Malik Ghazi was currently campaigning for control of the strategic Armenian city of Melitene and if he could be thwarted in this, it would be a serious check to his ambitions.

While the Turkish sultan once more rode across the entire width of his realm, one by one, the other Christian armies arrived at Constantinople. These were a far more dangerous threat to the Muslim world than the more lowly troops of Peter the Hermit. They were also a potential threat to the Byzantine emperor. Despite the fact that the crusading mission was ostensibly the emancipation of Jerusalem from pagan rule, Alexius was distinctly uneasy about having such powerful and effective armies gather at his capital. After all, back in 1082, Alexius had been general of a Byzantine troop against an invading force of Italian Normans led by Bohemond. In the course of a two-year campaign they had met twice on the field of battle, and on both occasions Alexius had been forced to retreat. Now here was his former enemy returning with another great Norman army. Is it any wonder that the Byzantines looked warily at the response to Urban's appeal for aid to the Christians of the East? The policy of the emperor in this unprecedented situation was to seek recognition from the leaders of the Latin armies that he was their overlord, to require from them a promise that all former Byzantine cities regained from their current Turkish rulers would be restored to the empire and, lastly, to avoid a situation where the crusading armies could unite together north of the Bosphorus. In return, the Byzantines would offer troops and logistical support to the overall expedition.

First to arrive, less than a month after the battle of Civitot, was Hugh the Great, brother of Philip of France. The presence of this group of knights presented no difficulties to Alexius, as Hugh's following, already small, had been further reduced by shipwrecks on the journey across the Adriatic. With due respect for his lineage, Hugh effectively became a prisoner at Constantinople, where he was obliged to take an oath of fealty to the emperor. Detained with him were a number of the rowdy knights of the army of Emicho who had terrified the Jewish communities of the Rhineland. Drogo of Nesle, Clarembald of Vendeuil and several companions had presented themselves at the border of the Byzantine Empire having survived the violent dispersal of Emicho's army by Coloman of Hungary. While most of Emicho's forces had either been slain or had abandoned the idea of the crusade, for these knights the adventure was only just beginning. Moreover, their period of forcible detention at Constantinople proved useful; Drogo and Clarembald now attached themselves to their royal companion and offered to make him king of Jerusalem if he would look after their interests. It was far too early to raise the extremely divisive question of who should rule Jerusalem, if, by some miracle, the crusaders captured the city, but Hugh was extremely proud of his lineage and no doubt enjoyed the daydream of being king of the Holy City.[16]

A more tense situation between a crusading army and the Byzantine emperor arose with the arrival, just before Christmas 1096, of the next Latin force, that of Duke Godfrey and the Lotharingians. Godfrey had been told that Hugh and several German lords were prisoners of the Greeks; the tale came in the exaggerated form of depicting these princes as being bound in chains. The Duke therefore gave his army license to pillage the Greek lands through which they were passing. Immediately, Alexius dispatched two Franks to appease Godfrey. Soon the Lotharingians were camped outside the walls of the Byzantine capital, while Hugh, along with Drogo, Clarembald and another illustrious knight, William 'the carpenter' of Melun, so-called because he prevailed in battle by hewing down men like an artisan, were all allowed to join their fellow crusaders, which they did with great enthusiasm.

Good relations between Alexius and Godfrey were still some way off and in their manoeuvres as to how they should meet and on what terms, the crusaders came to blows with mercenaries employed by the emperor, blows that at times were fairly serious engagements, with hundreds involved and many deaths on both sides. Just as Godfrey was showing a willingness to adopt the perspective of the emperor and it was being arranged to swap hostages in advance of a meeting, a messenger from Bohemond arrived in the Lotharingian camp. The Norman army was on the way and its prince promised that if Godfrey withdrew to spend the winter safely in Adrianople or Philippopolis, Bohemond would arrive by March and between them they could unseat the emperor. It was an interesting proposal, which Godfrey put to his intimates the following day. His reply to Bohemond, however, was unambiguous; he had not left his homeland or family for the sake of profit or the destruction of Christians. The Lotharingians were intent on marching to Jerusalem.

Bohemond's legation had the effect of making up Godfrey's mind with regard to Alexius, who in turn, when he learned of the contact between the Normans and the Lotharingians, was more conciliatory to the latter. Alexius's treasured son, John, was given over to Godfrey as a hostage. This gave Godfrey the confidence to gather his most prominent followers and, on 20 January 1097, enter the palace of the emperor. Alexius put on his most impressive display, sitting in a powerful throne, dressed splendidly and surrounded by precious items. The Lotharingians were invited to kiss the emperor, symbolic gesture of peace. But it was also a gesture of submission, for the emperor remained seated. First Godfrey, then the other German nobles, in order of seniority, bent the knee to Alexius. Praising Godfrey as a powerful knight and prince, Alexius declared him to be an adopted son, and showered all present with enormously valuable gifts. The crusaders placed their hands in those of the emperor, this was the act of homage, a public gesture that they had become his man.[17]

With plentiful supplies being sent to the Lotharingian army, which had now taken ship across the Bosphorus, soon all was harmony between the crusaders and the Byzantines. From Alexius's point of view, this was just as well, for the negotiations had dragged on for weeks and no sooner had they finished than Bohemond's army arrived in Byzantine territory, having sailed safely across the Adriatic. The Normans were marching at great speed along the road from Durrazo. And only a few days behind Bohemond were Count Raymond of Toulouse and Bishop Adhémar of Le Puy, whose Provençal army had taken the land route through Albania. After celebrating Easter, 1 April 1097, Bohemond left his army in camp at Hadrumetum to ride ahead to Constantinople with only ten companions, as if he hadn't ever schemed to destroy Alexius and apparently without the slightest concern for his safety. Around 10 April 1097, Bohemond met with Alexius in the presence of Godfrey and his younger brother Baldwin. Needing very little persuasion, Bohemond accepted the emperor's terms and to all appearances acted as a loyal vassal of Alexius, although it was noticeable that the Norman leader ate no food but that cooked by his own people.[18]

Not all the crusading nobles were so amenable to taking the oath to the emperor. One French knight had become furious at the sight of his lords having to stand while the emperor remained seated. When the opportunity arose, this knight went over to the emperor's throne and made himself comfortable in it. Did he recall the famous story of how Rollo, the leader of a Viking troop who became ruler of Normandy, met with King Charles the Simple? The bishops present insisted that Rollo kiss the king's foot. One of Rollo's comrades therefore went over to the monarch and raised the royal foot to his mouth, toppling the king onto his back. This scandal provided much amusement to the Viking army.[19] But by 1096 the whole legal system of homage, fealty and vassalage was far more rigorous than in the days of Rollo and his companions. Not only were the Greeks appalled by a barbarian seating himself in the imperial throne, but so too were the French and Lotharingian nobility. It was Baldwin who persuaded the knight that since they were now vassals of Alexius, they had to follow his customs and including that of standing while the emperor was seated.[20]

While Bohemond had gone on ahead to Constantinople, Tancred had been left in charge of the Norman army. The young knight had already experienced his first taste of battle on the crusade, when, on 18 February 1097, Turcopoles, the light cavalry mercenaries of the Byzantines, had attacked the rearguard of the Norman army once the majority of troops were across the Vardar river. Tancred had rallied a body of knights and swum back across the river. His arrival at the fighting scattered the Turcopoles and netted the Normans many prisoners, who revealed that the emperor's orders were to harass the arriving armies and keep them from plundering Greek lands. Bohemond let the prisoners go free before his departure for Constantinople. His nephew, however, had no intention of following a conciliatory policy towards Alexius. When nearly at Constantinople, together with his cousin Richard of the Principate, count of Salerno, Tancred disguised himself as a foot soldier and crossed the Bosphorus in secret. In this way, unlike the other prominent crusaders, he avoided having to take an oath of fealty to the emperor.

Another prominent crusading leader who had great difficulty with the idea of taking Alexius as his lord was Count Raymond of Toulouse. The Provençal army had made a rough journey winter journey through the forested mountainsides of Albania, where the locals had murdered their elderly, poor and sick stragglers for what little they carried. Coming to Durazzo and the first major Byzantine city on their route, the southern French army had been delighted, thinking that the worst of the journey was over. But they too had to contend with raids on their camps by Byzantine mercenaries. By the time the army had reached Constantinople, Raymond was seething. His rage was such that he contemplated assaulting the city, but all the other Latin princes insisted that it would be the height of folly for Christian to fight Christian and Bohemond went further, stating that he would take arms on the side of Alexius should it come to that. This was a rather dramatic profession of his newfound loyalty to the emperor and was likely to have raised a few sceptical eyebrows in the imperial court.[21]

When it came to taking an oath of fealty to Alexius, Raymond baulked. In part this was because in the politically fragmented south of France he was much more familiar with oaths of security, taken between equals, than oaths of fealty, taken between vassals and lords. In part, also, it did not seem right to Raymond that Alexius should be the leader of the crusade. After all, the Greek clergy had many practices that the Latin Church disapproved of. And it was Raymond who had first offered his services to the pope. If there were any overall leader of the expedition, it should be he. No matter how great the wealth on offer, no matter the entreaties, the furthest Raymond would go was to swear an oath of security with Alexius. The emperor was furious with Raymond and gave him little by way of gifts. But hindsight was to show that although the Provençal count was the most intransigent, he was also the most faithful to his promises.

The first contingents of the crusader army appeared before Nicea on 6 May 1097. Gradually, the other Christian armies converged on Qilij Arslān's capital, until the united army filled the land in all directions with tents and banners. The crusading force was about 60,000 strong with some 7,000 fully armoured knights. From the perspective of those who had sewn a cross upon their tunic and set out for the Holy Land, this was evidence of the divine hand at work. It was inspiring, so many people, with so many different languages, yet all united with a common purpose. In those heady days, everyone felt as one. Should someone lose his or her belongings, a mule for example, the owner would be sought and the property returned. Miraculously, all could make themselves understood, despite their different tongues. The clergy, of course, were in their element in this regard, with Latin the universal language of the army.[22]

One grim sight that had contributed to this sense of solidarity between all the Christians was the enormous scattering of bones at Civitot and the nearby paths. Many were in tears as they marched towards Nicea past the morbid remains of Peter's army. Those who had survived the catastrophe of the previous October told the tale of how Walter had been provoked into battle with the Turkish sultan and how he had died facing his enemies. Peter the Hermit was treated with respect by the leaders of the united army and still had some reverence from the poor. But much of his aura of saintliness had gone, stripped by a course of events that made his popular expedition seem reckless rather than divinely inspired.

From the perspective of those holding Nicea for Qilij Arslān, the situation was extremely frightening. The newly arrived Christian soldiers were nothing like those so easily defeated the previous October. They were far better equipped, far better organized, and as numerous as the grains of sand on a beach. Admittedly, there was still the lake, which meant a means of obtaining supplies for the garrison. But with the extraordinary manpower available to the besiegers, it was only a matter of time before tunnels undermined the walls or the increasing number of siege engines threatened to pound them down. Once he understood the gravity of the situation Qilij Arslān responded as swiftly as when he had first faced the Christians, bringing his *askar* back west across his lands and sending fast riders ahead. Two messengers attempting to get into the city were intercepted by the besiegers, one was killed, the other brought before Duke Godfrey and Bohemond. The spy revealed that Qilij Arslān intended to attack the following day, at the third hour, and that his message was intended to prepare the garrison of the city to attempt a sortie during this battle. Bargaining for his life, the Turkish messenger asked to be baptized and said that the proof of his words would be the arrival of the sultan by the stated hour. Should that fail to happen, then the messenger would willingly put his head under the axe.[23]

The crusading princes hurriedly prepared their troops and sent urgent messages back to Count Raymond, who had crossed the Bosphorus but was still a day behind. The Provençal army pressed on through the night, arriving as the sun cleared the horizon, prepared for battle behind their colourful standards. They had hardly established their camp when, at the third hour indeed, Qilij Arslān attacked. Thousands of Turkish riders pouring over the horizon and galloping down the valley of Nicea towards the city was almost a beautiful sight: their splendid banners and golden shields vivid against the newly risen sun. But the arrows that flew from the massed cavalry wrought cruel damage on the most recently arrived crusaders, for it was the troops of Count Raymond and Bishop Adhémar of Le Puy who had to bear the brunt of the charge.

It helped the Christian army that they had been forewarned of the attack. A division of responsibilities was clearly understood, and while those so designated held the lines facing the city, the remainder hurried to where the battle was thickest. The Normans came up fast, with Tancred rueing the fact that the Provençal knights and not his own had obtained the first opportunity to kill their Muslim enemies and thus earn the fame granted by song makers and history writers. The Lotharingians were equally swift, Baldwin, Godfrey's younger brother, at their head. Soon the arriving Christian knights were galloping through the melee, inflicting deadly wounds with their lances. If Qilij Arslān had expected to encounter the same poorly armed and equipped Christian troops that he had slaughtered in the autumn, he was now bitterly disabused. Optimism turned to dismay. No fool though, once the momentum of his attack had faltered, he understood it was better to save the army than risk losing both his striking arm and his capital.

The retreat was sounded and the bulk of the Turkish army extricated itself from battle. The cost of defeat was high enough though. The victorious Christians decapitated the slain. A thousand heads were taken by cart to Civitot, to be shipped from there to the Byzantine emperor as proof of the victory. The remainder, and there were still sizeable stacks of heads, were put on catapults and launched into Nicea. In a grim manner the attackers were demonstrating to the besieged that their lord had been defeated and they should expect no relief.[24]

In the aftermath of this clear-cut victory, morale was extremely high in the united Christian army. The spy, whose words had proven accurate, was a popular figure in the tents of the most senior Christian princes. Popular, that is, until he had relaxed his guards sufficiently to make a break for the walls of Nicea in the early light of morning. There he had a frightening moment. Those on the walls of the city were at first slow to respond to his frantic shouts, while from the Christian camp his captors raised a cry against the attempted escape. Just in time, a rope was found that allowed the spy to be hauled up into the city, while a hail of javelins kept the pursuit at bay. That day repeated cheers and taunts were directed at the besiegers as the Nicean garrison took heart from the first event of the siege that had favoured them. There were to be others, for despite their numbers and their recent victory, the Christian army had no way through the solid walls of the city.[25]

Two Lotharingian noblemen, still wealthy at this point of the journey although destined to become utterly ruined before the year was out, funded a 'fox' at their own expense. Count Hartmann of Dillingen and Henry of Esch commissioned a defensive structure that could hold 20 men, with the idea that it should be taken up to the walls of the city, where its triangular-shaped roof would deflect the heavy missiles that would undoubtedly be thrown at it, while those inside dug away at the stone. As the armoured men approached the city, however, uneven ground meant that the fox became caught. All straining together to push it on, the key beams were dislodged from their bindings and the entire structure collapsed, instantly crushing those inside without a rock having been flung against them. Hartmann and Henry buried their brave followers with all due reverence and lamentation, but with a certain relief that they had chosen not to accompany the attack in person.[26]

The Provençal army had been more effective under the direction of Count Raymond and the Bishop of Le Puy. The followers of the bearded legate looked upon Adhémar not only as a religious figure, but also a general in his own right. The bishop and the count had, at first, each built a mangonel. These rock throwers of ancient design were essentially massive wooden spoons, given energy by rope torsion. Having been hauled down into a horizontal position with the missile placed in the cup, the arm of the device springs up to a vertical position when released, where it is checked by a cross bar. This causes the contents of the bowl of the spoon to be flung forward at great speed, but a relatively low trajectory. After five weeks of chipping away at the same tower with such devices, it was clear that the two they had constructed were insufficient to seriously damage the walls. A number of other siege engines were built and, at last, cracks began to appear in the face of the tower. Encouraged by this, the crusaders charged the tower, with a wickerwork 'tortoise' over their heads offering some protection from arrows. Once at the walls, the crusaders set to work on the cracks with iron spikes, hacking away at the masonry. By inserting wooden props and burning them, the process of undermining the walls could be accelerated. But even so, this took time, too much time. It was nightfall before sizeable chunks of masonry were coming lose and the garrison were responding to the threat. Having pulled back due to the coming of night, the Provençals found that by the next morning the tower had been filled with rubble. To attempt to move these rocks was a disheartening and dangerous experience from which the Provençals had to reluctantly withdraw.[27]

At this stage of the siege Alexius was playing an active role in events. His generals, Taticius, Tzitas and Boutoumites, were camped with the Latin crusaders and it was Byzantine ships that contributed to a decisive tightening of the siege. That they were able to do was thanks to a very ambitious decision by the crusading army. On the night of 17 June at a large assembly of all contingents, the commoners agreed to take oxen, horses and their own considerable man-power, place themselves in harnesses and drag the ships seven miles from Civitot to the lake. Thousands of crusaders responded to the proposal with enthusiasm. Like a nest of ants, they poured along the paths to the sea and hauled the ships overland. Before dawn, the Byzantine navy was lying in wait on the lake waters, where they set up a blockade. The leaders of the city looked with horror at the unexpected appearance of these ships. Not only was this an end to their supply route, it was testimony to the tremendous determination of the army outside. This was warfare not just against fellow warriors, but also the many-handed creature that was the mob of Christian commoners.

Greatly encouraged by their success in setting up a complete blockade of the city, the united army tried once more to capture the tower that had been weak-ened by the Provençals. This time they brought up a battering ram, only to have it burned as a result of the grease, oil and pitch mixture that the Turkish troops poured from the walls and ignited with burning torches. Others working at demolishing the walls were smashed to the ground by rocks or pierced with arrows. One Turkish soldier, having been wounded and giving up on life, stood right out above the Christians and continued to throw rocks down with both hands, despite the many arrows that were sticking out of his torso. The true weapons of the nobility at this time were the lance and the sword. But the crossbow was becoming an effective tool and Duke Godfrey had learned its use, in fact he was an expert shot. Watching this soldier rage above those trying to dig away at the walls of the tower, killing many of them, Godfrey summoned two of his comrades, who provided cover with their shields. These three edged carefully into range, where Godfrey took aim, before sending a dart soaring right into the warrior's heart, killing him instantly. Once more, however, the sun set without a breach having been made and with many losses, mostly on the Christian side.[28]

The following morning, the attackers were disheartened to see that all their work of the previous day had come to nothing. More rubble had been piled up inside the tower. One knight, a follower of Robert of Normandy, tried to rally the crusaders to a further effort. Relying on the protection of his helmet, shield and chainmail hauberk, he ran to the walls and began to pull at the heaps of stones. But a deluge of rocks fell to replace each that was moved. To avoid the javelins being flung at him, this knight now stood directly under the walls where his dilemma was acute. Run back towards the Christian lines? He would almost certainly be caught in a hail of missiles. But standing still was not an option either. Already he was dodging heavy stones and deflecting them with his shield. Across the no-man's land, the Christians were gathering themselves, but no one wanted to charge across to the tower, risking death for what looked like a hopeless task. Yet more and more stones were falling upon the knight. Before he could realize his only hope was to run, the strength of Norman gave way beneath the crushing weight of a large rock and in an instant his formerly agile body was a broken-boned ruin lying right up against the wall. Not only did the watching crusaders mourn guiltily the loss of a hero; they also were dismayed about the probable loss of such precious armour. For the Turkish soldiers now had a new game, they had a chain prepared with hooks, which they flung down at the body. Eventually they caught hold of it and dragged the corpse of the knight up and over the wall. Soon it was on display, naked, hanging by a noose outside the walls, to the horror and shame of the Christian army.[29]

It was a master craftsman from Lombardy who ensured the prompt surrender of the city on 19 June. He came to the princes, promising to build a more effective covering protection than that of Hartmann and Henry, in return for 15 pounds of silver. The resulting fox was sturdy and yet mobile. Its constructor was sufficiently confident of the device that he was inside when it was manoeuvred right up to the walls of the city. There, despite the best efforts of the garrison, the steep slopes of the machine meant that rocks and flaming torches were deflected while those inside dug right down beneath the foundations of a tower. There they propped up the stone with enormous oak beams, while continuing to take earth away. Once satisfied with the digging, the Lombard had the space under the wall filled with kindling and carefully withdrew without taking any loses. The fire that resulted was unquenchable by those within the city. During the night both sides watched the orange glow, until, with a crash louder than thunder, the wall of the tower collapsed.[30]

On hearing this terrible sound, the wife of Qilij Arslān took to a ship with her two sons and tried to use the cover of darkness to escape to her husband by sailing through the blockade on the lake. The alert squadron intercepted her and handed her over to the Christian princes. The news of her capture was soon shouted across to those in the city, to dishearten them further. At this point Boutoumites, the Byzantine commander based at the lake, entered into secret negotiations with the Turkish officers. The terms offered by Alexius were generous. The family of Qilij Arslān would be returned to the sultan. None of the garrison would be harmed and, indeed, the officers would be given valuable gifts. The only stumbling point was the Christian army. Could Boutoumites speak for them? The Greek general contacted Taticius, who was camped with the Latin forces. Between them, the Niceans and the Greeks agreed to make it look like Boutoumites had broken into the city during a day of busy fighting.

The plan was successful if rather nerve-wracking for Boutoumites, who was inside the city with the relatively small numbers of his troops and at the mercy of the Turks, should they change their mind about the surrender.[31]

Once it was apparent that the blare of bugles and waving of Byzantine banners on the walls of the city meant the siege was at an end, the delight of victory quickly soured among many of the Latin crusaders, who had anticipated considerable booty on the sacking of the Nicea. The princes, however, were given generous gifts from Alexius and the very poor obtained a distribution of food. It was the foot soldiers especially who were bitter. They were envious and even hostile to their own princes, pointing out that they had done all the hard work but gotten none of the reward. With the Byzantines refusing to let the Latins into the city, except in groups of ten to visit the sacred places, there was nothing that could be done at this stage. But the lesson was not lost and the question of who had the rights to captured property was to become a central issue in the Christian army: to the cost of many Muslim and Jewish lives in the cities that lay in their path.

Chapter 2

Endurance

The fall of the seemingly impregnable city of Nicea should have been a moment of great satisfaction for the Christian forces. Instead it revealed fault lines that were to persist all the way to Jerusalem and affect the conduct of the siege there. First, was it proper that the Byzantine emperor should own the city? For the princes who had sworn oaths of fealty to Alexius, the position was an unambiguous yes. After all, they had agreed that Nicea and other formerly Byzantine cities were to be restored to the empire. For the great majority of crusaders though, the situation was less clear. It was the crusading army, not that of the Greeks, that had taken all the risks, surely it should be one of their own who was the new lord of the city? Many voiced the word 'betrayal' and continued to do so for the remainder of the expedition.

Secondly, what had become of the wealth of the city? The precious ornaments; the rich cloths; the abundance of food? It was all very well that Alexius had made gifts to the princes and set up a Latin monastery and hospice for the infirm. These were actions that benefited only a small minority at the very top and very bottom of the social hierarchy; the emperor had done nothing for the knights and foot soldiers who had risked their lives attacking the walls of the city. By word of mouth, by common accord – in other words, without consulting the princes – this sense of injustice translated into a new understanding on the question of booty. Next time, captured property would be dispensed differently. Next time, no matter what the princes said, the policy would be 'first come, first served'. One important consequence of the fact that Nicea avoided being sacked was that the crusading army now decided to take the question of loot into its own hands. This grim resolution was to lead to extraordinarily violent scenes on the subsequent capture of Muslim cities, not least in Jerusalem itself.

A source of great delight to the entire army was the release of many Christians from the prisons of Nicea. Survivors of the massacre at Civitot were enthusiastically reunited with the fragments of Peter the Hermit's following, swelling the numbers of poor crusaders willing to continue the journey. Even here, however, the collective joy was soured by a curious incident. A nun from the convent of St Mary at Trier had been captured at the time of the disaster at Civitot. The poor creature had been given over to a Turkish warrior as a bedroom slave and was thus a ruined woman unless she could obtain repentance. Thanks to the intervention of Henry of Esch, to whom she had tearfully appealed on recognizing him, Adhémar, as spiritual head of the crusading forces, granted her forgiveness. The weight of the nun's penance was relatively light, given that her defilement had been unwilling. All, therefore, was properly examined, adjudicated and enacted. The nun was restored to her former sacred condition with no blemish on her character. And yet the story had an unexpected turn. The Turkish warrior to whom she had been given had fallen for his prisoner. Following the surrender of the Nicea, he was temporarily a prisoner in the hands of the Byzantine emperor. Despite this, and confident in his future release pending negotiations between Alexius and Qilij Arslān, the warrior sent a messenger to his former captive. If she would escape the Christian camp and come to him, they would be lovers again and she would live a pleasant life with his generous support. Astonishingly, she agreed to the plan.[1]

Here was a woman who had been filled with enthusiasm for the crusade by Peter the Hermit, who as a penitent pilgrim had survived the chaotic rout of Peter's army in Hungary, the hardship of hunger, the massacre of her friends at Civitot. What greater fears could she have held than to be a slave of those pagans whom the Christians marched against? And yet this enormous dedication to the Christian cause evaporated in the light of her actual experience as a captive. The incident was rather demoralizing to the Christian army as her actions stood in such stark contrast to their own faith. Did she really believe that life with a Turkish soldier was better than one dedicated to Christ? In the end, her defection was rationalized by those who said her Turkish captor had promised to become a Christian in order to marry her, or the less charitable who believed that it was the sin of lust that had conquered the nun.

A week after the fall of Nicea, on 26 June 1097, the crusade set out southwards. They fell into two distinct forces, already a sign of deeper rivalries to come. The main body of the crusading army, with Robert of Flanders, Hugh the Great, Godfrey of Lotharingia, Raymond of Toulouse and Adhémar of Le Puy was some two miles behind the vanguard. Those in the lead were Robert of Normandy, Stephen of Blois, Bohemond and Tancred, who at this moment was in a rage at his uncle. It had not escaped the notice of the Byzantine Emperor that Tancred had failed to perform an act of homage to him and had made no oath to return the former Byzantine cities to the empire. Alexius therefore insisted to Bohemond that Tancred must take the oath of fealty. This placed Bohemond in a very difficult position. Although the trick of crossing the Bosphorus in disguise had made Tancred the champion of those hostile to the emperor, Bohemond decided it was better, at this stage, not to alienate Alexius. Despite being cursed by Tancred for weakness, Bohemond brought the young prince before the emperor. Here, though, despite his youth, Tancred rose to the occasion. In his speech the Norman prince made it clear that his oath of fealty to Alexius was conditional: it was taken on the understanding that the emperor acted as the common leader of the crusade and should the promised material support fail to appear, then the oath was void. The suggestion that the Byzantines might cease to support the crusade was treated with indignation by the Greeks, but there was a clamour of approval from those Latins present at the scene.

Better still, as far as the followers of Tancred were concerned, was his answer to a very generous offer by the emperor. In an effort to conciliate the young knight, Alexius asked Tancred to name anything belonging to the emperor, no matter how precious, and it would be given to him. After all, Alexius had a treasury beyond compare. The emperor was stunned, however, at the impertinence of Tancred's reply. Rather than ask for a gold, silver, horses or precious cloth, Tancred responded by saying that he would take the emperor's tent. Not only was this impertinent, it was absurd. The emperor had a tent with a turreted atrium that looked like a city. It required 20 heavily burdened camels to carry, held a multitude and soared above all other tents like a cypress above roses. It was unique in the world. At the time of his request, Tancred did not have enough followers to fill such a tent, nor could he realistically hope to use it on campaign, there would not be enough time each day to raise it. But the symbolism of the statement was immense. Tancred was effectively declaring an ambition to be as great a lord as the emperor. His point was not lost on Alexius, who rather astutely replied that the Norman should remember the tale of the ass who put on a lion skin and thought he was better than he was, only to be killed by farmers after they discovered its true nature upon hearing it bray. The ceremony terminated in acrimony with Alexius' refusal to grant such a gift. The youthful knight had effectively shaken off the harness that the powerful emperor had tried to place upon him.[2]

As the crusading army marched through Anatolia towards the old Byzantine fortress at Dorylaeum with a potential dangerous division between the vanguard and the main body, Qilij Arslān awaited them. The Turkish sultan had thoroughly reappraised his policy in the light of the defeat outside Nicea. There was no longer any question of underestimating his new enemies. In fact, so serious was his response to this invasion that Qilij Arslān was prepared to make concessions to his current enemy, the Danishmend ruler, Malik Ghazi. The two

Muslim leaders agreed to join forces against the common enemy and mobilized all their vassals. Their army consisted entirely of mounted warriors and was some 10,000 strong. Enough to destroy the Christian knights if they could be separated from the infantry, or to defeat a vanguard so foolishly distant from the main body of the army.

At the merger of two valleys, where wide spaces would allow them maximum room to manoeuvre, the Muslim riders set up their camp. On the night of 30 July 1097, the first knights of the Christian army came in to view and Qilij Arslān was careful to keep the main body of his army out of sight. It was vital not to forewarn the Christians and have them send messengers back to their main army. Not until the Christian vanguard left camp early on the following day, 1 July 1097, did the entire Muslim army appear, flowing over the horizon into the shadows of the hills, ready to destroy the crusaders in front of them while they were still in the confused state of having recently dismantled their camp.

Qilij Arslān knew full well that it would be several hours at least before the larger section of his enemies could arrive, during which time the army in front of him could be annihilated. Howling like wolves, his forces charged at the Christian knights, wheeled, and released volley after volley of arrows into their mass. Clouds of dust rose in all directions. The foremost Christian knights lined up as though preparing to counter-charge. This was exactly the tactic that would destroy several crusader armies in the future, for unless the terrain helped or there was an element of surprise, the heavily armoured Christian knight invariably failed to strike home against the fleeter Muslim riders. Remarkably, however, the bulk of the Christian forces behaved with extreme discipline and held their position. While the compact mass of knights stood their ground, beyond them the foot soldiers and poor hurried to set up camp: so that tents and carts would act as a barrier towards the rear.

The source of this composure among the Christian troops was Bohemond. The dawn of 1 July 1097 probably witnessed the greatest test of generalship in the Norman prince's long military career. Any one of the other princes could have led a suicidal charge of the willing knights. In fact, it was far harder to restrain them. Only a general with nothing to prove and a grasp of the dynamics of the crisis could have acted so decisively and yet so defensively. On seeing the enormous black masses of cavalry moving against him, Bohemond had instantly understood that the crusaders' only hope of victory lay in surviving until the remainder of the Christian army arrived. He dispatched his fastest riders to summon the rest of the army, ordered the establishment of a camp near some swampy ground, and had his most reliable officers repeat again and again the command: stay together and hold your ground. By way of encouragement Bohemond added the words 'because today – God willing – everyone will be made rich'.[3] Optimistic words, but the fact was that the crusading knights were pinned against their camp, fighting in heavy dust, each soldier under constant threat from arrows that flew among them. While the chainmail armour of the Christian knight could deflect a spent arrow, those fired from close range or those flying into unprotected flesh – such as an eye – began to take their toll.

The sun slowly mounted the sky, obscured by the dust and a mist created by the heaving breath of thousands of horses. Again and again, clashes along the front line led to casualties, until even the hardiest of the Normans were wavering. Robert of Normandy, though, was in his element. Seeing a growing reluctance among the Italian knights around him to take their place in the battle line, he tore off his helmet, so all could recognize him, before shouting that no one could hope to return to the towns of their birth by retreating: flight meant death. They would either be victorious or die at this spot; there was no choice but to battle on. This rallying cry spread down the line and encouraged the Christian knights to renew their efforts. It was of enormous help also that the women of the army, on their own initiative, brought water up to the battle lines and refreshed both men and horses.[4]

Among those for whom the strain of being on the defensive was too much was Tancred. Along with his small band of followers and against the direct orders of Bohemond, who was worried that the rashness of the younger knights would undermine the order of the whole force, Tancred, still feeling disdainful towards his uncle, decided it would be valuable to take a nearby hill. The charge was a success in that Tancred scattered the Muslim archers from the hill and could plant his ornamental banner at the top of the rise. But soon the arrows came like a heavy rainstorm on to the youthful troop. Even though the main Christian army was close by, Bohemond refused to allow anyone to go to the assistance of their fellow crusaders. It was tantalizing and desperate, but the gap was just too much: to bridge it would disperse the compact formation of knights that was their only hope of survival. Realizing only a small number of crusaders had taken the hill, the nearby Muslim warriors drew their swords and tried to overwhelm them. The young Normans held their ground and, despite the great disparity of numbers, overthrew their attackers with their lances. Regrouping, the Muslim forces then drew their bows again. This time the relentless fall of arrows was decisive. But only when his brother, William, died under the storm of arrows, did Tancred realize the folly of his position and order a retreat, barely able to extract himself alive from the hilltop. Obliged to abandon his banner, the Norman prince was fortunate to survive the adventure.[5]

The greatest losses to the crusading army, however, came among the poor. Large numbers of Turkish cavalry rode around the central area of battle, to come across stragglers who had failed to reach the defensive camp in time. They were quickly run down and slaughtered. The camp itself offered poor protection and lacked armoured defenders. Inside the ring of carts, priests huddled together, giving each other confession, and preparing for death; it seemed inevitable that at some point a large body of Muslim cavalry would charge in among them. Some of the younger women prepared for this by putting on make-up and their finest clothes, so that they would be appealing to their captors and become slaves instead. It was not very devout, to prefer captivity with Muslims to a martyr's death, but, after all, the story of the nun of St Mary of Trier showed that life after captivity might not be so harsh.[6]

For six hours the hard-pressed Christian army endured, never far from complete destruction. Every hour that passed, however, meant severe attrition for the forces of Qilij Arslān and a danger that the remaining Christians would arrive. Surely, though, those before him, outflanked and so outnumbered would have to break soon? The clashes continued, with considerable numbers of bloody corpses from both sides strewn around the defensive line. Yet the Christian knights did not break to flee, nor lose their discipline in hopeless charges. Around midday, the sight he had imagined with dread became real. Clouds of dust from the arriving Christian forces were seen in the east. Victory, which would have been costly but certain, was now in doubt. Nevertheless, Qilij Arslān persisted; after all, his army still had more mounted troops than the Christians.

From the perspective of those who had been persevering in the face of constant deadly arrow fire, repeated enemy charges, and growing fatigue, the arrival of the Christian reinforcements meant the return of hope that they were not yet at the end of their lives. Hugh the Great was first to reach them and with him those grim knights who wished to make him king of Jerusalem, now anxious to cover themselves in fame and the blood of their enemies: Drogo of Nesle, Thomas of Marle and Clarembald of Vendeuil. Joining Hugh was Robert of Flanders and soon after came the Lotharingians. Godfrey had ridden ahead with just 50 knights so as to arrive as quickly as possible. This hand picked force was enough to drive back outlying Turkish riders. With the arrival of Raymond of Toulouse and his Provençal knights, Bohemond finally allowed his battered forces to take the offensive and the everywhere the Christian lines troops began to advance.

Despite this enormous change in the dynamic of the battle, its outcome was still in doubt due to the ability of the Turkish riders to retreat while continuing to fire arrows. That it became a decisive Christian victory was due to Adhémar, the papal legate. The bishop of Le Puy had brought his Provençal knights along a higher route than that taken by the other Christian princes and this meant that while he was delayed, when he did arrive to take Qilij Arslān's army unexpectedly in the flank, the impact of his charge was devastating. Suddenly the Turkish riders were routing, shattered, and with all order lost. Their baggage and supplies were abandoned as they fled, south and west and without halt, until they were safely away from the path of the crusading army. As they fled they took with them the news of the true strength of the Christians and the calamity of the defeat alarmed the Muslim world.

For a western army to have won a decisive victory against a Turkish one was unprecedented and the troubadours on the crusade immediately began to compose verses to celebrate the outcome. Bohemond was the hero of the hour, of course, but each of the leaders got a mention and the stars of Robert of Normandy and Hugh the Great in particular glowed brighter. For those intending to stay in the Holy Land, perhaps as king of Jerusalem, making political capital out of the victory was essential. Yet having come joyfully through the hardest fought battle of entire crusade, the celebrations of Christian army were only temporary. They now faced a new enemy on the Anatolian plateau, one more implacable and almost as dangerous as the Turkish warriors: thirst.

Having exhausted all their supplies, the crusaders had hoped to be able to live off the land until they reached the relatively wealthy cities to the southeast. But the Christians found that the region they were travelling through had been stripped of all obvious sources of sustenance. They had plenty of coins and military equipment from the looting of Qilij Arslān's army, but nothing to eat or drink to sustain them as they crossed arid highland during the hottest time of the year. Hunger and thirst drove many to seek sustenance from cacti, which they gathered and rubbed between their hands. The human suffering was wretched enough, but many of the army's horses died through lack of fodder. Rather than give up on the enormous gulf in social status between those on foot and those with mounts, some knights even resorted to riding upon oxen. Desperate to drag arms and armour along with them, goats, sheep and even dogs were harnessed as beasts of burden. Thirst brought about premature labour in pregnant women, leading to very distressing scenes.[7]

During this difficult passage, Count Raymond became so sick that the Bishop of Orange administered the last rites to him. A Saxon count in the Provençal contingent, however, comforted Count Raymond, saying that he would not die of this illness. The Saxon claimed to know this directly from having interceded with God on behalf of Raymond. Count Raymond accepted this divine intervention as a genuine miracle and not only was he restored to health, but also his belief in his special role a divinely appointed leader of the crusade was reaffirmed.[8]

At last, in early August 1097, the crusade came to fertile country again and found that the important city of Iconium had been abandoned by its Turkish garrison. Heraclea was reached by the end of the month and was taken with similar ease. This brought the Christian army out of the domain of Qilij Arslān, who was only too pleased to see the back of them and begin the slow process of reassembling an army capable of restoring his sultanate. The lands the crusaders now travelled through were mainly inhabited by Armenians, a Christian people over whom the Seljuk Turks had established a relatively insecure rule.

At this point two small breakaways took place from the main crusading forces. Tancred departed the expedition on 15 September 1097 with a few hundred knights. Baldwin hurried after him with a force that was twice as strong, some 300 to 500 knights. Both bore away to the west in the hope of capturing towns that they could become rulers of, above all, the major city of Tarsus, ancient capital of Cilicia. First to arrive at Tarsus, Tancred drew the Turkish garrison out by a ruse. He had some light cavalry loot cattle outside the city, only to turn and flee as the Turkish forces emerged from the gate to chase them. This chase led to woods in which the full strength of the Norman cavalry was hidden. The ambush was effective and Tancred was able to break the Turks, many of whom had not had time to put on their armour. In the panic at the city gates only so many of the garrison could get back in due to the press; the rest had to ride around the city or be cut down. During the night, the survivors of the ambush fled, allowing Tancred to enter the city, to a great welcome from the Christian population.[9]

The very next day, however, Baldwin arrived and insisted upon obtaining the governance of Tarsus. Now there was an important source of income at stake, the Lotharingians and Normans were as much rivals as comrades. Outnumbered, Tancred departed, furious. In doing so he just missed the arrival of some 300 Norman foot soldiers, who turned up at the city the following day looking to join Tancred's forces. Despite the pleading of his own people, Baldwin did not trust these Normans enough to let them inside the city walls. As a result they were slaughtered during the night by the Turkish cavalry that had been skirting the main Christian forces since their abandonment of the city.

On seeing the bodies and pools of blood around the walls of the city the next morning, a great uproar broke out and even Baldwin's own troops fired arrows at their lord as a result of this incident. He had to take refuge in a tower until their anger had been assuaged. And an even greater clash between crusaders was to follow. At Mamistra, early in October, Tancred had once again ousted the Turkish garrison with the help of the local Christians. This time when Baldwin's army drew near, Tancred attempted to resist his rival's demands for the city and battle took place between them. It was an extraordinary moment: two crusading leaders marshalling their troops to fight one another. In part the conflict was fuelled by the fact that both the leaders were princes with an insecure position. Not yet in command of substantial forces and serving under more prominent lords, both Tancred and Baldwin were desperate for the streams of revenue that control of cities could bring to promote them to equal status with the senior princes. Neither therefore was willing to back down and their knights charged back and forth, inflicting casualties on each other's army. Not until the Lotharingians captured Richard of the Principate, to match the fact that Tancred held the sick Conan of Montague prisoner in the city, were negotiations begun to exchange prisoners and establish peace.[10]

Ironically, Baldwin's efforts to establish dominion over these cities was soon abandoned in favour of a much more attractive prospect further to the east. He received an invitation to come and fight for the major city of Edessa, governed by an Armenian lord, Thoros. On the 6 February 1098 Baldwin arrived at the city, with a relatively small number of knights. Nevertheless, the population saw in him the possibility of an alliance with the Christian army that offered freedom from the threat of a Turkish take-over. Their enthusiasm was so great that Baldwin was in a strong position to insist that he had not come as a mere mercenary, but as an ally. Thoros was obliged to adopt Baldwin as his son and heir. The ceremony was a curious one but it made the point clearly: bare-chested, Baldwin had to wriggle under the same garment as Thoros and the two embraced. The fact that Baldwin was now in line for succession only created further momentum for the idea that Baldwin as ruler was a better guarantee of independence for the city than the current lord. On Sunday 7 March 1098 a crowd stirred up by a council of leading citizens attacked the royal family, who sought and obtained refuge from Baldwin. By Tuesday, however, this protection was either unable or unwilling to stand in front of the popular forces of revolt. The palace was stormed, Thoros – Baldwin's new father – was killed, and the Lotharingian prince declared ruler.[11]

This massive turn in fortune for Baldwin had important implications for the leadership of the crusade. Baldwin now had access to a regular and ample source of revenue from which he could attract followers and support his brother Godfrey. While other lords were slowly sinking into complete destitution, the Lotharingian brothers were not only able to maintain their vassals, but assimilate others willing to take service with them in return for sustenance. Their star was on the rise.

Meanwhile, the main body of the Christian forces had arrived at Antioch on 21 October 1097. Situated on the Orontes river, Antioch had once been one of the great cities of the ancient world. The circuit of walls that defended the city was vast, climbing up a mountain to encompass the high ground on which the citadel was built. Although past its most glorious days, Antioch was still a major trading centre and a near autonomous Seljuk garrison was based there under the command of Yaghī Siyān, a former slave. A major goal of the crusade, at least as far as the Byzantine emperor was concerned, was to regain such an important city for the empire. The Latin Christians too considered the capture of Antioch essential. It would not be possible to safely march south towards Jerusalem if an active Muslim army remained in the city.

Arriving at the city when the recent harvest had been gathered meant that a great quantity of foodstuffs existed there to seize or buy cheaply from Armenian merchants; the crusaders set up camp in some comfort. But as the readily available food was consumed and autumn turned to winter, the siege began to take its toll on the Christian army. A famine developed that devastated the ranks of the poor and diminished the whole army. The poorer people were desperate enough to seek grains found in manure. They also began to organize themselves into bands in order to march together in search of food, with the agreement to share all captured booty. The most notorious of these bands were the *tafurs*, who prided themselves on their poverty. They marched barefoot, without arms or money. They were naked, needy and filthy, living off the roots of herbs and any worthless growth. Their leader was a well-born man from Normandy who having become a foot soldier after losing his horse, wished to give them direction and had himself declared their king. These *tafurs* were so wild that even the Christian princes did not dare to approach them.[12]

During the course of the siege three major battles took place. The first, on 31 December 1097, was blundered into by both the contending armies. Robert of Flanders and Bohemond had united their forces to lead a major foraging expedition to the regions south of Antioch. Accompanying their knights and foot soldiers were a body of poorer crusaders hoping to be able to loot food-stuffs from the fields and villages they passed through. With the crusaders having spread out in search of supplies, encumbered by their booty, and returning slowly towards Antioch with captured beasts, an alarming report was brought by some of the Christian poor who had been attacking a village. A large Muslim army was in the vicinity and closing on them fast.

The army that was hurrying to confront the crusaders was the *askar* of Damascus, led by its young emir, Duqaq, his atabeg (governor and tutor) Tughtigin, and Janāh al-Dawla, atabeg of Homs. Once it was clear that the Christians had arrived at Antioch in considerable strength, the Turkish governor Yaghī Siyān sent his son Shams-ad-Daulah to Damascus to plead for assistance. It suited the Damascene nobility to strengthen their ties to Antioch, which until recently had been allied to their bitter enemies at Aleppo. The *askar* was therefore mobilized and having joined with Janah, they were surprised to learn from Muslim farmers fleeing the raid that a Christian army was in the vicinity of Albara, some 25 miles south of Antioch.

Once more the Muslim forces had the upper hand for the early part of the fighting and once more Bohemond showed his grasp of the tactics required in this new pattern of warfare. Anticipating that the Muslim army would attempt to ride around the crusaders, he formed a substantial rearguard and attempted to fight off the envelopment. When Robert arrived with the Flemish forces, a cross prominent upon his chest, displayed proudly as it was every day, the safety of the Christian knights was assured. The Muslim cavalry that had sought to encircle Bohemond's knights broke off from the hard fighting that did not favour their light armour. The position of the crusading foot soldiers and poor was another matter. They had been left behind by Bohemond's manoeuvre and now tried to make a run for steep mountain slopes or hidden valleys. For many of them though, the return of the Muslim army meant a sorry death, cut down as they fled. Robert and Bohemond made the decision not to risk even greater losses and abandoned the foot soldiers, not to mention all the booty, for a safe passage back to Antioch.[13]

From Duqaq's perspective, the mauling his troops had gotten when they closed with Bohemond and particularly the losses after the arrival of Robert were enough. He had plenty of captives and had rescued the stolen herds. And so he too turned about, bringing the booty back to Damascus. Both sides claimed the victory. Tactically, Duqaq had done the better, in that he had come away with the crusaders' much needed supplies, but strategically the outcome of the battle favoured the Christians. The siege of Antioch still continued; Bohemond and Robert had done enough to discourage another relieving expedition from Damascus, despite the pleas and protestations of Shams to Duqaq.

The failure of Duqaq to relieve the besieged opened the way for his hated elder brother Ridwan to pose as the defender of Antioch. Rejected at Damascus, Shams now travelled to Aleppo to appeal to its lord, who was only too happy to respond. The second important battle of the siege of Antioch took place between the *askar* of Aleppo and the crusading knights on 9 February 1098. News of the arriving force had reached the Christians the previous day; they were shocked and alarmed to learn that a force of some 12,000 Muslim riders was already at Harem, only 20 miles away. An emergency council of the princes took place in the tent of the papal legate. At this crisis meeting all divisions, even those increasingly bitter ones between Norman and Provençal, were forgotten. All agreed that the emergency called for one person to command the entire crusading forces and that person should be Bohemond.

The Norman lord rose to the occasion. His plan was risky. He ordered all the available knights to mount up that night and ride out in darkness in order to ambush the arriving enemy forces, while the foot soldiers remained at the siege to ensure that those inside Antioch were unable to break out of the city and assist their co-religionists. Under the direction of Godfrey of Lotharingia, Stephen of Blois and Bohemond, the crusading nobility left camp; among them were knights riding asses, such was the desperate shortage of horses. Their total force was less than 1,000 riders and there was some bitterness directed at the Greek general Tatikius, who had recently given up hope of a successful conclusion for the siege and departed in order to return to Constantinople. Robert of Normandy was also missing; he certainly would have happily joined in battle but missed it because of his reluctance to participate in the daily grind of the siege. The Norman Duke preferred wine, women and hawking to the dirt and hunger of Antioch. Ignorant of the desperate situation faced by the others, Robert was enjoying slumber and idleness at the costal city of Latakia, excusing himself on the grounds that he was safeguarding supplies arriving from Cyprus. Only after the battle against Ridwan, at the third summoning, with the population of the city growing restless at his exactions and under threat of excommunication, did Robert return to his tent.[14]

The day of battle, 9 February 1098, was a grey and wet day. It was just the kind of weather that the crusaders would have been praying for; the heavy rain seriously slackened the force of the Muslim bow and could even make it unusable. It also served to assist in their concealment. For while Ridwan's army approached, the crusader cavalry were deployed behind a large hill, some 15 miles from the city. The trap was sprung and the Christian knights galloped down upon their enemies, like a falcon upon its prey. To create the impression that the crusaders were there in great numbers, all the banners had been brought from the camp. This ruse and the unexpected descent of these glittering knights was a complete success. The vanguard of Ridwan's army recoiled back upon his main force, adding confusion to fear. Not that victory was assured for the Christians. Sheer weight of numbers began to tell and although the Muslims were suffering far greater losses than their opponents, the much smaller body of knights began to waver after the momentum of their attack was spent. With precise timing,

Bohemond now committed his reserves, riding among them in a ferocious charge. The sight of the Norman banner flying high, moving deep among the Muslim army rallied the whole Christian army and in equal measure demoralized Ridwan's troops, who assumed that such recklessness meant they were engaged with only a part of a much larger force. Abandoning all hope of victory, the Muslim riders scattered, now anxious only to escape the remorseless toll of sword and spear. Their casualties were nevertheless considerable and the victors collected over 700 heads to take back to Antioch and display to the garrison.[15]

The third major battle during the siege of Antioch took place on 6 March 1098 with Yaghī Siyān's own last desperate attempt to break the grip of the siege: a sortie from the garrison of Antioch. The timing of the Muslim breakout was near perfect. Having learned that Bohemond and Count Raymond of Toulouse along with Everard of Le Puiset and Warner of Grez had led a substantial force westwards to escort supplies back from the port of St Symeon where an English fleet had recently arrived, the Turks stole out of the city on its mountainous north side and prepared to ambush this force on its return. Careful not to alert the main body of the Christian army camped on the low lands to the east of the city, the garrison of Antioch crept over the one bridge that the Christians had been unable to blockade. As a result, 4,000 Turks were awaiting the returning Christian troops and their attack out of the thorn bushes and scrub was entirely successful. Taken by surprise, the Christians foot soldiers scattered, to be hunted down with bow and sword. The more disciplined bodies of knights were hampered by the terrain and their own dispersed formation. In fact, there was a danger that they too would be caught up in the rout. Bohemond, Raymond and Warner retreated in order to secure an escape route through the mountains.

While the Turkish forces rejoiced and began collecting heads – there were hundreds of corpses to decapitate – Christian survivors had reached the main crusader camp where there was uproar. Those carrying the news of the ambush were uncertain as to what the army should do; the Turkish garrison was out in such force that to attack it risked a further defeat. But Duke Godfrey and the Lotharingians had no doubts. They rode from the camp as soon as they could and were delighted that by the time they had organized themselves and were making progress up the mountain, Bohemond, Raymond and Warner arrived safe and sound, with their core force of knights in good order. Perhaps there was a chance to reverse the misfortune of the day.

The united Christian army cautiously approached the site of the ambush. Ten Christian scouts took up position on a ridge, where they soon had to retreat, spotting 20 Muslim riders manoeuvring to cut them off. Turkish riders now occupied the ridge and were the target for attack by some 60 Christian knights. Not realizing that the bulk of the crusading army was nearby, more and more Turks committed themselves to this fight, turning a skirmish into a major battle.[16]

Now that the opportunity for revenge was before them the crusading princes were not slow to seize it. The violence of their charge quickly routed the Turkish horsemen. During the fighting an incident took place, which was to spread the name of Godfrey of Lotharingia across Europe as it was told and retold in songs and histories. Riding up to an armed opponent, Godfrey dealt him such a mighty blow that metal, leather, skin and bone all gave way before his sword. The top half of the Muslim warrior slid to the ground, while his horse bore away little more than the man's legs. As the Christian knights rejoiced in this deed, the Turks galloped for safety. But the situation of the garrison of Antioch had suddenly come disastrous. Their losses in the actual fighting were not that great; less, in fact, than they had earlier inflicted on the Christians. The problem was: where to turn?

The bridge back to Antioch was completely congested with soldiers trying to force their way back into the protection of the city. An enormous slaughter now took place. Burning with the anger of battle, Duke Godfrey, having dismounted, planted himself in the line of retreat, hacking out around him with huge and deadly blows of his great sword. Those wishing to flee past the spot were forced to part either side of him, like a stream around a rock. No Turkish warrior delayed to stand and fight the wild Lotharingian lord.[17]

On the bridge itself the press was such that crusaders could rush at the crowds with sections of railing, pushing 20 soldiers at a time over the lip and to their death. Afraid that the city might be breached, Yaghī Siyān ordered that the gate be closed, condemning all those still outside to their deaths. Secretly, from walls and windows, Armenian women applauded the actions of their fellow Christians as they watched the river turn red with the blood of the slain. One measure of the effect of this massacre on the Turkish army inside the city was the silence that thereafter reigned at night. Throughout the siege the Turks had kept up a jubilant tone to try and discourage those outside. Jeers and cries would come from the walls all through the long winter nights. From this day though, the city was still with trepidation.[18]

Antioch fell on 3 June 1097. A former Christian by the name of Firouz was the guardian of a section of the walls that contained three towers. Firouz had approached Bohemond with an offer to allow the Christians in to the city in return for rewards and protection. In a manoeuvre that revealed that all his bowing to the Emperor had been an act of expediency rather than a genuine commitment to be a servant of the Byzantine Empire, Bohemond hid the knowledge of this offer from the other princes. Only after the rest of the Christian leaders were worried by reports of the imminent arrival of an enormous Turkish army under Kerbogha, atabeg of Mosul, did Bohemond call the princes together for a special announcement. Even then he simply hinted at the situation. Bohemond asked all the others swear an oath that whoever could deliver the city should become ruler of it. Many of the army had never agreed with the terms of the Byzantine alliance. Now Bohemond appealed to this sentiment and secured agreement from the majority of princes that if he could get them inside the city walls, he deserved to become ruler of Antioch.

A nerve-wracking moment still lay ahead though. Firouz claimed that he was bitter with the Turkish ruler of the city, Yaghī Siyān. Firouz had kept a certain amount of grain stored to feed his family, but on discovering this, Yaghī Siyān had it confiscated and redistributed, as well as punishing Firouz for failing to share his grain as decreed. This certainly seemed a plausible enough reason for him to become a traitor, but was it all a trap, perhaps intended to capture Bohemond? In the early hours of 3 June 1098, while it was still dark, a large body of knights, predominantly Normans, made their way as quietly as possible up the hills to the north of the city and around to the walls guarded by Firouz. There, the agreed signal was given and a knotted rope was lowered.

Who was willing to climb it? From the top of the walls Firouz was urging them on in urgent cries, using Greek as a common language. But there was a great reluctance among the Christian knights to risk their necks in the possible trap. At last, a knight from Chartres, Fulcher and his 60 companions offered to go ahead. Fulcher's friends included Drogo of Nesle, Rainald of Toul and Gaston of Béarn. These knights were already establishing a reputation for heroism, albeit that it was rooted in a callous disregard for life that had already seen Drogo conduct massacres of civilian Jews. Drogo, Rainald and Clarembald, the supporters of Hugh the Great, had earlier been singled out as the unanimous choice of the captains of the army when riders were required to investigate reports that Kerbogha was arriving with a great army. No better squadron of warriors then, to risk their lives and to conduct bloody slaughter in the event of success.[19]

When Firouz saw that instead of an army only 60 knights had climbed the walls he panicked, crying out in Greek for Bohemond and exclaiming that there were too few Franks. One of the knights, having seen that this betrayal of the city was no ruse, climbed back down and ran to Bohemond's concealed troops to get them moving. His fervour convinced those still wavering. 'God wills it!' was heard from above, as those already in the city called down to the knights now gathered at the foot of the wall and they were met with the same happy cry in reply. But for a moment it seemed that God did not will it. The knotted rope broke under the strain of too many knights climbing at once. Fortunately for the handpicked vanguard inside the city, there was a gate within the stretch of walls controlled by Firouz. From both sides this gate was assaulted until it gave way and there was no stopping the flow of Christian soldiers entering the city. At dawn the entire camp woke to hear trumpets and see the waving of Bohemond's red banners on the towers of the city walls. They came running as fast as they could to join the slaughter.[20]

The scramble for booty in the city led to the first open social breach between rich and poor on the First Crusade. While the knights continued to seek out and kill Turks, obedient to military priorities, the poor ran around seizing everything they could in a disorderly manner. They had not forgotten the lesson of Nicea and were not going to leave the distribution of booty to the princes. The uncontrollable mob surging through the conquered city were prefiguring the even bloodier scenes that would be enacted at Jerusalem.[21]

Within four days of Antioch having fallen to the Christian forces an enormous army led by Kerbogha arrived to trap the Christians in the city. A Turkish garrison still held the citadel inside the city, putting the crusaders under pressure from two directions. This was the period of greatest crisis for the expedition, where it seemed to be on the verge of disintegration. The capture of the city had hardly alleviated the hunger of the Christian poor, as those inside the city had very little food to plunder. Famine conditions continued after the fall of Antioch, with people being compelled to devour the leather from skins of animals and even their own shoes, or else abandon the city in the hope of reaching the Christian controlled port of St Symeon.[22]

The real danger for the poor, however, was that knights were lowering themselves by ropes from the walls of Antioch in order to escape the crisis and if this were to continue the Christian forces would melt away to the point that battle against Kerbogha was impossible. As early as 20 January 1098 William Carpenter, one of Drogo's companions in the attacks on the Rhineland Jewish community, had attempted to abandon the crusade, only to be hauled back by Tancred. Tatikius, the envoy of the Byzantine Emperor, made his excuses and abandoned the siege shortly after the return of Tancred. Just before Antioch had been captured, Stephen of Blois had departed, giving rise to a great deal of acrimony at his conduct. Now, while besieged by Kerbogha, many more knights were stealing away from the Christian army. Guy Trousseau of Montlhéry was the ringleader of a party of deserters, which included William of Grandmesnil, Aubrey and Ivo his brothers, Lambert the Poor, and many others, who let themselves down from the wall secretly during the night and fled on foot towards the sea. But for the fact that the Bishop Adhémar of Le Puy and Bohemond had closed the gates to the city very few nobles would have remained to face Kerbogha. Rumours began to spread that even the most senior princes were considering flight.[23] The phenomenon of knights slipping away by rope was sufficiently widespread that within a generation, from Constantinople to England, those who fled were being remembered by the mocking sobriquet 'rope-dancers'.

Under these desperate circumstances, on 11 June 1098, two humble men came forward, both with a similar story: they had been blessed with a divine communication, whose main content was to let the army know that God would aid the Christians if they sought battle with Kerbogha. The first of these visionaries, Stephen of Valence, was a respectable priest. He mounted the hill in Antioch, to where there was a gathering of the princes near the citadel, and reported his vision. Stephen said that he had taken refuge in the Church of St Mary in a fearful state of mind. Christ had appeared to him and, although expressing anger at the lust of the Christians following the fall of Antioch, Christ had relented following the intervention of Our Lady and St Peter. The Lord promised that if they sung *Congregati sunt* (Psalm 47:5) in the daily Office he would return within five days with mighty help for the army. Christ ordered everyone to accept penance and with bare feet make procession through the churches and give alms to the poor. To prove the truth of this vision, Stephen offered to throw himself from a tower but Adhémar, who instead had the priest swear on the Gospels and a crucifix, did not consider this necessary. As a result of Stephen's vision the princes assembled and took an oath that they would not flee, although they added the qualification, 'unless by the common counsel of all', a testimony to the low morale among even the most determined of the princely leaders of the crusade. Nonetheless, as the news of the oath spread it greatly encouraged the broader body of Christians who rejoiced on the news of the oath taking by the princes.[24]

The other visionary who came forward at this time was Peter Bartholomew, a servant of William Peyre of Cunhlat, from the Provençal region of France. Peter was not a particularly credible candidate for divine approval, due to his lowly status. How was it, people later asked, that God deserted princes and bishops to speak to such a rustic? Poor, Peter nevertheless had tried to contribute to the military activities of the crusade and had nearly died on 10 June 1098 when the arriving forces of Kerbogha caused Christians outside of Antioch to rush back to the protection of the city. In the crush at the gates Peter had almost perished between the horses of two knights.

It is understandable then that Peter Bartholomew initially approached the senior princes in a very deferential and cautious manner. He returned from several wide-ranging foraging expeditions to seek a meeting with the papal legate, Bishop Adhémar of Le Puy, Count Raymond of Toulouse and Peter Raymond of Hautpoul, one of the Count's leading vassals. The servant claimed that St Andrew had appeared to him during the night and that this was the fifth such visitation. After a lengthy recounting of the circumstances that obliged such a lowly person as himself to approach the princes, Peter came to the point. He declared that he had a tangible proof of divine aid, the Lord's Lance, whose hiding place had been revealed to him by St Andrew. Adhémar was extremely sceptical of the news brought by Peter Bartholomew, not least because, the legate was well aware of Constantinople's much more convincing claims to house the same lance. But Adhémar also wanted to encourage the nobles to stay and fight, so he was not going to press his doubts too hard. Furthermore, one of the themes of the visions of Peter Bartholomew was that God had allocated a special role in the expedition to Count Raymond of Toulouse. Raymond himself believed that God had chosen him to play a special role on the journey and welcomed the new visionary's confirmation of this. Peter's bid for the support of the elderly count was therefore entirely successful and Peter Bartholomew was taken into the care of his chaplaincy.[25]

On 13 June 1098 a meteorite fell in the direction of the camp of Kerbogha, giving material for the clergy to offer further encouragement to the Christian forces. The following day digging began in the Church of St Peter in order to unearth the Holy Lance. Initially Count Raymond of Toulouse himself, along with his more powerful vassals, undertook the work. But by evening they were overcome by tiredness. Fresh workers dug furiously until they too became tired. At this point Peter Bartholomew dropped into the deep hole and urged everyone to pray at length. While everyone else present was above the pit, praying, Peter alone discovered the Lance. Not all the crusaders were credulous believers in miracles and later, especially among the Normans, they would express their scepticism. But at the time all the crusading princes united behind the discovery of the Lance. Cries of immense joy and impromptu parades rallied the Christian knights and made them more willing to do battle. The commoners were revitalized by the oath of the senior princes and these apparent signs of divine favour. They now began to agitate that the princes should stop being so passive and initiate battle without delay.[26]

The princes responded by sending an envoy to negotiate with Kerbogha. The commoners, however, showed their mistrust of this embassy by insisting that the envoy be their guardian, Peter the Hermit. The resulting scene was almost as strange as that when the lowly hermit met the Greek emperor: the mighty Kerbogha, surrounded by powerful emirs and atabegs wearing the finest clothing in the Mediterranean world, meeting with a scrawny, emaciated man in bare threads. Peter had two offers to make to the leader of the united Muslim army. One was that the city would be given to Kerbogha and the Christian princes would be willing to serve under him, providing that he become a Christian; failing this, the Christians offered to settle the ownership of the city through a trial by combat of 20 champions on each side. Kerbogha, of course, refused, although he did make a counter-offer: to provide lands and castles in return for the city, so that those knights impoverished by famine and years of travel could regain their former status.[27]

On 28 June 1098 the small and weakened Christian army rode out of Antioch to give battle with the huge and well supplied army of Kerbogha. The Christians were in such desperate a condition before the battle that even Duke Godfrey of Lotharingia had to borrow a horse from Count Raymond of Toulouse, while a bowl was carried from inn to inn on behalf of Robert of Flanders whose constant fighting during the siege had seen him lose all his own horses. As the various divisions of the Christian army emerged one after the other from the city gates, Kerbogha played chess, publicly demonstrating his composure. Should he attack swiftly, while the Christians were not fully formed? No, let them come out and have his enormous army surround them and wipe them out with arrows. But Kerbogha failed to appreciate that half of his army were more than willing to abandon the battlefield as soon as decently possible.[28]

For decades the rulers of Damascus had adopted a fiercely independent policy from those of Mosul and the young emir Duqaq felt he had more to fear from a victorious ruler of Mosul, capable of taking Antioch under tight bonds of control, than the threat posed by a Christian advance towards Jerusalem. Moreover, Kerbogha had displayed his ambitions already, sending a messenger to those in the citadel of Antioch announcing the deposition of their commander and ruler, Shams, the son of Yaghī Siyān. The former lord of the city had met a miserable end, clubbed to death by a peasant, who had recognized Yaghī Siyān on his own, hiding in a bush, having lost his nerve and run from Antioch on the morning of 3 June 1098 when the Christians broke in to his city. Shams and Duqaq were former allies and the arrogance of Kerbogha towards them was deeply alienating. Worse again, Kerbogha was known to be conducting friendly negotiations with Duqaq's murderous elder brother, Ridwan, emir of Aleppo.

Unlike the battle of Dorylaeum, where the fighting lasted for a great part of the day on 1 July 1097, the serious fighting at Antioch was a relatively brief affair and no major losses occurred among the Christian knights. Under the command of Bohemond, who was given two weeks of absolute authority over the crusaders, the Christian knights engaged with only the minority of Kerbogha's army that was directly ahead of them, while monitoring the enveloping movements of the Turkish riders, turning their reserves to face them. Given the failure of Kerbogha's allies on the wings to commit themselves, his centre soon disintegrated and began to flee, except for a few devout adherents of Holy War who fought to the last. Kerbogha had suffered a shameful defeat; the Seljuk Turks had lost Antioch and would no longer be in a position to prevent the Christians marching on to Jerusalem. That task would now fall to the Arab princes of the costal cities, rulers who short-sightedly relished the humiliation of their hated schismatic rivals.

Not only was the result of the battle an indication for contemporary eyes of God's judgement, but also during the course of the battle, Stephen of Valence's predicted divine aid was said to have materialized in the appearance of three fighting saints with white banners leading a detachment of troops on white horses. Meanwhile, those marching in the vicinity of Adhémar and the Holy Lance thought that the relic was protecting all near it. With almost no losses, the Christians had routed and slaughtered an immense multitude. Surely God had strengthened their arm? The authority of the two visionaries, Peter Bartholomew and Stephen of Valence, was greatly enhanced by the victory and the surprisingly light number of casualties. What the crusaders didn't appreciate, therefore viewing the result as miraculous, were the deep divisions that existed among their enemies.

United as one under Bohemond for the victory on 28 June 1098, the Christian forces quickly dissolved into their respective regional factions in its aftermath. Of the major princes, Stephen of Blois had already abandoned the undertaking, returning to Europe in the belief that the Christians would be destroyed at Antioch, only to be greeted with such ignominy that he set out for Palestine once again, where he earned what was considered a martyr's death in 1101. Hugh the Great was sent to Alexius Comnenus in order to convey the news of the fall of the key city of the region. He never returned, having struggled to reach Constantinople by the autumn after facing ambushes and an arduous journey through Anatolia. The abandonment of the crusade by Hugh was a big blow to those knights who had aspirations to make him king. Without the resources to remain independent, this faction – including Drogo of Nesle, Rainald of Toul, Fulcher of Chartres and Gaston of Béarn – now made their way to Edessa to take service with Baldwin. This left as the leaders of the expedition: Bohemond, and Tancred, his second in command; Godfrey of Lotharingia, with his brother Eustace; Raymond of Toulouse; Robert of Normandy; Count Raymond of Toulouse, Bishop Adhémar of Le Puy and Robert of Flanders.

Bohemond's perspective was clear enough. On 14 July 1098, even though no one Latin prince had been made ruler of Antioch, Bohemond signed a treaty with the Consuls of Genoa, granting them a market, a church and thirty houses. As far as the Genoese were concerned, he was the rightful prince of the city. Count Raymond of Toulouse, however, could not disagree more. Not only was the Provençal commander holding on to a major gate and section of the city, but also he reminded all the other princes of their oaths to Alexius. They should assign the city to the Byzantines, who would appoint a ruler of their own choosing. The Christian commoners watched the manoeuvres of the princes with growing bitterness as their poverty increased.

Plague broke out in the city at the end of July, thriving on the weak conditions of the human beings within the walls. The princes, wanting to avoid the plague and to consolidate their local gains, scattered throughout the region, securing the income of nearby towns and villages. The disintegration of princely leadership of the crusade was an opportunity for some and a Provençal knight, Raymond Pilet, rallied the poor to lead an expedition against Ma'arra in July 1098. The lack of knights among the participants of this adventure resulted in Raymond Pilet's forces being thrown back by Ridwan of Aleppo.

On 1 August 1098 Bishop Adhémar of Le Puy died of the plague. The papal legate had been a key figure in maintaining harmony between the princes and the poor. No sooner was Adhémar dead, than Peter Bartholomew stepped forward try to offer leadership to the poor and shape the direction of the crusade. He reported a vision in which the dead bishop appeared accompanied by St Andrew and promised that he would continue to assist the crusade by offering advice from the afterlife, that is, through the policies expressed by Peter Bartholomew. The ghostly Adhémar and the saint were particularly anxious that Bohemond and Count Raymond of Toulouse not come to blows over the ownership of Antioch. Already by the time of the vision Bohemond had violently ousted Raymond's troops from the citadel of Antioch and was tightening his grip over towers and gates. St Andrew's message in response was that peace was essential as disunity could lead to disaster. Peter's visions had a consistent message, the crusade should continue on to Jerusalem and Count Raymond had a special role assigned to him by God. This message straddled two political positions. On the one hand it was a vital demand of the poor, who had nothing to live on but booty, that the crusade continues. On the other hand, Peter was consolidating his position in the entourage of the Count. So long as the two positions were not in opposition, the visionary was a popular figure. But before long he would have to decide whether he was with the Count or the poor, and the conflict of interest between the two would cost him his life.[29]

On 5 November 1098 the senior princes and their immediate followers met in the Cathedral of St Peter in Antioch. It soon became clear that a deep division remained between Count Raymond, who reminded Bohemond of the oath they had taken to the Byzantine emperor, and the Norman prince who was determined to hold the city. Such frustration grew among the poor that they threatened to choose their own leader to lead them onward and even to tear down the walls of the city if no resolution was come to. A compromise was resolved, which in practice favoured Bohemond. Oaths were taken and the expedition resumed by the princes with agreement that their first goal should be the reduction of Ma'arra. It was Count Raymond and Robert, count of Flanders, who led the first army out of Antioch on 23 November 1098, accompanied by a great number of poor Christians, delighted that the expedition was moving onwards again.

On 11 December 1098 the defences Ma'arra were breached, with the Provençal knight, William of Montpellier, playing a famous role in hurling stones down from a siege tower onto the walls of the city. But just as the Christians gained a foothold on the defences, sunset halted the fighting. The poor took advantage of the 'first come, first served' looting policy to steal into the city at night to secure all the plunder and houses. When the knights entered the next morning they were dismayed to find little they could take away with them. The situation for the Muslim population was extremely grim as they were tortured for information about their wealth. Some pretended to lead their captors towards treasure, only to leap down wells and die of the fall rather than at the cruel practices of the Christian conquerors. Bohemond did well out of the sacking of the city though. The Normans had arrived late to the siege and having promised the citizens he would spare them, he robbed those who surrendered to him of all their belongings, killed some, and brought hundreds back to Antioch in chains for the slave market of his new city.[30]

That the plunder gained by the poor at Ma'arra satisfied their needs for only a short interval was demonstrated within the month by acts of cannibalism. At first the crusaders began to split open the bodies of the pagans, because they came across bezants in the stomachs of corpses. These small gold coins had been swallowed by some of the inhabitants of the city in order to hide them. Others, such as the notorious *tafurs*, then fell to the flesh on these unearthed bodies for scraps of food. Disgusted and concerned about plague, the princes had the bodies stacked up into a mound and burnt.[31]

It was at Ma'arra that a major political upheaval took place in the Christian army, one that would have important consequences for the question of who should rule Jerusalem. Count Raymond had hoped to use the town as a base for a principality that he could hold as a vassal of the Byzantine emperor. But in the harsh circumstances of December 1098 this was an ambition that was deeply unpopular with the poor and those knights who were not attached to him, amongst whom were the Provençal followers of Adhémar. After the death of the papal legate his knights had nominally placed themselves under the command of Count Raymond, but with the expectation he would lead them to Jerusalem. Around Christmas 1098 at a council of the Provençals they sided with the poor in insisting that the Count lead the way to the Holy City, failing which they demanded that he hand over the Holy Lance and the people would march to Jerusalem with the Lord as their leader.

Count Raymond subsequently arranged a conference with the other princes to negotiate the terms on which the expedition would continue. This meeting took place at Chastel-Rouge, probably on 4 January 1099, but came to nothing. In the meantime, the Count had allocated a significant number of his knights and footmen to garrison Ma'arra. But the poor crusaders could see the danger in this. What would happen if the Christian forces were diminished by the allocation of a garrison to every captured city between Antioch and Jerusalem? They resolved upon an extraordinary policy. They took their hammers and picks to the walls of their own city, thus rendering it defenceless and unsuitable as a base for Raymond's local operations. As a policy this proved to be brilliant, despite the fact that it was not far from insanity. The recently created bishop of Albara, acting for the Count, used threats and force to prevent the poor, including the sick and infirm, from destroying the city defences. But as soon as his guards passed by, the people returned to their task. Count Raymond on his return to the city was furious but helpless. He bowed to the alliance of poor pilgrim and knight and set off southwards.[32]

At last they were moving through fertile terrain, and day by day the poor regained health, the knights became stronger, and the army seemed to multiply. Again during the course of the march, on 28 January 1099, the poor once more grabbed plunder from under the noses of the knights, this time during an attack upon Hosn al-Akrad. While Count Raymond and his most loyal followers were committed to the battle, the commoners ran off in search of booty and, when they had obtained it, one after the other began to leave the fighting. Their success in obtaining loot led to foot soldiers joining in the search for foodstuffs, prisoners and coin. Soon even the common knights, seeing their comrades pass them by with their plunder, started to leave the front line for the same goal.

Count Raymond was unaware that he was gradually being abandoned by the army and having pushed forward too far, came closer to death than in any of the major battles he had fought in. As the Muslim fighters drew closer to him, Raymond faked a charge, causing his opponents to hesitate and in that moment the count wheeled and with his bodyguard escaped towards safety. The following day, having received a furious lecture from Count Raymond, the entire Christian army came to attack the city, only to find it a ghost town. The inhabitants had fled, in such a hurry that they had left their dead unburied.

Although he was marching south, Count Raymond still harboured an ambition to form a principality in the region. He proposed that the Christian army attempt the capture of Jabala at which point Peter Bartholomew found an unexpected supporter. As the voice of the poor, Peter had been constantly urging the army press on to Jerusalem. Now Tancred, leader of a troop of Normans, the most sceptical faction with regard to the Holy Lance, spoke up, saying that it was evidently God's will, expressed through his visits to the commoners, that no one should turn aside from the journey. Count Raymond was obliged to abandon that idea, but his ambitions grew again following the delivery of a huge amount of gold and silver from Jala al-Mulk ibn Ammār, emir or Tripoli, who was anxious to buy off the danger of an attack on his city. With this coin, Count Raymond was able to offer to pay sufficient knights that it was agreed to attempt to take the city of 'Arqā. The crusaders reached 'Arqā on Valentine's Day, 1099. They were not to leave it for three months, even though the support for this action quickly became lacklustre, especially after the emir of Tripoli ceased his payments.

On the night of 5 April, during the now deeply unpopular siege, another vision occurred to Peter Bartholomew, one which cost him his life. Christ addressed the visionary and demanded great effort in attacking the city. Those who were lingering in their tents were compared to Judas and Pontius Pilate. Christ urged that some of the malingerers be executed to make an example to all. This vision was a political misjudgement by Peter Bartholomew. The former servant had kept his influential position by striking a balance between enhancing the authority of Count Raymond and by articulating the needs of the commoners. By siding with the unpopular perspective of the count at 'Arqā, the visionary had made a fatal mistake. The attitude of the Norman contingent abruptly hardened against him. Worse, the last message that the now politically active body of poor crusaders wanted to hear was that they must bestir themselves in this siege or risk execution for cowardice. For the sake of endorsing Count Raymond's strategy, Peter Bartholomew had alienated himself from his supporters and allowed his enemies the chance to bring him down.

On learning of this vision the legitimacy of Peter's Lance was immediately challenged by Arnulf of Chocques, the friend and chaplain of Robert of Normandy. At first it looked like Arnulf had misjudged the mood of the army as many of the clergy rallied to Peter. Arnulf began to retreat and prepared to make a confession of error to the visionary. But it was close. There was enough support for the challenge to Peter that Arnulf rallied and once more threw down the ecclesiastical gauntlet. Arnulf proclaimed Peter and the Holy Lance a fraud, with Peter then offering to undertake an ordeal by fire to prove his testimony.[33]

Medieval ordeals were not as absurd as they sometimes seem to modern eyes. Often they were more a test of public opinion than of the presence of divine intervention. Just how hot the blacksmiths' irons were that a woman must run over to prove her innocence of the charge of adultery, for example, depended on the ill will or otherwise of the clergy in charge of the proceedings. In this case, Peter's sympathizers were very influential in the building of two great bonfires with a narrow space between them.

On 8 April, a beautiful day with clear blue skies, Peter Bartholomew, clad only in a tunic, carried the Holy Lance along the narrow path between two ferocious pyres. The flames, however, shooting up into the sky, left him relatively unscathed and he even took a moment to pause right in the centre of the blaze as if in prayer. Emerging from the fires Peter held the Lance aloft and screamed 'God help us!' It should have been a moment of great triumph for Peter and his supporters. But those less enamoured of Count Raymond's goal of capturing 'Arqā were ready. They mobbed the visionary as if delighted, but during the tussle delivered several deep stabs to the would-be saint and crushed him until his back was broken.[34]

With the death of the visionary came the final disintegration of the hegemony of Count Raymond's entourage over the crusade, particularly because those Southern French followers of the Bishop of Le Puy who had joined the following of the Count after the death of their lord no longer co-operated with their Provençal comrades. In fact, it was with the return of William Hugh of Monteil, brother of Adhémar, with a piece of the true cross that Adhémar had carried that a new mutiny broke out against Count Raymond. A great commotion took place in which Count Raymond's followers set fire to their own tents and departed from the siege. The count broke into tears and attempted to halt the movement, but once a part of the Provençal contingent was underway the other crusaders needed little encouragement to join in.[35]

As the army approached Tripoli, around 13 May 1099, Count Raymond made one last effort to gain control of the leadership of the army by offering gifts to the other princes, so that they would support him in an attack on the city. This proposal drew upon the count the wrath of another visionary, the priest Peter Desiderius, who reported that St Andrew had come in the night with a strong rebuke for the count: 'do not be a plague to yourself or to others because unless Jerusalem is captured you will have no help. Let the incomplete siege of 'Arqā not trouble you, it is not to concern you that this city or others which are on the route are not at present captured.' This vision encouraged a further mutiny, this time by the poor, who could no longer restrain themselves. Irrespective of sensible military formation, they set out at evening and enough soldiers came with them that the rest of the army soon followed. The resumed march was enthusiastic but hard on those who could not keep up. A trail of bodies lined the route. But at last, over three years since Peter the Hermit had set out from Cologne, the Christian army was approaching Jerusalem.[36]

Chapter 3

Factions and Schisms

That a Christian army could travel on foot successfully all the way from Nicea to Jerusalem in an era when the region was dominated by Muslim princes was due to one fact above all: a deep and bitter split between Cairo and Baghdad. Two different administrative systems and two different versions of Islam bordered each other, with the fault line precisely that area of Palestine through which the crusaders marched.

To the east, the once dynamic Abbasid dynasty adhered to the Sunni religious tradition. At the height of Abbasid authority, around the year AD 800, the caliph had theoretical authority over territory stretching from the southern part of Spain, across North Africa, through Persia and nearly reaching to the Indus. But maintaining a unified jurisdiction over such an extended and culturally disparate region proved impossible and before long the Abbasid administrative system fragmented, to the benefit of more localized lordships. It seemed that a centrifugal decline in Abbasid sovereignty was inevitable and irreversible, until a new force capable of centralizing the authority of the caliphate swept down from central Asia from the 1040s, a Turkish tribe, the Seljuks. Conquering Iran, Iraq, Anatolia and Syria, the Seljuks – who had earlier adopted the Sunni form of Islam – recognized the caliph at Baghdad as their spiritual head.

Not that this was the old dynasty restored to its full vigour. The deference shown by the Seljuks to their caliph was limited to religious matters; the practical governance of the region lay in the hands of Turkish 'emirs', senior military commanders, who had considerable local autonomy and dynastic ambition. When a powerful enough figure could command widespread obedience from several emirs he took the secular title of 'sultan' and to all intents and purposes governed independently of the caliph. In Christendom at this time the papacy was attempting to emancipate itself from local secular aristocratic influence, aspiring to become an autonomous voice capable even of commanding kings. The Sunni caliphate was evolving in the opposite direction, being reduced to a political tool for the strongest Seljuk military faction and being revered only as the voice of religious judgement.

A similar trend was at work in the region controlled by the main Islamic rivals of the Seljuks, the Shia Fatimids of Egypt. The caliphate of al-Mustansir at Cairo had experienced massive political turbulence, which was stabilized only after the repulsion of a Seljuk invasion of Egypt in 1077. The Egyptian victory was led by Badr al-Jamālī, an Armenian governor of Acre, who had been invited by the Fatimid caliph to come to Cairo as his 'vizier' or chief minister. Badr's harsh measures against rival factions secured his position and he quickly obtained titular authority over the army of Egypt and also the direction of the missionary activity of the Shia clergy. On the death of Badr in 1094 the accession of his son, al-Afdal, demonstrated that – in Cairo as in Baghdad – the ability of the caliph to rule was being undermined by those who controlled secular authority.

Of the two caliphates, the Fatimids appeared the weaker, not least due to a renewed bout of political instability in the 1090s. When al-Mustansir died, in 1094, soon after al-Afdal had come to power, the vizier was able to prevent al-Mustansir's heir, Nizār, from becoming caliph, instead promoting the younger son al-Musta'li to the succession and subsequently reinforcing his control over the politically isolated youth by marrying al-Musta'li to his own sister. Nizār, however, had a substantial body of supporters and while this manoeuvre by al-Afdal may have enabled him to control a weak caliph, it also led to a new schism in the Shia clergy, with the enterprising Hasan ibn Sabbăh leading the opposition to al-Afdal and creating a following, the Bātinī (called by later Western writers the 'assassins'), which by recruiting among the lower social classes of the Shia populations of Syria and Iran was to grow to a become a movement capable of threatening the authority of a number of Near Eastern rulers, both Shia and Sunni.

The most important conflict in the region though, overriding the internal divisions in their respective caliphates, was that between the Fatimids and the Seljuks. To a large degree the rivalry of al-Afdal, vizier of Cairo, with the various Turkish emirs of Syria and Iran for control of the cities of Palestine can be portrayed as religious rivalry between Shia and Sunni, but this should not suggest that the cities of the Near East were religiously homogeneous; far from it. All the major Muslim-controlled cities at the time contained mixed populations of both Shia and Sunni worshippers and most rulers were unwilling or unable to persecute the opposite sect. The battles and sieges that took place in the 1080s and 1090s arose from the clash of ruling elites much more than from popular religious antagonism.

The bitterness of the conflict between Fatimid and Seljuk rulers led to a distortion in their understanding of the implications of the arrival of the crusading army. Over 100 years after the fall of Jerusalem to the Christians, it was still being said in the Sunni world that the arrival of the crusaders had been the work of the Fatimids. Once the Seljuks had reached Syrian lands and controlled cities as far south as Gaza, wrote the Sunni intellectual Ibn al-Athir, there was no buffer state between them and the Fatimids, who therefore sent to the Franks to invade Syria, to conquer it and separate them from their Muslim rivals. Ibn al-Athīr himself doubted this story; he was writing c.1212, long after the true nature of the Christian enterprise had become clear, but the basis for many Sunnis believing that the crusades were a Fatimid conspiracy was rooted in the actual historical experience. For it was undeniably the case that the Fatimids were initially well disposed towards the crusaders, seeing them as potential allies, allies capable of checking the hated Seljuks.[1]

At the time that the various strands of the Christian army set out in 1096, al-Afdal was struggling with the Seljuk threat to the Fatimid coastal cities of Palestine, the Bātinīd schism, and the effects of several years of plague in Cairo. Thoroughly misunderstanding the unique nature of the crusade – that it was as much a pilgrimage as a conventional army – al-Afdal saw only the possibility that he might be able to direct the Christians against his Seljuk enemies. The fact that crusaders had worked closely with al-Afdal's ally, Alexius Comnenus, the Byzantine Emperor, in order to capture Nicea from the Seljuks of Rum suggested that it might be possible to come to an understanding with them. Indeed, late in June 1097, some members of the Christian army sailed south to contact the Shia ruler.[2]

In return, ambassadors from Egypt arrived at Antioch during the siege just as the Christians celebrated their major victory over a sortie by the garrison, the day that Duke Godfrey had famously cut an opposing rider in two. The victorious Christian army put on a good show for the Fatimid delegation; they spruced up their tents and demonstrated their riding skills by marking out an arena for quintain by placing their shields on stakes. Quintain was a challenge that required a knight to ride at speed past a target that he aimed to strike with his lance. The target swung on an arm that was counter-weighted and the trick was to be moving fast enough that after you had smitten the target you were past the device before the weight could spin around and give you a belt, potentially throwing you from your horse. It was good practice at a skill that, along with their heavier armour, gave the Christian knight an advantage over his Muslim counterpart. Not that the crusaders were attempting to intimidate the ambassadors from Cairo; the possibility of a mutually beneficial agreement was recognized on both sides. After all, it was their common enemy the Seljuks who ruled Antioch and Jerusalem.

While the knights most proud of their riding prowess displayed their fighting skills and later their skill at chess, the senior princes behaved in a less competitive manner: hosting the delegation in their tents, holding lengthy and serious conversations about the political and military situation, and, eventually, sending their guests home on the best of terms, with a large cart full of Seljuk heads. Quite what the Fatimid ambassadors thought of the Christians digging up a Muslim cemetery to decapitate the corpses of those of the garrison who had been killed on 6 March 1098 is not left on record. But they bore away the grisly present with good grace.[3]

On the return of his embassy to Cairo and their report that the siege of Antioch was proceeding well for the Christians, al-Afdal took his *askar* and considerable quantities of wood needed for making siege equipment and marched towards Jerusalem, confident that his Seljuk enemies would be unable to mobilize against him. Already, in 1097, he had taken advantage of the disarray in the Seljuk world to regain the powerful maritime city of Tyre for the Fatimids and the time looked propitious for a strike at Jerusalem. Al-Afdal's advance could not, in fact, have been more opportune; for while the Egyptian army was being mobilized, his greatest rival, Kerbogha, atabeg of Mosul, suffered a catastrophic defeat at the hands of the Christians on 28 June 1098 outside of Antioch. If there was one Seljuk ruler capable of exerting sufficient hegemony over the various Seljuk emirs of Syria to lead a major army against the Fatimids, it was Kerbogha; with him out of the picture, there was a wonderful opportunity for the Fatimids to expand their realm and, in particular, to capture the prestigious city of Jerusalem.

Economically, as it stood some distance from the important trading routes to the coastal cities, Jerusalem was in decline. Had military or economic considerations solely determined the issue, al-Afdal might have prioritized other goals than the conquest of Jerusalem. But from its capture by Caliph 'Umar I in 637 the city had been treated with reverence and pride by Muslim rulers. This was most obviously demonstrated in the construction of the Dome of the Rock, the nearby al-Aqsā mosque and several other religious complexes in the years that followed. The Dome of the Rock is a spectacular example of Islamic architecture and it was completed in 692, possibly the earliest monumental work of art of Islamic civilization.

These buildings did not, however, decisively establish the importance of Jerusalem in Muslim theology. For three centuries Jerusalem was eclipsed by the overwhelming importance to Islam of Mecca and Medina. That Jerusalem came to be seen as the third most holy city for Muslims was due, above all, to the spread of the idea that the Dome of the Rock and the al-Aqsā mosque, whose complex formed the 'Haram', were connected with a miraculous nocturnal journey by the Prophet Muhammad from Mecca to Jerusalem. This journey, it was believed, saw the Prophet ascend to Heaven from the rock now covered by the Dome. During his ascension the Prophet conversed with Moses, after which he prayed. The five daily prayers observed throughout the Muslim world therefore became associated with Jerusalem. The definite connection between the night journey and the Haram came relatively late; it was not incorporated in the mosaics of the al-Aqsā mosque until the end of the tenth century.

In 1098, to own and control Jerusalem, therefore, was a great prize for the Fatimid caliphate, which, after all, had previously ruled the city and had been responsible for much of the original Islamic building and, indeed, rebuilding following the effects of earthquakes. Delighted by the opportunity created by the problems of his enemies in the north, al-Afdal brought his army before the walls of the city to face the Seljuk governors, Suqmān and Ilghāzī, sons of the previous governor, Artuq, who had died in 1091. With them were their cousin Savanj and their nephew Yāqūtī. Suqmān was the more able of the family, as Ilghāzī was prone to disastrous bouts of drinking: 'when Ilghāzī drank wine and it got the better of him', wrote a contemporary Damascene chronicler 'he habitually remained for several days in a state of intoxication, without recovering his senses sufficiently to take control or to be consulted on any matter or decision.'[4]

The crusaders who had been sent from Nicea to Cairo to liaise with al-Afdal watched the subsequent siege with a great deal of interest. Al-Afdal's strategy was simple and effective; he used his advantage in resources to build twice as many mangonels as his opponents could bring to bear. Then, from the north side of the city, his machines toiled away for over a month in a missile duel, until the wall was sufficiently breached that, in August 1098, Suqmān accepted terms. By this time both sides had learned of the defeat of Kerbogha and it was clear that there would be no assistance coming to the garrison from their co-religionists.

The surrender of Jerusalem to al-Afdal on 29 August 1098 was a relatively amicable affair. On his arrival in July, al-Afdal had sent letters to Suqmān and Ilghāzī, appealing to them to avoid bloodshed and surrender the city. The fact that there had been casualties in the exchange of missile fire over the month did not sour negotiations once Suqmān realized the situation was hopeless. Al-Afdal let the two brothers leave the city, along with their family, their followers and a large body of Turks.

The expectation of the ruler of Cairo was that the advance of the Christian army had more or less finished; after all, they were nearly at the limits of the old Byzantine borders. They had done very well to capture Antioch and would surely wish to consolidate their position in that region. This undoubtedly would have been the case if al-Afdal was dealing with a Byzantine army. But this was a Christian army of a very peculiar nature. It was driven by a theological commitment to the idea of Jerusalem and while there were several princes with whom sophisticated negotiations could take place, these lords within the Christian army were unable to speak for or control the masses of foot soldiers and non-combatants. Understandably, al-Afdal misinterpreted the dynamics of the situation. He left Jerusalem in the hands of his competent general, Iftikhār al-Dawla ('pride of the nation'), and returned to Cairo.

It must have been surprising therefore, when news of a southward moving Christian army was brought to al-Afdal early in the following year. Surprising, but not necessarily alarming. The Christians perhaps had their eye on targets on wealthy cities like Tripoli. Jalāl al-Mulk, the 'qadi' there, the spiritual and political governor, was nominally subject to the Fatimid vizier, but to all intents and purposes was ruling on his own account. Its loss could be borne.

On 13 May 1099, shortly after Count Raymond of Toulouse had been forced to abandon the siege of 'Arqā and the crusade had begun marching south again, a second embassy from Cairo came to the crusader camp. They offered continued friendship and should unarmed groups of Christians wish to journey to Jerusalem to visit their holy places, the Fatimid coastal cities would grant them safe passage. It was a civilized and respectful offer. But at the time of the previous embassy it was the Seljuks who controlled Jerusalem; now the Fatimids held the city and they were no longer allies in the eyes of the Christians. They were the enemy. This time there was no gaming, no negotiation, no exchange of presents. Rather, the ambassadors left with an unambiguous understanding of the state of affairs. They were at war.

The city of Jerusalem is built on a very uneven V-shaped ridge of land between two gorges, both steep sided and rocky (see Figure 3). Inside the walls of Jerusalem, the land rises and falls due to the presence of a valley that effectively divides the city into east and west. The Haram es-Sharif (the Noble Sanctuary) complex, containing the Dome of the Rock and the al-Aqsā mosque, is on the higher ground to the east, walled off from the rest of the city. Adjacent to the Haram, running along the entire eastern side of the Jerusalem is the Kidron Valley. Across the south and – as it turns northwards – across part of the western side of the city runs the Hinnom Valley. These two gorges merge just some two kilometres south of the city, creating cliffs and rocky slopes that gave the old city very strong natural defences around more than half of its walls. When the Roman general Pompey came to besiege the city in 63 BC, his assessment was that it could only be taken from the north, a policy that every subsequent attacker adhered to. This is because from the north the city has less of a natural defence, as there the spur of land on which Jerusalem is built connects to the broad plateau of central Judea.

In 1099 Jerusalem's defences were contracted compared to how they had stood in ancient times, reflecting a decline in the city's economic importance. As a consequence, it had become more vulnerable to attack in that the high ground – which had formerly been enclosed – only some 200 metres to the north now overlooked the current city walls. The southern wall of Jerusalem, too, was not as extended as it had been in 63 BC and as a result no longer took full advantage of the natural defences. Between the southern walls of Jerusalem and the cliffs of the two gorges there was a potential weakness: Mount Zion. This was a hill that had formerly been enclosed inside the city's defences, but now whose peak was just higher than the facing walls and from where attackers could move downwards to attack.

As the crusading forces arrived at the city, approaching from the northwest, there would have been a number of experienced soldiers present among them, whose first thought was to appraise the military geography of the city. But this was no ordinary army and no ordinary city. For many, the feelings evoked by the proximity of the city would not have been conducive to a clinical examination of its fortifications. For the devout Christian, Jerusalem was the ultimate pilgrim site, the centre of the world. The most sacred places of their religion were close, tantalizingly so. Everywhere the crusaders looked were places that evoked the life of Christ. Even the nearest gate to them, the 'Nablus gate' was, said those who knew the city, Pilate's judgement-seat, where Christ was judged by the chief priests. Not far beyond it could be seen the domed roof of the Church of the Holy Sepulchre. This, along with the nearby Golgatha, the site where they believed Christ to have been crucified, was their goal: a goal that had kept them marching through famine, thirst and the ever-present danger of attack. Now it was nearly theirs. Perhaps God would cause the walls to tumble for them? As they set up their camps, the overwhelming feeling among the army was that it would not be long before Jerusalem was in Christian hands. But which of their princes, if any, would be the new ruler of the Holy City?

The Christian army that arrived before the walls of Jerusalem on 7 June 1099 was a fragment of the massive force that had united at Nicea, some two years earlier. There had been many casualties on the way, from battle, but also from plague and starvation. Then, too, there had been those who despaired of victory, or personal safety, and had abandoned the expedition in a state of demoralization. Even greater losses in strength had arisen from the decision of Bohemond to remain at Antioch and Baldwin at Edessa, both retaining a substantial number of followers.

At its height the crusading army had, very approximately, 100,000 participants, of whom 7,000 were knights. Outside of Jerusalem, the Christians had
1,200–1,300 knights, 12,000 foot soldiers, and several thousand non-combatants,
perhaps 20,000 crusaders in all. It might have been expected that the bonds
created amongst these survivors of such an extraordinary journey were powerful ones forged by solidarity in face of death and hardship, strengthened by
common purpose and belief. Surely, now that they were at the place they had all
worked so hard to obtain, a sense of awe and fellowship would unite them?
Such sentiments existed within smaller groups of crusaders, but the army as a
whole was riven by divisions so great that effective leadership had broken down
and bitter regional rivalries soured all sense of unity.

The Normans were putting it about that the Provençals were experts at
foraging, to the neglect of fighting. Their children had a refrain with which
they taunted their southern French counterparts: 'the Franks go to fight, the
Provençals to food'. Far worse, given the vital importance of cavalry, the
Normans believed that the Provençals had a technique of wounding a healthy
horse through its rectum, so that the cause of death was impossible to deter-
mine. In times of hardship at the siege of Antioch they had deployed this trick,
so that fearing disease, the Norman owner of the carcass would decline to eat
the meat, leaving it for the Provençals to flock to it, like a pack of crows.[5]

Relations between the Lotharingians and the French, both north and south,
were little better. At Antioch, the Lotharingians had been caught resting while
guarding a wall that protected the Christians from attacks by those Turks still
in the citadel of the city. They had concentrated their troops on night duty, little
expecting a daytime attack. Having realized that there was a certain complacency among the guards of the wall during the day, the Turks in the citadel
stormed out in bright daylight, raiding deep into the Christian camp and inflicting many casualties before retreating safely back to their defences. As a result of
this failure by the Lotharingian guards, the French and Italian crowds had
roamed the streets shouting 'Germans are shit'. Duke Godfrey's men were still
smarting at the insult.[6]

The single largest faction of the Christian army was that lead by Count
Raymond of Toulouse, but not only was the elderly count unable to exert his
will over the other princes, even his own following had become insubordinate.
The depth of the discontent among the Provençals had already been revealed
by their shocking action in burning their own camp at 'Arqā, then setting out
for Jerusalem. Now, at the Holy City itself, the fact that this discontent remained
was made manifest as the Provençals set up their new camp.

In the west wall of the city, standing just to the southeast of the Jaffa Gate
was the major defensive structure of Jerusalem, a very massive tower from

Herodian times. Known as the 'Tower of David', it was build over a natural spring out of a red stone too hard to be vulnerable to undermining. The base of the tower consisted of large dressed stones sealed with cast lead. It was large enough to hold hundreds of people, having dwellings and a mosque within, and its defences had been supplemented by a deep ditch, which meant having to use a bridge to cross to the small gate that gave access to the ground floor of the tower.[7]

When the Provençal army had arrived at Jerusalem they had taken up a position opposite this strongpoint. But although their camp was secure enough, the prospect of launching attacks on this, the most well defended part of the city, was intimidating. Count Raymond therefore scouted further south, searching for a better position for his troops. Opposite the southern gate of Jerusalem he came to the very promising position of Mount Zion and immediately appreciated its potential. From here a southern force could realistically threaten the city. This was a much more favourable position from which to launch attacks than the west, not least because the intervening ground was flat enough to allow a siege engine to be moved up to the walls of the city. The great disadvantage of making camp at Mount Zion, however, was its vulnerability to counter-attacks. In fact, as they later proved, should the garrison of Jerusalem employ a powerful enough mangonel, they would be able to launch missiles right into the besiegers' defences.

Count Raymond announced that the Provençal camp would be at Mount Zion. He did so, however, not by arguing for the military advantages of the position, but in a manner that revealed that he still clung to the notion of his being a champion especially chosen by God to lead the crusade. There were ruins on the hill, those of the largely intact Church of the virgin, and those of a much more fragmentary structure, a synagogue known as 'David's Tomb'. Taking on the mantle of a prophet, Count Raymond announced that the sight of the ruins of the Church of St Mary on the hill had inspired him. 'If,' he asked, 'we should give up these sacred places that God handed to us here, will the Saracens not then occupy them, to take them from us? Might they not defile them and ruin them because of their hatred of us? Who knows, it could be that God has given us this trial, so as to prove our love of Him? Certainly, this above all I know: unless we carefully protect these sacred places, God will not give to us those that are in the city.'[8]

Count Raymond and the clergy in his entourage would have been very familiar with the deeds of Judas Maccabeus. This biblical commander, who had campaigned against the Seleucid Empire as military and religious leader of the Jewish people, was seen by the Latin clergy – especially those intellectuals associated with the papacy of Urban II and his predecessor Gregory VII – as the model of a 'knight of Christ'. According to the Old Testament, Judas Maccabeus had built a sanctuary on Mount Zion. Count Raymond was therefore echoing the deeds of this Christian champion and once more casting himself as a divinely approved leader, this time adding to his credentials by proclaiming knowledge of the will of God.

The other leading Christian princes thought it more advisable that the Provençal army remain facing the west wall, and thus be in on the right flank of a united army in direct contact with one another's camps, exerting pressure on the northwest and north walls of Jerusalem. The count's own soldiers were equally unconvinced of the need to move. In fact, they protested both at the relocation of the camp and also at the corresponding requirement that they would have to organize watches throughout the night. Very few Provençal knights came voluntarily to Mount Zion, the majority remaining on the west of the city. Fortunately for Count Raymond he was in control of a considerable amount of coin, gathered as tribute from the coastal cities that the crusaders had passed en route. With large payments from these funds, the count was able to attract a sufficient garrison of knights and foot soldiers to make the southern camp viable; viable providing he also use precious timber to construct a defensive palisade and gate between his camp at the city walls. The Christian army was now physically split in two, a potentially hazardous distance between the Provençals facing the south gate of Jerusalem and the other princes on the north side of the city.

The Lotharingian brothers, Godfrey and Eustace had the single biggest army on the north side and pitched alongside them were Robert of Normandy and Robert of Flanders. Nearby, too, were those with a smaller following, notably Tancred and Gaston of Béarn. The latter, being from Provençe, might have been expected to join the southern camp, but Gaston now thought his fortune would be better served in association with Tancred. His calculation was not mistaken, as he would shortly be given the important responsibility of overseeing the construction of the northern siege tower.

The association of proud and warlike knights who had once banded together under Hugh the Great also took to the northern camp. Drogo of Nesle, Everard of Le Puiset, Raimbold Crotton, Thomas of Marle and others had been first into Antioch at the storming of the city; they had been assigned the daring task of scouting for the arrival of Kerbogha's army as it approached Antioch; they had been among the most fervent in insisting that the army press on to Jerusalem; and now that they had reached their goal, they looked forward with eager anticipation to one final act of destruction, the glory of which would lead to their names being sung throughout Christendom.

The poor, both male and female, who in many cases had organized themselves in bands independently of the princely leaders, on the whole took to the southern camp. It was dangerously close to the city, true, but their religious spokespersons were in the southern camp as part of the entourage of Count Raymond. Peter Bartholomew was dead, but there were others, such as the priest Peter Desiderius, whose visions continued to express the importance of attending to the poor. Peter Desiderius was an ally of those Provençal knights who had come with the papal legate, Adhémar of Le Puy, and who now looked to his brother, William Hugh of Monteil, as well as Isoard I, count of Die, for leadership. Disillusioned as they were with Count Raymond, these lords were willing to accept his payments in return for their military activity. As the count was liberal with his money, paying for the filling of ditches, the serving of night duty and the hauling of timber, his camp offered greater attraction for the non-combatants than that set up on the north side.

There was another faction among the Christian army that crossed regional boundaries, creating a division as great as that between rich and poor: the clergy. Now that the expedition had arrived at Jerusalem, the clergy on the crusade were beginning to feel that their moment had come. They demonstrated their knowledge of scripture and of the pilgrim trail to show the laity the spiritual significance of the landscape around them. Here, for example, on the Mount of Olives, the hills to the east of the city, was where Christ ascended to heaven. There, at the ruins on Mount Zion, was where Mary departed the world, the place that the Lord broke bread with the disciples, and the place that Holy Spirit entered the disciples. Proud of their role as intermediaries between the army and God, the clergy were beginning to unite as a political force across their respective geographical contingents.

On 6 June, the day before the Christian army had reached Jerusalem, Tancred and his knights had ridden ahead into Bethlehem. There, according to the custom that evolved over the course of the expedition, he had raised his banner to signify the fact that he claimed the town. The most appropriate building for his purpose was the Church of the Lord's Nativity. But the sight of a military banner flying over the church, as if it were a temporal possession akin to a castle, scandalized the crusading clergy. After all, this was an expedition called for and organized by the pope. Moreover, what did Tancred's claim mean in the context of the seizure of Jerusalem?

By the start of July this discontent among the clergy had surfaced in the form of a major assembly at which the bishops and leading clergy made their case that the next ruler of Jerusalem should be a Latin patriarch. It would be wrong to elect a king where the Lord had suffered and was crowned. Yes, a

noble warrior could play an important role as servant of the Church and pro-
tector of Jerusalem, but they, the clergy, should rule. This division, between the
clergy and the princes, was potentially an extremely serious one, capable of
paralysing the army. It would have strengthened the clergy's ability to influence
the outcome of the crusade if Jerusalem had been promptly and miraculously
delivered to the Christians. Why, they told one another, shouldn't God, who was
able to make earth to tremble, shake down the walls of the city now that they
had arrived? Their hopes for divine intervention in the taking of the city per-
meated the whole army.

Soon after the crusaders had arrived at Jerusalem, Tancred had ridden up to
the top of the Mount of Olives – the 830 metre tall hills to the east of Jerusalem,
across the Kidron Valley – in order to study the city below him. From there he
could see the streets busy with people making preparations for the coming
siege. The Mount of Olives was home to several Christian hermits and one of
them approached Tancred. To their mutual surprise, they discovered that the
hermit had set out on his travels as a result of the destruction of his home lands
by Tancred's grandfather, Robert Guiscard. Now, however, the hermit took
Tancred's presence at Jerusalem as a sign of penitence by the Guiscardians and
was eager to help the Christian army. He predicted that if the city was attacked
on the 13 June, it would fall.

Their conversation was interrupted by the sight of five Muslim riders making their way up the rough terrain of the hill towards them. As these riders were
some distance from one another, Tancred declined to flee, but rather charged
the foremost, sending his body crashing from his mount. Turning on the second
rider, Tancred severely wounded the horse, which in its death throes brought its
rider to the ground, wounded and stunned from having smashed his head on
the ground. The third Muslim rider now arrived; having rushed on as fast as he
could to join battle while Tancred was still engaged; but too late. The young
Norman prince had time to round on him and slay him too. The last two riders
had seen enough, they turned and made their way as rapidly as they could back
to the safety of the walls, all the while being chased by Tancred, shouting war
cries.[9]

The other princes of the Christian army appreciated the value of the Mount
of Olives as a position from which to overlook Jerusalem and they were also
interested in meeting the hermit who had promised them victory in a short
space of time. On 12 June the hermit repeated his prophecy to a group of leading crusaders, insisting that if they attacked the city the following day until the
ninth hour, it would fall to them. 'But', the princes pointed out, pragmatically,
'we do not have the equipment needed to storm the walls.' To this the hermit

answered that 'God is omnipotent, if He desires it, someone with just a ladder can rush the walls. He is at hand for those who are working for the truth.'[10]

That evening the entire Christian army was full of talk and enthusiasm generated by the hermit's message, an enthusiasm that was fuelled by their proximity to the holy places. If Godfrey, Raymond, Robert of Normandy, Robert of Flanders, or any of the lesser princes thought the proposed attack absurd, they nevertheless dared not stand in opposition to the mounting excitement. During the night the army made ready to assault the city with whatever they could make from the limited materials at hand. Their effective equipment the next morning though, amounted to just one ladder. It is testimony to the fever-ish state of mind of the Christian forces and their hope in divine intervention that, regardless, they charged towards the walls on the morning of the 13 June.

What did the garrison and townspeople of Jerusalem think of this mob, carrying only one ladder, hurtling towards them? Contempt, no doubt, for their enemies' evident lack of the knowledge of the military arts; but perhaps fear also crept into their hearts. A fear not that this wild crowd might obtain some kind of miraculous aid, but a shiver of trepidation about what it might mean should this ferocious army somehow get into the city.

Volley after volley of arrow fire, a constant hail of sling stones, and the thun-derous release of large stones from mangonels took a heavy toll of the attacking forces. Nevertheless, the Christians reached an outer wall, which gave them cover while they took their mattocks and iron hammers to it. Throughout the morning, the ringing blows of the crusader tools struck against stone, until with a crash of rubble and dust, a section fell that was large enough to allow the attackers to press on to the inner wall of the city. By this time the initial giddy excitement of the attackers had become tempered and it was helmeted knights in chainmail who led the way, shields over their heads in a 'tortoise' formation. They bore the onslaught of missiles well, despite losses from arrows finding eyeholes and the blows of heavy masonry that crushed both shield and knight. Gaining the foot of the walls, these knights then raised up their ladder and stood it against the walls of the city.

For one glorious moment the eyes of the entire army, from the most senior princes to the lowest peasant, were raised enviously at the knight who now ascended the ladder and gained the honour of being the first to the top of the walls of the Jerusalem: Raimbold Croton. Raimbold had earned the right to try to be first into the city by his actions on the crusade thus far. He had been among those who risked climbing on to the walls of Antioch and entering the city on 3 June 1098, the night it was betrayed to Bohemond. After the incident where the Turks of the citadel had successfully raided the crusaders in the city proper, Raimbold was among a select few praised for taking responsibility for guarding the wall that protected the Christians. But now, above him, hardy Muslim warriors were pressing around the ladder. It would have been miraculous if under the circumstances Raimbold had managed to fight his way through them to stand on to the walls of Jerusalem. In fact, as soon as he placed his left hand on the wall of the city, one of the defenders chopped down upon it, so that the hand was almost severed. Raimbold fell back and was carried away.

He did not die of this wound, surviving to earn a reward from Godfrey the following year. For his bravery in mounting the ladder on 13 June, Raimbold was given a fragment of the True Cross, preserved in a cross-shaped reliquary covered with worked gold, a relic that stayed in his family for centuries. Indeed, his family adopted a white cross on a red background as their coat of arms in honour of their crusading ancestor. Verse makers relished this extraordinary incident and before long songs of Raimbold's bravery were being proclaimed across Christendom, with later legend ascribing to him the role of being first into the Jerusalem on the day that the city finally fell.[11]

Not that the actual warrior was as saintly as his later reputation was to suggest. On Raimbold's return to Chartres directly after the crusade, he became embroiled in a dispute with Bonneval Abbey in the course of which he castrated a monk who had beaten some of his servants, having caught them stealing hay from the abbey. As a result Raimbold was given 14 years' penance, which, on appeal to Pope Paschal II, seems to have been lifted in time for him to get himself killed at another siege, that of Montmorency in 1101, fighting with Louis VI of France against dissenting lords.[12]

While Raimbold escaped with his life there were other notable knights killed in this reckless and ill-prepared assault on the walls of Jerusalem, including Reginald, seneschal of Hugh of Liziniac. Despite the failure, the overall mood of the army was nevertheless optimistic. The feeling in both northern and southern camps was that but for the lack of a few more ladders, they could indeed have climbed into the city with no more strategy than the head on assault.[13]

The princes, though, settled down to a more sophisticated plan and one that relied less on the advice of hermits and visionaries. The truth be told, theirs was not a comfortable position. The greatest danger and one that they were already being warned about was that al-Afdal was assembling an army to come from Cairo to Jerusalem. There could be no question of conducting a long and protracted siege, such as that of 637 when Caliph 'Umar I took nearly a year to wear down the resistance of the defenders. In any case, if the siege turned into a test of attrition, there was no guarantee that the inhabitants of Jerusalem would run out of supplies before the crusaders. The question of keeping the army supplied with food was a difficult enough one, but the issue of water was more urgent still. No, if the Christians were to gain Jerusalem they had to do it swiftly, time was not on their side. Their instructions the day following the failed assault were to scour the land for timber in order that they could build the siege equipment that was so demonstrably needed.

Chapter 4

Thirst

When you lose two per cent of your normal water volume, you feel extremely thirsty and your mouth is constantly dry. With the loss of five per cent of your water volume, you have bouts of dizziness and painful attacks of cramp in your limbs caused by a rising concentration of sodium and potassium. Although the pain might make you want to cry, your eyes are too dry for tears to form. As your intestines dry out, you get bouts of severe abdominal cramps. A further symptom of protracted thirst is a constant feeling of lethargy. With the loss of ten per cent of your water volume, your lips begin to crack and dehydration of the mucous membranes causes nosebleeds. Your brain begins to shrink and you experience constant headaches and occasional hallucinations. While your body temperature rises – due to lack of sweat – your hands and feet feel cold; the body's circulation having withdrawn to the vital organs. With the loss of 15 per cent of your water volume you have only a matter of hours to find water before falling into a coma and dying. In the summer of 1099, so close to their goal, thousands of crusaders experienced exactly this progression of dehydration and many of them expired of thirst outside the walls of Jerusalem.

Both the crusaders and the Fatimid garrison understood that access to drinking water was the key logistical issue of the siege. Lack of water had the potential to force the Christian army to abandon the undertaking. Control of the water sources could be far more effective in the Fatimid cause than arrows and blades. Just how seriously the crusaders took the matter was evident as they turned away from the coast in their march towards Jerusalem. At Ramla, in the first week of June 1099, a special assembly of the Christian army was convened to discuss whether a siege of Jerusalem was viable. There was a body of opinion that argued against an immediate attack on Jerusalem, precisely because of the lack of water available to them. These crusaders proposed instead that the army stay close to the sea and attack Egypt. Reasonably enough, the majority of army were having none of this: their small force could not possibly mount an expedition to such remote regions. But to have even contemplated marching off towards Cairo shows how anxious were some of the crusaders over the question of water supply. The problem for the majority who wished to press on to

Jerusalem was that they had no answer to the question of where they expected water to be found. God, they conjectured – rather hopefully – would take care of the question.[1]

To stave off the effects of thirst an active male in a warm climate requires six litres of water a day. A horse in the same circumstances needs about 50 litres a day. Where were the Christian army to find a daily source of 200,000 litres of drinking water? The problem was that despite their swift advance from 'Arqā to Jerusalem, Iftikhār, the general commanding the defence of Jerusalem, had acted more swiftly still. For a distance of up to six miles from the city, the wells and many cisterns around the city were broken and their precious contents allowed to drain away, with filth and refuse thrown in to make them unusable. The less powerful springs that could be closed off or hidden were smothered under piles of rocks. Roman aqueducts bringing water to the city were broken at source. In the winter there was a creek at the bottom of the Kidron valley, but that was stone dry now and Iftikhār must have been satisfied that he had done all he could to exacerbate the difficulties of the besieging army.[2] The Muslim civilians of the region affected by Iftikhār's measures had to abandon their fields and vineyards, but at least they could obtain fresh water from the cisterns of Jerusalem. They entered the city as refugees in advance of the crusader army. The local Christian population had to fend for themselves as well as they could and they tended to gravitate towards Bethlehem and its ample water supply (see Figure 5).

Once they had set up their camps outside the walls of the city, the Christian predicament grew with each day of bright sunshine and soaring temperatures. July is the hottest month of the year for Jerusalem, with average high daytime temperatures of 31 degrees centigrade. In 1099, the suffering experienced by crusaders lacking shade and water was made worse by strong winds. The whirling dust from the rocky land around the city was choking. There was one source of hope, however, and that was En-Gihon, a spring that flowed from the southeast spur of the city. It lay below the ridge that held the very first human settlements in the area, known in ancient times as Zion, a very long bowshot from the current southern walls of the city. This spring, Gihon, was the reason why the area had become inhabited in the first place. Gihon was a powerful spring and during the wettest months of the year over a million litres a day flowed from it.

The problem with Gihon though, was that it was a siphon-type karst spring, that is, a spring that provides water which, having collected underground from sinkholes and sinking streams is siphoned to the surface each time a critical point is reached and the subterranean spaces filled. The rocks beneath and around Jerusalem are porous limestone. When it rains, a great deal of the water disappears underground into fissures in the rock, and, over the centuries, this flow has formed subsurface channels and caves. The conduits carrying water from each point where water sinks are joined together beneath the hills of Jerusalem to form a complex and erratic flow, which eventually pours forth at Gihon. Often the quality of the water coming from a karst spring is very poor, bringing with it a high level of sediment and minerals, and this is true for Gihon, especially in the summer months when the overall flow drops considerably. In a typical month the spring gushes for about 40 minutes, then ceases for six to eight hours. But both the frequency and volume of the Gihon's flow is irregular and considerably affected by the season. In the summer of 1099 it poured out its life-giving water only once every three days.[3]

The ancient city of Jerusalem was considerably larger than the medieval city that the crusaders arrived at in 1099, in particular, the southern walls of the First Temple period reached all the way to the sides of the Kidron valley. At the end of the eighth century BC, desiring to bring the water from the Gihon spring to a pool inside the walls, the Judean king Hezekiah took advantage of the natural fractures in the limestone to organize an impressive feat of Iron Age engineering. Pickaxe-wielding workers dug a tunnel over 500 metres long that brought the flow of the Gihon to the west and the Siloam Pool. By 1099, however, the wall of the city had retreated, to where the pool was nearly out of bowshot range. The crusaders could access the flow of the Gihon spring as it emerged in the Siloam Pool without too much danger. During the siege of Jerusalem, the scenes around this pool were nevertheless pitiful (see Figures 5 and 6).

No sooner did the water come gushing out from the rocks, turning an expanse of filthy paving into a deep pool, than a massive and chaotic ruck formed. Driven by their desperate thirst, the crusading army lost all discipline. The strongest among them got to drink clean water; the weaker, the dirty water escaping along the swampy course; and the weakest had to beg pitifully for whatever they could get. Sprawled on the ground they lifted outstretched arms, pleading to be allowed a mouthful of water. Thirsty pack animals and cattle also pressed towards the water on the days that the Gihon flowed. The crush was so strong that some of these animals died and their corpses added to the barrier through which the struggling crowds strove to pass. And if the flow came during the daylight hours, archers on the city walls would amuse themselves by launching long, speculative, shots towards the crowd.

Those unable to force their way through the mob to the clean flow of water were so desperate that they drank the filthy liquid that remained after the crowds around the pool had dispersed. Resorting to such sludge was dangerous. Muddy water consumed by the desperate could perhaps prevent their death by thirst, but at the cost of a new danger: suffocation. There were leeches in the dirty water, leeches whose suction allowed them to fasten hard to the throat. As the irritated flesh swelled, the throat closed and, gasping, the victim expired as though choked by a powerful and implacable hand.[4]

The nearest Christian prince to these scenes was Count Raymond of Toulouse. His authority was not great enough to impose any kind of order or systematic attempt to ration the fresh water when it came gushing forth. No one, especially those half way to death by thirst, could contain themselves when the fresh water gurgled into the pool. They elbowed their way through, fighting as much as their weakened bodies allowed, to slake their thirst and fill their water skins. Not that the Christian army was well equipped to store and distribute the water even if there had been greater discipline among them. The skins of dead oxen were sewn into crude bags to store and carry water, but these festered and the warm water from them was so rancid as to be nearly undrinkable.[5]

One curious result of mob rule over the waters of the Gihon was the appearance of a market for water. Sufficient water for a day for one person cost five or six *nummi*, bronze pennies. A mouthful of water was one penny. For an endeavour that emphasized charity and fellowship among the Christians, the crusade was surprisingly ruthless. If you couldn't afford the money, or weren't strong enough to fend for yourself, or in an association that protected its members, you died. Dozens of animals too, whose owners could not afford the cost of the water they needed, became so weak that they could not take another step and expired where they stood. As these creatures shrivelled and decomposed in the searing heat, the sickening – yet slightly sweet – odour of death spread over the crusader camps. It was the mules, oxen and sheep of the army that died in this way. Horses were too important to the army to allow them to suffer and the Christian knights could ride them to more distant sources of water, but it was camels that came into their own at the siege. Ever since their victory over Qilij Arslān near Dorylaeum on 1 July 1097, exactly two years earlier, the Christians had brought captured camels along with them. Despite their inexperience with such naturally uncomplaisant creatures, the value of having done so was now shown, as the camel's tolerance of the near desert conditions made it the most important pack animal of the siege.[6]

The princes of the Christian army, wealthy with tribute that they had extracted from Muslim cities on the march, had no great difficulty purchasing water from locals willing to supply them. Indeed, if you had the money, there were deliciously fresh fruits and fine wines to be enjoyed. Moreover, early in the siege an unexpected delight came to the princes. The exiled Greek Patriarch of Jerusalem was living in Cyprus at this time. When the news reached him that a Christian army was besieging Jerusalem, he eagerly sent a ship with a great quantity of grapes and wine to the Christian princes, who shared the refreshing gifts between them. More gifts – of pomegranates, fat bacons and other costly foodstuffs – arrived from Cyprus before the sea route was closed by the activities of the Fatimid fleet. Not that the crusading princes had any intention of restoring Simeon II to his office; the new Patriarch of Jerusalem would, of course, be one of their own: a Latin cleric. Still, the goods were very welcome and were enjoyed by the princes and knights, while the foot soldiers and poor of the Christian army looked on with envious eyes.[7]

Having a certain amount of wealth, the princes and their immediate followers had a much more luxurious lifestyle than the poor crusader. For the crusading elite there was no danger of death by thirst. But even they were not living in the manner that they would have been accustomed to on their own lands. Quite apart from having to share with the entire army the difficulties of heat and dust, after the grain from Ramla had been used up, none of the crusaders, prince or pauper, could obtain bread, apart from gluey and dissatisfying corn bread. Eventually that too ran short and for ten days the army began to experience hunger again with the possibility that, as at Ma'arra and Antioch, the poorest might once more die from starvation. For those dying of thirst, the pangs of famine actually gave some relief, which says a great deal about the agony of water deprivation.

The hardships experienced by the poor, who all the while were just a few hundred yards from the Holy Places they had walked over 2,000 miles to reach, proved to be too much for some. Desperate to earn heavenly reward and despairing of life a new pattern of martyrdom appeared in the Christian army. Many a semi-delirious crusader would expend their last energy in a dash to the walls of Jerusalem, where, unable to cry due to their dry tear ducts, he or she would spend their last moments kissing the stone before falling rocks smashed the life out of them. The garrison and townspeople of Jerusalem were quite encouraged by such signs of demoralization among the Christians and there was no need to waste arrows on such targets when a good heavy rock did the trick. One distasteful feature of this suicidal behaviour by the Christians though, was that the smell of death from the corpses, especially frequent along the south wall of the city, was making guarding the walls an unpleasant experience.[8]

Others crusaders showed their desperation in less suicidal a manner. They tried digging through the sandy soil, down to where the earth was damp, and they would put the dirt in their mouths, hoping to extract some of the water before spitting out the gritty earth. Even a lick of moisture was worth struggling for. Clusters of poor Christians formed wherever there were large lumps of smooth rock, such as marble. Although the atmosphere was generally dry, dawn brought a hint of dew; enough to encourage the crusaders lick the stones they were guarding, searching with their dry tongues for the slightest sensation of dampness.[9]

By contrast, the inhabitants of Jerusalem met all their needs from the deep cisterns that supplied the city with its water whenever – as was the case in 1099 – the supply from Roman aqueduct systems was interrupted. The largest of the open cisterns, Hezekiah's Pool, just to the west of the Church of the Holy Sepulchre, was 240 feet long, 140 feet wide. It had once been fed by aqueduct and could hold up to 18 million litres of water. Another great cistern – the Pool of Israel – was that immediately to the north of the Haram complex. It had an arched roof and marble pillars. Every time it rained, gutters from the roofs of many buildings directed the flow to this cistern. In addition to the major pools, hundreds of smaller cisterns were located in the city under houses and court-yards, fed by a system of pipes and channels from flat roofs and paved streets. Further away, between the Haram complex and the north wall, were two great cisterns that Iftikhār had ordered to be filled to the brim by the water brought in from outside the city. One of the pools was known as the Sheep Pool, because it was once used for washing the animals destined for sacrifice.

Tens of millions of litres of water gathered in the rainy season, from November to March, gave the population of Jerusalem confidence that they could last out the summer. The citizens prayed that the sky would remain clear and that the daytime temperatures continue to soar. They took hope, also, from the desper-ate scenes at the Pool of Siloam; perhaps thirst might defeat the Christian army. Given the presence of 400 extra horses and their riders as a supplement for the garrison plus an accretion of the civilian population – as villagers from the lands around Jerusalem sought protection in the city – Iftikhār decided there was no room for complacency and as a precaution ordered that the water be rationed and guarded. But all the same, those who presented themselves to the troops at the cisterns obtained the water they needed. There were no unruly scenes inside the walls of the besieged city, all the hardship and corresponding tumult was in the Christian camps.[10]

The siege of Jerusalem was an untypical medieval siege for many reasons, one of which was the fact that the besiegers were cut off from any military or logistical support. Apart from nearby Ramla and Bethlehem, themselves vul-nerable to Muslim raids, the nearest friendly city, Bohemond's Antioch, was impossibly far away, back through either Seljuk territory around Damascus or Fatimid territory along the coast. There was no prospect of supplies coming to the Christian army by an overland route. But the sea routes were hardly any more promising. It was true that ships from Cyprus could land at the port of Jaffa – a full day's march to the west – ever since the Fatimids had evacuated the town at the time of the approach of the Christian army. The walls and towers of Jaffa had been demolished, but the port and citadel still served. Yet to use it was risky. The large Fatimid navy of Cairo was at sea and seeking to intercept ships coming to aid the Christians and in any case the line of march from Jerusalem to Jaffa was very insecure.

The truth was that the spiritual lure of Jerusalem had drawn the Christian army into a very dangerous position, one that no commander looking only at the military factors would have considered viable. Indeed, nearly 100 years later, whilst at Jaffa and considering whether to strike inland to Jerusalem, Richard I of England, despite enormous pressure from the desire of his crusading army to capture the Holy City, decided that to attempt the siege would be disastrous. Logically, Jerusalem should only fall after several of the coastal cities and after a secure line of communication had been established. Al-Afdal, for example, had no difficulty the previous year keeping his army supplied with food and water while he spent a month eroding the north wall of the city with stone-throwing equipment because he controlled all the coast to the west of his army. But in 1099 the dynamics of the Christian army were such that not even Count Raymond of Toulouse, with his large following, was able to restrain the crusaders from rushing on to Jerusalem, despite the fact they had no secure lines of supply. And it was not just the poor and the foot soldiers who refused to countenance a more long-term strategy involving the capture of coastal cities, there was a great impatience among even quite senior figures to fulfil their vows and return to Europe.

The crusaders therefore had to conduct the siege of Jerusalem while being limited in supplies and vulnerable to attack, particularly as they dispersed their forces in search of water. Whilst the Gihon spring, in its erratic and mysterious manner, could intermittently keep the crusading army refreshed, it clearly was inadequate for their overall needs. This meant the Christians, especially knights anxious for the survival of their mounts, had to look further afield for water sources. Approximately four kilometres northwest of Jerusalem, on the far side of the watershed and therefore flowing away from the city, was the Mei Nefto'ah (the Waters of Nephtoah) spring. This was another abundant source of water in 1099, emitting some half million litres of water daily along a narrow channel, comfortably enough to satisfy the needs of the crusaders and their animals. But those four kilometres were extremely dangerous.

Knowing the territory well, Muslim soldiers set ambushes at the springs that they had been unable to block and at cisterns outside the six-mile radius of Jerusalem that still contained water. The garrison of Jerusalem was unable to ride out in large numbers undetected, but the fact that the Christian forces only faced approximately half the circuit of the city's walls meant that it was relatively easy for small numbers of soldiers to slip out and make their way through the rough terrain of the valleys east or west and then escape out to the countryside. Moreover, as word of the siege of Jerusalem spread, not only did al-Afdal's scouts from Ascalon ride through the region, so too smaller groups of local inhabitants gathered together, more interested in stealing the animals of the Christian army than picking off human beings. Not that they had any hesitation about killing crusaders if the opportunity presented itself. Many a group of crusaders were shocked to find the decapitated bodies of their colleagues at a watering spot and no sign of the animals that had been with them. The landscape was rocky, full of caves and hidden crevasses, the animals could be close but impossible to detect. On the hills of Jerusalem the early grapes were ripening and the vineyards too provided both a lure for the thirsty Christian and places for successful ambushes by local Muslim fighters.[11]

Despite all the dangers from ambush, the internal rivalries in the crusading army meant that reckless fighting sometimes broke out among them at these water sources. Local Christians from Bethlehem and Tekoah were eager to show the army where they could find water and led them five or six miles to the uncontaminated springs and wells. But sometimes when a band of thirsty Christians had formed up and marched through the heat of the day to their longed for goal, they would come across a great throng already ahead of them. Under such circumstances quarrels were frequent and escalated to full blown conflict, something that was all the more likely if the bands were from the opposite sides of the city.[12]

The Christian army had set up camp at Jerusalem on 7 June 1099. On the 13 June they had tried to storm the city with their one ladder. In the following days it became evident that information about the siege had spread to the nearby cities, whether controlled by Fatimid or Seljuk governors, and bands of Muslim riders roamed the hills. What little food and drink had been coming through to the Christian camp from merchants willing to trade with them was cut off and the signs of famine among the crusaders grew stronger. It was impossible to leave the camps without a sizeable escort, but to stay passive in the heat was to despair of life. Only a minority of the army were concentrating on the needs of the siege, the rest were simply attempting to preserve their energy and their lives. On the 17 June, however, a messenger reached the crusaders with exciting news. Six ships, four of which were Genoese, finding the port of Jaffa empty, had put in there and the sailors wished an escort for the dangerous 35km march to Jerusalem, so that they could fulfil their pilgrim's vows. They also requested a garrison for the citadel of the port, to guard the ships in their absence.

Count Raymond was first to react to the messenger and the French knight Geldemar Carpinel hurried out of the southern camp at dawn on the 18 June 1099 with 20 knights and 50 foot soldiers, while his colleague Raymond Pilet followed on as soon as he could make ready with 50 knights and after him William Sabran with his own entourage. The reason for their haste was that the princes of the northern camp were also interested making contact with the Genoese and Godfrey of Lotharingia had dispatched Baldwin of Bourq (not to be confused with Godfrey's brother Baldwin, who in 1099 was consolidating his rule of Edessa) westwards. Accompanying Baldwin was Thomas of Marle.[13]

This was a very illustrious race. Many of the most important Provençal knights were on the march. In Geldemar's party were the Burgundian prince Gilbert of Traves and a castellan of the same region, Achard of Montmerle. The latter knight already had a great reputation for piety and military prowess. Achard had mortgaged his patrimony to the monastery of Cluny in return for 2,000 solidi and four mules in order to join the crusade and his donation charter included a clause covering the possibility he might stay in the Holy Land. In the years to come he would turn into a legendary figure, with epic songs composed in his honour and it is clear from them that local traditions indicated Achard had already earned a reputation for bravery before departing on the crusade.[14]

Hurrying after Geldemar and the Burgundians came Raymond Pilet, lord of Alès. Whenever Count Raymond of Toulouse found it necessary to detach troops from the main Provençal army, his commander of choice was Raymond Pilet. After Kerbogha had been defeated and while crusade was at a standstill due to the dispersal of the princes to nearby cities, Raymond Pilet had even led an army of his own. Recruiting many knights and foot soldiers he had marched southeast from Antioch with some initial successes. Raymond Pilet's army was, however, defeated in an attempt to storm Ma'arra, 27 July 1098. Thereafter he resumed a place among the army of Count Raymond. In the company of Raymond, vicomte of Turenne, he temporarily took Tortosa on behalf of his lord, and earlier at the siege of Jerusalem he had given great encouragement to the Christians when, on 10 June 1099, again with Raymond of Turenne, his patrol encountered 200 Arabs whom he put to flight, returning to the southern camp with 30 captured horses.

The two leaders of the northern troop were equally notable. Baldwin was a kinsman of the duke of Lotharingia who had been among the followers of his namesake, Baldwin of Boulogne on the detour to Tarsus in 1097 that had seen the Lotharingians come to blows with Tancred's Norman army. Later Baldwin of Bourq would go north to serve with Baldwin at Edessa and in time not only inherit the lordship of that city, but also the crown of Jerusalem. With him in the ride towards Jaffa was the notorious Thomas of Marle. Thomas was out to prove himself as a valiant knight and was already celebrated in the Christian army for his role at the battle of Dorylaeum (1 July 1097); for being among those who risked going ahead on to the walls of Antioch on the day of its capture (3 June 1098); and for his vigorous fighting in the battle against Kerbogha (28 June 1098).

There was a dark side to Thomas' valour though; he had been prominent in the savage attacks on the Rhineland Jewish population in 1096 and on his return from crusade he cruelly tortured his enemies, including the clergy, as he strove to build up his power in the vicinity of Laon, Reims and Amiens. While popular songs of a later era celebrated his crusading deeds, the stories circulated about Thomas by contemporary clerical authors were grim and it was said that his preferred method of torture was to hoist a man by his genitals and leave him hanging until the soft flesh was torn away.[15]

Throughout the long day's march Geldemar pushed on hard for Jaffa. This celerity was a mistake. On a plain near Ramla Geldemar's small troop were shocked to encounter 600 well-equipped Fatimid horsemen from Ascalon. How did the tiny force of 20 Christian knights respond to the presence of large numbers of enemy light cavalry before them? As was almost inevitable, they charged. Whilst this bravado might have surprised the Muslim cavalry it was exactly what they were trained to deal with. Given enough room – and here there was plenty – they could scatter while firing over their shoulders, before circling back, always just out of contact. This was Dorylaeum in miniature. Geldemar's best hope would have been to hold his knights in check behind a defensive line of foot soldiers until the following crusader knights came to assist him. In the event, Geldemar's attempt to rout the Muslim cavalry was a failure; the clouds of arrows that assailed the Christian knights and their horses began to take their toll. Before long, several crusader corpses lay in the dust, including those of Achard and Gilbert. The foot soldiers, although many were equipped with bows, were no match for the hundreds of mobile archers all around them; lacking the chainmail armour that was preserving the lives of the knights they were shot at mercilessly, until every one of them was dead.

The surviving Christian knights fled in disorder back towards Jerusalem and straight into the company of Baldwin and Thomas. On seeing their fellow knights, regional differences were forgotten and the survivors of Geldemar's troop were invigorated by Baldwin's eagerness for battle. Straight away they returned to the site of the conflict and, still heavily outnumbered, once more charged in among the Muslim riders. This time the struggle was more evenly matched and for a long time a running engagement took place. The outcome remained in doubt, especially after Baldwin was struck in the chest and wounded: surviving thanks only to the protection of his armour.[16]

A cloud of dust from the east announced the arrival of Raymond Pilet's experienced troop of Provençal knights. They had been spurred on by the news from a messenger, urging them to come to the assistance of Geldemar and his men, who, the messenger cried, might already all be lying dead. The Arab and Turkish riders from Ascalon did their best to cope with the new balance of forces. They attempted to form two divisions, in order to draw the crusaders on with one, while encircling them with the other: their favoured manoeuvre for larger scale battles. But in the heat and dust, while still engaged with the earlier body of knights, this proved impossible. As the Provençal knights thundered into the engagement the line between orderly withdrawal and panicked rout was crossed. Suddenly Muslim riders were fleeing in all directions and over the course of four miles a great many of them were slain.[17]

A lamentable encounter from the Christian point of view, one that had led to the death of Achard of Montmerle, a great hero of theirs, had, nevertheless, ended in a most encouraging victory. In time they would return to the camps at Jerusalem with striking proof of their success, they had taken 103 horses and a captive. The prisoner fell to Baldwin of Bourq and had been kept alive amidst the general slaughter because of his visibly noble bearing. For one thing, the Fatimid warrior was very stocky and only the nobility were corpulent. He was elderly and bald headed: a most promising prize. Baldwin brought his captive back to the northern camp where he kept a rather elegant tent complete with couches covered in precious purple cloths. His captive took to the extravagant seating as if in his natural element, another sign of his illustrious status. Over the next few days, as Baldwin recovered from his wound and talked to his prisoner with the aid of an interpreter, it was clear the Muslim was a wise, noble and vigorous man. They talked a great deal about one another's customs and life-styles. The Christian clergy were hopeful that this dialogue might encourage the Ascalonite noble to convert to Christianity, but when this was put to him, the elderly Muslim was scornful.

While the overall mood in the Christian camp was celebratory following the victory of 18 June, their cheer was spoiled by the news of the death of Achard and Gilbert. The bodies of these two knights had been recovered in the after-math of the skirmish and they were placed by priests in a sepulchre outside the walls of Jerusalem that was given over for Christian burials. A large crowd assembled to watch the funeral rites and it was no doubt partly to appease their anger as well as to demoralize the jeering figures on the walls of the besieged city that the harmonious and civilized relationship between Baldwin and his captive came to an abrupt end. The elderly Muslim nobleman was taken to a spot right in front of the strongest point of Jerusalem's defences, David's Tower, and forced to kneel forward. There, in full view of both the garrison of the city and a huge gathering of crusaders, Baldwin's squire stepped up and hacked off the prisoner's head.[18]

Meanwhile, with the booty having first been divided, the Provençals under the leadership of Raymond Pilet had pushed on to Jaffa to represent the crusad-ing army to the Genoese. The sun was setting on the far side of the Mediterra-nean as the Christian knights rode through the dismantled walls of the city. A merry evening lay ahead as the Genoese, led by William Embracio and his brother, hosted the successful knights with a meal of fresh bread and fish and all the wine they cared to drink. It was a welcome relief for the knights from the thirst and hunger of the siege camp and the joy of their victory earlier in the day gave them all the more license to indulge themselves.

The following morning, 19 June 1099, the Genoese arose to find their joy turned to utter dismay. Spread across the western horizon, allowing no possi-bility of escape, was the great Fatimid fleet. Even now the enemy ships were coming on the tide and if the wind had been more favourable, they might have overwhelmed the port before the sailors had stirred. How they rued their lax behaviour of the night before and their failure to post proper lookouts from dawn, lookouts that might have seen the approaching sails in time to give the Christian ships the chance to flee the harbour before they were penned in. As it was, they had to hurry to load the knight's horses with as much of their supplies and equipment as they could before the Fatimids landed.

Belatedly climbing the tower to confirm their situation was hopeless, the lookouts gazed enviously to the north, where one of their comrades was in the fortunate position of having sailed in search of plunder before the arrival of Raymond Pilet. Although laden with pirated goods, this crusading ship was outside of the trap and made good its escape to Byzantine-controlled Latakia, 500 kilometres away. From there they were able to send news to Bohemond at Antioch and Baldwin at Edessa, stressing the difficult state of affairs at Jerusalem. But in the summer of 1099 neither of the northern Christian princes was willing to undertake the hazardous journey south to assist their co-religionists.[19]

From Raymond Pilet's perspective, the situation was not so disastrous, far from it. There was, admittedly, the prospect of a dangerous journey back to Jerusalem. With most of the horses burdened with the sailor's goods it would be a long slow march. But the victory of the previous day had been so complete there was little danger of encountering a substantial body of Fatimid cavalry en route. Furthermore, these sailors were skilled in craftsmanship. The Provençal detachment could return with priceless equipment salvaged from the ships: iron hammers and nails, carpenter's axes, rivets, pick axes and smaller hatchets. Best of all they carried great lengths of good quality rope, essential for the making of mangonels, trebuchets and siege towers. Confident he could speak for his lord, Raymond Pilet promised William Embracio that he would be well received by Count Raymond and well paid for assisting them in making equipment for the storming of Jerusalem.

Once they had arrived safely at Jerusalem, the spirits of the sailors lifted. They hurried on to the famous river Jordan where they gathered palms and had themselves baptized. This had been their goal since taking the pilgrim's vow, and having bathed in the Jordan their intention had been to find their way home by ship, in whatever way they could. But their ships were now at the bottom of the harbour in Jaffa. In any case, the Provençal clergy assured them, it was clearly God's will that the sailors remain to assist in the taking of Jerusalem. To put the matter beyond doubt Count Raymond did indeed promise William Embracio wages from the treasure chest and a place at his camp in Mount Zion. It was a coup for the Provençal camp to have the sailors with them, but one they had earned through Raymond Pilet's victory against the large body of Muslim riders from Ascalon. The prospect that the crusaders, and Count Raymond in particular, could capture the city had dramatically improved, for they could now set to work on the ambitious siege equipment necessary for an assault on the walls.

Chapter 5

Siege Warfare

Two days after the failed attack on Jerusalem on 13 June 1099, the over-optimistic assault in which Raimbold Crotton had momentarily laid a hand on top of the wall of the city, the senior figures of the crusade – north and south – met to discuss their strategy. Once it was clear to the army the city was not going to be given to them by the miraculous intervention of God, more sober and calculating voices could be heard. The time for wishful thinking was over and any honest assessment of the position of the Christian army had to admit that it was a difficult one. Already, in the week since they had arrived at Jerusalem, it was clear that the situation favoured the inhabitants and garrison of the Holy City.

The issue of water supply, as the pessimists had foretold, was a nightmare. Those who died of thirst or who were ambushed while seeking water in the hills around the city could not be replaced. If the siege were to become a war of attrition then the crusaders would lose, their strength and morale eroded by the difficulties of obtaining enough fresh water each day to keep themselves and their beasts alive. At Antioch the Christians had suffered a great deal, but they had been able to sustain a nine-month siege thanks to the proximity of friendly or conquered towns and the possibility of reinforcement by sea. At Jerusalem, as the fate of the Genoese ships was to make clear, no further troops or equipment could be expected from the coast, while the land route was impassable to all but a major army. Left to their own resources, it was hard to imagine the siege lasting several months; especially given the blazing heat of the Palestinian summer.

Moreover, the lack of nearby water supplies was not the only reason for thinking that the siege would have to be brought to a swift conclusion. Rumours were already reaching both the Christian camp and the garrison of Jerusalem that the vizier of Cairo, al-Afdal, was assembling a great army to come to the relief of the Holy City. The capital of the Fatimid Caliphate was 264 miles from Jerusalem. Supposing that al-Afdal's preparations were nearly complete, that might give the crusaders as little time as a fortnight to take the city or else having to risk battle with an active enemy either side of them.

The morale of the army was a cause for anxiety too. For the moment every-one was deeply committed to the siege, but with the flush of excitement at having arrived at their long yearned for destination having passed, dissention was already spreading through the separated camps. Not unreasonably, it had dawned on some crusaders that the reward for their extraordinary march might not be a triumphant entry into Jerusalem but their own destruction. They began to complain to one another that all the battles had been in vain. All their hunger at Antioch had been in vain too. And while the more spiritual crusader took consolation in the thought that the additional hardship they were now experiencing would help earn them salvation in the end, the battle-hardened military leaders focused their discussion on the necessary steps required to launch an attack on the city, measures that had a realistic prospect of breaking through in the short space of time they had at their disposal.

Among the leaders of the Christian army were knights with a great deal of experience at siege warfare. Robert, duke of Normandy, had fought for three years against no less a figure than his father, William the Conqueror. The Vexin in northern France, the location of their sieges and battles, was at the forefront of castle-building technology and no warrior pursuing a career there would have failed to pay attention to the science of siege warfare. Similarly, standing on rocky heights that dominated the River Semois, was the heart of the domain of Duke Godfrey of Lotharingia: the castle of Bouillon. Soon after his succes-sion to the city, in 1076, Godfrey had been obliged to fight for his life and his patrimony by defending the castle and town from an attack from a powerful local rival, Albert III, count of Namur. Not only did Godfrey successfully defend himself, but he was able to take the offensive, attempting to establish his authority through battles and sieges against his enemies. The lesser princes in the northern camp also knew much about the techniques for the capture of cities. Tancred had come away from the siege of Bari to join the crusade with his uncle. Even more relevant to their current situation, Gaston of Béarne had previously campaigned against Muslim cities in Iberia. On the southern side of Jerusalem were Provençal leaders with just as much experience in the strategies and tactics that had to be employed in the capture of towns and castles; although Count Raymond's own experience of siege warfare was limited to rather minor conflicts in Languedoc. In any case the entire army, from the veteran com-manders of wars between the European nobility to the lowliest pauper, had seen how those who had expertise in such matters had successfully set about Nicea, Antioch and Ma'arra.

Once the prospect of conducting a long siege that would starve the garrison into surrender was ruled out, there were essentially two ways to capture the city: batter down a section of the walls down or climb in over them. The defences of the city were strong, but not as intimidating as those of Nicea or Antioch. The main obstacle preventing the capture of Jerusalem was its inner wall, a tall – between 12 and 15 metres in height – but not especially thick wall, the course of which had been drawn up by Fatimid governors following an earthquake in 1033. The foundations of sections of the walls, especially on the east and west sides, might have been Byzantine, or even more ancient, but the line as it stood in 1099 reflected the decline in the population of the city. Rather than try to encompass all the advantageous terrain at the cost of having to enclose a great number of abandoned buildings and empty spaces, the Fatimids drew the wall much closer to the city, taking stones from ruined buildings and Christian churches outside the new boundaries. One drawback of this new shape to the city was that Mount Zion and the Pool of Siloam were outside the defences, but this was more than offset by the sturdy new wall and a shorter perimeter that could be more easily manned.

After their conquest of Jerusalem in 1073, a succession of Seljuk governors – Atsiz b. Uwaq, Turtush, Artuq and his sons Īlghāzī and Suqmān – not only maintained the wall with stone obtained by destroying monasteries and other remaining buildings outside the city, but they also considerably improved the defences of Jerusalem. To help protect the walls of the city from being scaled or approached by a siege tower a deep ditch was constructed that ran outside for most of the circuit. There was no need for a ditch on the east side of the city; the Kidron valley more than served the purpose there. But, initially to strengthen the defences of David's Tower, a substantial dry moat was dug around the tower, cutting off the stronghold from the city proper: to cross from the city to the tower now meant using a bridge. This ditch was then extended northwards along the west wall, around the corner and east as far as the 'Goliath Citadel', a sturdy defensive point on the corner with the northern wall. As the land along the north wall became less rocky and a little softer, the ditch was continued as a formidable obstacle, up to 7 metres deep and 19 metres wide, stretching along to the Kidron valley. A similar ditch, too, protected the southern wall, so that where nature had not provided defence through height, human engineering had done all it could to deter assault upon the walls of the city.

Moreover the Seljuk governors had completed an extra line of defences just inside the ditch in the form of outlying strongpoints – salients – and an outer wall. The outer wall was not a great obstacle to attackers, on the twelfth of June the crusaders had brought down a section with pick axes, before running on to the tall inner wall with their one ladder. It did serve, though, to obstruct the line of flight of stones cast on low trajectories from mangonels, preventing the missiles from striking low down on the inner wall. This smaller outer wall was not free standing, but connected to the city at various points, creating narrow areas of enclosed 'no-mans land' between the two walls.

In 70 AD, when Titus Flavius Sabinus Vespasianus (later Emperor Titus) brought his legions to besiege Jerusalem, the technology of stone throwing machines was not advanced enough to throw missiles of sufficient weight to damage the walls. Their *tormenta* were mainly anti-personnel devices, such as *ballista*, which flung round stones and darts with a fair degree of accuracy. They could keep up a discouraging fire against the defenders of a city, but they were not heavy enough missiles to cause a breach in the walls. For that the most effective Roman device was the heavy ram. A thousand years later though, as the crusaders had proved at Nicea, stone-throwing machines were capable of flinging sufficiently heavy rocks against the walls of a city, over and over, until they began to crack. In part this was due improvements in the mangonel, the device driven by rope torsion that flung its rocks forward from the release of a giant wooden spoon. But even more effective at weakening defensive walls was the trebuchet.

The trebuchet was essentially a giant sling. It stood upright from the ground and had a sling dangle from one end of an arm that was attached to the frame of the machine by a pivot. Pulling down sharply on the other end of the arm caused the sling to swing up and over, casting its contents forwards. The knowledge of such devices came from China, where they were used as early as the fifth century BC. The early versions of the trebuchet relied on raw human power for energy. Teams of people would haul on ropes to bring down the arm as fast as they could and so cast the missile from the sling. The rocks thrown in such a crude fashion, however, were not so heavy as to threaten the walls of cities; they were best used against formations of foot soldiers. The full potential of the trebuchet would be realized about a hundred years after the First Crusade, when instead of human muscle powering the device it was discovered that releasing a great weight – first ratcheted high off the ground – would bring down the arm of the sling with far greater violence but also, vital for repeatedly hitting the same spot, with far greater accuracy.

Such 'counter-weight' trebuchets were unknown in 1099, even to the crusading engineers and sailors most adept at construction. But they did know that a balancing weight on the other side of the arm to the missile made it a lot easier to fling the contents when they hauled on the ropes. These devices were 'hybrid' trebuchets, they used weights to assist in the pulling down of the throwing arm, but they still relied on teams of people hauling on ropes to set the sling in motion. Trebuchets, because of their advantage in range over the mangonel, were what the Christian army needed for the artillery battle ahead. Of course mangonels too, would be useful. But unless the crusaders were able to make very many machines they would be at a disadvantage. For inside the city Iftikhār had a great many mangonels left in the city after al-Afdal's bombardment of Jerusalem the previous year. Enough that he could form a considerable battery and, if the Christians brought their machines into range, defeat them in a rock-throwing duel.

Along with the stone-throwing machines, the leaders of the Christian army also wanted to construct a ram. Josephus' account of how Titus had broken into the city was well known to literate members of the Christian army and the inner walls, while tall, were not so thick as to discourage the idea of using this most direct form of attack on them. A good stout timber with an iron head could do a great deal of damage to such stonework, provided it could be positioned at the wall and provided those working it had protection while they swung the heavy ram back and forth. Above all, however, the crusading princes wanted siege towers. Even with trebuchets and a ram, it could take precious weeks, months even, to create sufficient damage to the walls that they disintegrated to the point where an assault could hope to succeed. With siege towers, on the other hand, it would be possible to try to storm the city whenever they chose.

At the end of the council of 15 June there was unanimous accord among the Christian leaders. No more futile attempts would be launched at the city, instead the priority of the crusader army was the construction of the machines necessary for a serious assault. This was all very well, but for two problems. The poor, both non-combatants and foot soldiers, were too distracted by their struggle to meet their daily needs to attend to such constructions and moreover, there was no wood available for the crusaders to fashion into the necessary devices.

The Christian army at Jerusalem was severely hampered in its newfound resolution by a lack of timber for the construction of siege equipment. This was a consequence of the Fatimid siege of the city the previous autumn. Not only were all orchards and major copses cut down for miles around Jerusalem, but even nearby buildings had been left derelict and depleted of timber. The local Christians, currently gathered for their safety in Bethlehem, reported of two sources of wood. The nearest was a copse some six or seven miles away that had a number of trees; the quality of the wood, however, was barely adequate for serious construction. More useful was a trail that led to over the hills north of Jerusalem to a good-sized wood near Nablus. This wood had cypress trees, silver firs and pines, but it was over 60 kilometres away in territory where there was a significant danger that large numbers of Muslim cavalry from Damascus would be encountered. Nothing was done, therefore, until the arrival of the

Genoese sailors and their equipment at the southern camp galvanized the whole army.[1]

Count Raymond set to work at once on a massive siege tower. The sailors were brought to the southern camp by Raymond Pilet to be greeted with enthusiasm by the grizzled Provençal leader. William Embracio shook hands on an agreement that offered him and his men a generous allowance from Count Raymond's treasury. In return, they would build a most impressive wooden tower. With the arrival of the sailors and their willingness to serve him, the count enjoyed the very tangible prospect of becoming the knight who captured Jerusalem for Christ. The sailors had brought all their tools with them from Jaffa, but they had only modest supplies of timber. The count had a solution to this difficulty. Suffering more than any Christian from hunger and thirst were throngs of captive Muslims brought along with the Provençal army to be ransomed or sold as slaves if circumstances permitted. Circumstances had not permitted and a use was now found for these unfortunate prisoners. They were set work in slave gangs of 50 or 60, carrying on their shoulders timbers that even four pairs of oxen would have struggled to drag.[2]

The person assigned with the responsibility of leading the slaves out to bring timber to the Provençal camp was Peter of Narbonne, the recently created bishop of Albara, appointed following the capture of the city by Count Raymond (12 December 1098). Peter was formerly a chaplain to the count and as his candidate for the bishopric remained loyal to him. When the poor had mutinied, concerned that placing garrisons in every captured city would lead to the disintegration of the main army, they had torn down the walls of Ma'arra so that there could be no question of a garrison remaining safely behind. Peter had done his best to prevent this, touring the walls with his men and using force on those they caught tumbling the walls. But no sooner was the bishop out of sight, than the crowds had set to work once more; no matter how elderly or infirm, they had crawled the walls to assist in their destruction. As a result, Peter abandoned his new see and – on the orders of Count Raymond – having sent for the 7 knights and 30 footmen he had left to garrison Albara, took up a position with Tancred at the head of the Christian army as they all marched south.[3]

Peter of Narbonne was a good choice of commander for the labour needed to bring timbers to the southern camp. He had the military resources to protect his charges, but as one of the most senior voices within the clergy, he also was in a position to encourage a major voluntary effort by the considerable numbers of poor who clung to the Provençal contingent. His urgings met with willing hands, for it was clear to the entire Christian army that the sooner the siege tower was built the sooner their hardship would end. As a consequence it seemed like the will of God was at work among them. From having made only a desultory contribution to the siege, a renewed optimism filled the poor and fuelled a considerable effort by the Christians to bring to the camp all the materials that the Genoese sailors needed. Even though only the sailors and the knights protecting the camp were being paid, many enthusiastic volunteers from among the poor laid out the foundations of a giant wooden tower. By the end of June, Count Raymond could cast his eye over the proceedings with a certain sense of satisfaction.

In the northern camp a similar sense of urgency galvanized the army, with an additional desire for haste injected by a desire not to fall behind the achievements of the Provençals on Mount Zion. Robert of Flanders and Robert of Normandy took camels, now the most invaluable pack animal of the crusade, to the hidden copse a few miles from Jerusalem to cut the timber that had been shown them by a local Christian. Accompanying the two Roberts on this journey was a notable warrior among the Christian forces, Gerard of Quierzy.[4]

There were many French knights who had come on the crusade as independent figures, owing vassalage to none of the major leaders and, indeed, sometimes bringing a few followers of their own. For a while they had been loosely affiliated to Hugh the Great, brother of the king of France. But Hugh had never returned from an embassy to Alexius after the defeat of Kerbogha. These knights therefore gravitated towards the company of one or other of the senior princes. For reasons of language and temperament Gerard preferred to ride with the two Roberts, where he was very welcome. He had a fine reputation among the Christian army, partly for the excellence of his horse, but also from his deeds at the battle of Dorylaeum. There, after the main body of Qilij Arslān's troops were scattered, a particularly bold Turkish warrior remained on a ridge, refusing to retreat. Gerard rode for this defiant cavalryman and skilfully deflecting a potentially lethal arrow with his shield, plunged a lance into the warrior's lungs.[5]

The story of Gerard was to echo that of Agamemnon, particularly in regard to the manner of his death. For after his triumphant return to France, his energy in pursuit of war made him a great man, despite his small stature and lean body. He was one of the barons of the region of Soissons and held the title of guardian of the convent of Saint-Jean of Laon. Gerard's tongue, however, was rather too free and the fact that on getting married he spurned his former lover, Sybille, countess of Coucy, earned him the fierce hatred of the countess. Plotting with Bishop Gaudry of Laon, Sybille arranged for Gerard's murder. On 7 January 1110, Gerard, who was known for his devotion to the Church, rose at dawn and made for Notre-Dame Cathedral. There, two carefully chosen knights were ready to ambush the veteran warrior. But they still feared the celebrated crusader. Waiting until Gerard was praying, they rushed to him and pulled his purple cloak tight around his body, to prevent him from wielding his sword. Slashed in the throat and legs, Gerard screamed out for help in the nave of the church, but the poor in the church and the clergy who were not involved in the conspiracy were too afraid to come to his assistance. This hero of the First Crusade, celebrated in song across Europe, bled to death before the altar: a squalid and ignominious end to a proud military career in the service of the Church.[6]

The short expedition by Gerard and the two Roberts was entirely successful in that they returned to camp without injury. The quality of the timber they brought with them, was, however, disappointing. It was too soft to serve for the construction of sturdy siege equipment and the northern camp therefore had to plan on making a major undertaking to obtain timber from the woods around Nablus.[7] Of the northern leaders, the prince most dedicated to the spiritual aspect of the crusade was Robert of Flanders. Every day he proudly displayed his cross over his armour and he harboured no ambition to be ruler of Jerusalem. Rather, he wanted to worship at the Holy Sepulchre, to restore the Holy City to Christian rule, then return to northern Europe with his men. When he offered to lead a body of woodsmen to Nablus it was not, therefore, an act prompted by a desire to win popular approval for the sake of his future ambitions in the region. He simply accepted that the risky journey had to be undertaken by someone and was prepared to volunteer.

Robert's was a force of 200 soldiers, enough that he feared no attack from Fatimid scouts or the ambushes of local Muslims. His concern, however, was that by straying some three days from the main Christian army, he might encounter the full *askar* of one of the stronger Muslim leaders of the region. In particular, the greatest danger lay 150 kilometres to the northeast, where Duqaq, the powerful emir of Damascus, was quite capable of bringing his troops south on learning of the proximity of a small Christian army.

In the event, the actual experience of those who undertook the hazardous search for timber turned out to be pleasant rather than dangerous. The Christian detachment was undisturbed by any alarms or any sightings of Muslim troops. They were in a region with plenty of fresh water and, at last, both man and beast could slake their thirst as often as they pleased. Having set up camp, the woodsmen chopped down the trees, lopped them, and cut them into stout lengths of timber, while the knights enjoyed their favourite pastime: hunting. Away from the hardship of the dry siege, the knights from Flanders were in their element. Their daily hunting expeditions provided fresh meat at night for everyone, worker and soldier alike. For a few days their hardships outside the walls of Jerusalem were forgotten. But this idyll could not last, time was against the Christian army and as soon as they had prepared all the wood their beasts could carry, they set off on the return journey. The slow-moving convoy laden with timber was sent ahead with some of the soldiers while the majority of knights formed the rearguard. Their safe return to the northern camp several days after their departure was received with great jubilation and a universal increase in belief that it would be possible to take the city.[8]

Moreover, the northern camp had just benefited from a stroke of great fortune. Tancred, who regularly rode on patrol with his 40 knights, had been suffering from dysentery. On one of these patrols, he had been struck by a sudden need for privacy in order to relieve himself; consequently Tancred dismounted from his horse and retreated to the dark shadows of a rocky outcrop. Astonishingly, he discovered 400 lengths of timber hidden in the darkness. This was wood that had already been smoothed and prepared for use. Al-Afdal's army had hidden the wood the previous autumn, as surplus to their needs following the surrender of Jerusalem. A celebratory procession greeted Tancred as news of his discovery spread through the army. In the space of a few days, the outlook of the Christian army had improved dramatically. The northern camp had secured the essential supplies of wood that they needed, while the southern camp had acquired men with the expertise and tools to make that wood into the finest siege equipment known in the art of warfare.[9]

For the first time since the arrival of the Christian army, Iftikhār was seriously perturbed. The signs of vigorous activity and the sounds of construction coming from the crusaders' camps gave a new, more professional, tone to their armies. Messengers were sent to Cairo, encouraging al-Afdal to hasten his preparations to come and lift the siege while the Christians were still outside the walls and vulnerable to attack. At the same time Iftikhār attempted to dispatch spies to gather more information as to what was afoot. That his initiative was unsuccessful, however, was due to the fact that the Christian army had its own spies in the city. Just as Bohemond had cultivated contacts inside the city of Antioch, so his nephew, Tancred, was attentive to the local Christians whom he had been the first to encounter thanks to his dash to Bethlehem on 6 June. These sympathizers of the crusaders were able to slip up to the city in the darkness and whisper to their friends on the walls. Neither the Christian army nor the Muslim garrison were sizeable enough to secure the entire boundaries of the city and in particular the eastern side of Jerusalem, which dropped away so quickly to the rocky Kidron valley, was a place where a careful person could make their way undetected.

Tancred learned from his contacts that Iftikhār was communicating with Cairo through the use of this valley and that messengers were moving back and forth in secret. He took this information to a private meeting of the most senior princes of both camps. There it was agreed to co-operate in a nighttime ambush. Keeping the plan to just those knights whom it was necessary to mobilize, once the sun was down small groups of crusaders took up their places. They stationed knights on the Mount of Olives, on all the approaching paths, and stole quietly down along the bottom of the valley itself. Their plan was entirely successful. Not long after nightfall, two Muslim messengers who had journeyed from Ascalon with communications for Iftikhār from al-Afdal ran straight into one of the ambushing parties. They were quickly restrained, but an overeager Christian knight nearly ruined the value of the operation by stabbing one of captives with his spear and killing him. The other unfortunate was brought to the camp, where the princes came hurriedly to interrogate him.

What could the messenger do? He might not have believed the promises of the Christian princes to reward him with his life, but there was no doubting that when the crusaders put it to him bluntly that unless he co-operated they would torture him, they meant it. The Fatimid messenger told them all he knew. The main content of the information he carried was that al-Afdal was on the march and expected to be at Jerusalem within 15 days. The defenders of the city were therefore not to show any fear or make any agreement with the Christians, but to stand firm in the knowledge that a great army was coming to liberate them.

Once they were satisfied the messenger had no other information of interest, the princes gave him back to the group of knights who had made the capture. These soldiers amused themselves throughout the night with arguments about what to do with their prisoner. By the next day they were decided. It was time to test one of the new mangonels. Binding the poor man's feet to his hands, they trussed him up and placed him in the throwing cup of the machine. Then they aimed the machine at the city, hoping to toss their prisoner over the walls. The game was a disappointment to them, however, as the man's weight was too great for the machine to cast any distance. The Fatimid messenger fell far short of the walls, shattering his bones on impact with the stony ground.[10]

Inside the city the tempo of the siege also rose. If the Christians were at last conducting themselves like a serious army, there would soon be a duel of stone-throwing machines. Iftikhār had been with al-Afdal the previous year when the

Fatimid attack on the city had been victorious because they considerably outnumbered the defenders in such devices. He was determined that the crusaders
would not be allowed to wear away at the city walls in the same manner. All
available timber and rope was marshalled in the construction of additional
mangonels for the city. Furthermore, bags were sewn and stuffed with straw,
before being piled up at strategic points beside the walls. If the crusader
machines proved to be capable of damaging the stone, these bags could be lowered on ropes in order to cushion the impact of the flying rocks.

When Iftikhār had learned that the Christian army might come to Jerusalem
he had done all he could to make the city secure and to make sure that no
resources, whether water or wood, were available for his enemies in the vicinity
of the city. The other important measure he had taken was to expel many
of those Syrian Christians who might be sympathetic to the crusading army.
This had the advantage of reducing the possibility of acts of betrayal within the
city, but it also led to the Christian army having – at their camp or in nearby
Bethlehem – a body of local supporters keen to supply them with information
about where water and wood could be found. Additionally, unknown to Iftikhār,
information from within the city was coming to the crusader camp through
these intermediaries.

All the Fatimid soldiers from nearby fortresses along with Muslim inhabitants of the countryside around Jerusalem had hurried to the city in the first
week of June and they were quartered in the empty houses. Since Iftikhār
remained suspicious as to the loyalties of the remaining Christians, to keep a
watch upon them he placed the refugees from the surrounding areas in to the
Christian households. This solved two problems at a stroke. The responsibility
of feeding the hundreds of displaced Muslims was given to the host household
and at the same time a constant scrutiny could ensure there would be no repeti-
tion of the events of Antioch, where ultimately the city fell due to the discontent of Firuz, a guardian of a stretch of the walls.

The situation for the Christians within Jerusalem was extremely difficult.
Hated and mistrusted by everyone else inside the walls, they were also the
targets of official hostility stemming from the commands of Iftikhār. Not only
did households barely able to feed themselves have to share what little food
they had with strangers, but also they were subject to new and heavy duties.
Large payments of money were demanded from them and to encourage com-
pliance, several prominent figures were led off in chains. When there were
heavy loads to be moved, it was the Christian population that was aroused and
compelled to do the carrying. At any hour, day or night, they were liable to be
summoned and if they delayed at all Muslim soldiers would grab hold of their

hair and beards to drag them out of their residences. Those who had skills in any of the trades were obliged to work for the defence of the city. Where stone or timber was lacking, it was Christian homes that were broken down to supply the materials.

Most dangerously of all, the Christians inside Jerusalem at the time of the siege were vulnerable to the accusation of spying for the crusaders. It was later said that Gerard, the founder of the Hospitallers – the guardians of the Christian hospice at Jerusalem – was in the city at the time of the siege. He did his best to assist those outside by pretending to throw rocks at them, but his missiles were in fact loaves of bread. On being accused of treachery and taken to Iftikhār, the loaves of bread in his clothing, which were to act as evidence against him, had miraculously changed to stones and he escaped punishment.[11]

The less romantic fact of the situation was that there were indeed some Christians who did their best to assist their co-religionists outside the walls. Tancred, in particular, was working with the Syrian Christians outside the walls to develop contacts within the city. Suspicion of such treachery fell upon the entirety of the Christian community. Every unfortunate accident was attributed to the Christian enemy within the walls. It became dangerous for them to leave their houses without rousing suspicion. No Christian dared ascend the walls or appear in public unless carrying some burden. Even then, the Christian citizen was subject to constant insults. An accusation arising from the whim of anyone who felt like playing informer could quickly see the Christian being carried off to imprisonment, whether the accusations were true or not.[12]

By contrast with the Syrian Christians, the Jewish population of the city, both Rabbanite and Karaite, were considered entirely reliable. They had once inhabited the southern part of Jerusalem, around Mount Zion, but when the lines of the city walls were redrawn, their communities were outside the new defences. As a result a new Jewish quarter had been established in the northeast sector of the city. Among them were famous scholars, theologians, grammarians, philosophers, lawyers and students who had travelled to Jerusalem from all over the Mediterranean. Indeed, the city was such an attraction to the Jewish population of Spain that a distinct Spanish colony existed within the city. Those from the Jewish community who could fight did so. Those who could assist Iftikhār with the administration of the siege performed that service and were stationed at the citadel. And those who could not give direct aid to the Muslim ruler did what they could to help in the construction of siege equipment. They had just as much reason to dread the fall of the city to the Christian army as any Muslim citizen, as the entire course of the crusade had demonstrated, from its origins in northern Europe to the massacres at nearby cities such at Ma'arra.

The news of the horrific pogroms perpetrated by these crusaders on the Jewish communities of the Rhineland had reached Jerusalem and the Jewish population knew they could expect no mercy in the event the city was taken.[13]

Iftikhār had a more ambivalent attitude towards the smaller Samaritan community, a religious group who were similar to the Jewish community in that they based their beliefs on a version of the Torah. By medieval times Samaritans were considered to be closer to the views of the Muslims than the other religions of Palestine. As al-Dimashqī (writing c.1300) put it: 'some say that if a Muslim and a Jew and a Samaritan and a Christian meet on the road, the Samaritan will join the Muslim.'[14] Samaritans participated in the Fatimid administration, but they had also, like the Christians, suffered at times from bouts of heavy taxation. The common experience of being discriminated against by the Muslim authorities made the Samaritans potential allies of the Christians and even though the crusaders were unlikely to distinguish between the Samaritan and Jewish communities, Iftikhār considered them as neutrals in the current situation.

All in all, the Fatimid governor had done all he could to mobilize the resources of the city against the besiegers and exert effective control over the population. Thanks to the presence of skilled workers and ample supplies of equipment, his stone-throwing machines were more than a match for those of the Christians. In particular, there was a large mangonel under construction whose missiles, he hoped, would be able to reach to the enemy camp on Mount Zion. If he could burn that down, then concentrate his artillery on the north side, he had every reason to hope that the city would remain intact until the arrival of al-Afdal.

Chapter 6

Preparing for the Assault

As June turned to July, matters were clearly approaching a crisis point. Working hard in the dust and heat, with an enthusiasm generated by their recent luck in obtaining timber and skilled woodworkers, the crusaders were near to completing a whole array of siege machines: mangonels; 'hybrid' trebuchets; a ram; and, most crucially, two enormous wooden towers. Inside the city the garrison and the citizens – with the exception of the remaining Christians – were determined to match every effort of their enemies beyond the walls. They laboured continuously to ensure that they would outnumber the crusaders in stone-throwing devices and both soldiers and civilians collected rocks to pile them up beside the machines for ammunition. Everyone, both inside and outside the city, was spurred on by the knowledge that a few more weeks would see the arrival of the vizier of Cairo with a great army.

Day by day, the two wooden towers grew in height. Both were built so that their top platform was higher than the walls of Jerusalem, putting them at over 15 metres tall. They were huge affairs, which the defenders of the city gazed upon with considerable anxiety. That built by William Embraico on Mount Zion was the more impressive of the two; efficiently jointed, it had an air of solidity that the northern one lacked. The advantage of having proper tools and skilled workers showed in the way that those who climbed to the top to survey the city ahead of them barely felt it stir. By contrast, the creaks and swaying of the upper reaches of the northern tower did not entirely inspire confidence.

The princes of the northern camp had decided to nominate Gaston of Béarn as the person responsible for the construction of their tower. This was a political, rather than military, appointment. Gaston had travelled on crusade with Raymond of Toulouse and the Provençal knights and was a very welcome member of their company; he brought with him his own small following of knights and a wealth of experience in warfare against Muslim opponents from his campaign in Iberia in 1087. But Gaston was rather independently minded and certainly no vassal of the count. Although he camped beside the great Provençal warrior William of Montpellier at the siege of Nicea, he was attracted to the spirited company of Drogo of Nesle, Thomas of Marle, and their friends, with whom he fought at the battle of Dorylaeum. At the time of the battle, these French knights were loosely aligned to Hugh the Great.

During the siege of Antioch, Gaston agreed to a request from Raymond of Toulouse that he join William of Montpellier and the boldest of the Provençal company in garrisoning a castle built outside the city to prevent sorties from the west of the city. This successful alliance continued for the famous battle with Kerbogha, where Gaston fought alongside William of Montpellier. But the mutual respect that existed between Gaston and William was not enough to bind him to the wider Provençal contingent of Count Raymond, for soon after the victory Gaston left the main army with those now famous for being first into Antioch – Fulcher of Chartres, Drogo of Nesle and the other champions – and rode east to seek service with Baldwin, now lord of Edessa. Thereafter Gaston did his best to remain independent from the authority of any lord. Since his escapade in the raid on Jerusalem alongside Tancred's small company, Gaston had decided to maintain his association with the Norman prince and set up his tents beside those of his new ally on the northern side of the city.[1]

The question of who among the Christian princes would become ruler of Jerusalem once it had been conquered was never far from the thoughts of the senior knights. The leading contender for the honour was Count Raymond of Toulouse. If the Provençal contingent stuck together, they would probably be able to impose Raymond upon the captured city due to the fact they were the single largest regional grouping among the crusading forces. But there were signs of severe tensions among the Provençal contingent between the more loyal followers of the count and less dedicated knights, in particular the former followers of Bishop Adhémar who although stationed in the southern camp were there more to avail of the regular payments from Count Raymond's huge war chest than out of enthusiasm for the would-be Moses. Furthermore, the great numbers of poor and non-combatant crusaders who camped with Count Raymond at Mount Zion were a law unto themselves. All in all, it was far from guaranteed that Raymond could rally everyone around him to ensure he would be the future ruler of Jerusalem.

In the northern camp, even though the composition of the crusading army was extremely diverse with many different languages and regions represented, the mood was much more harmonious. Because Robert of Normandy and Robert of Flanders were anxious to fulfil their vows and return home there was only one clear candidate for the lordship of Jerusalem: Godfrey of Lotharingia. Of course Tancred, in his heart, aspired to rule towns, cities, principalities, kingdoms and eventually empires. But right now he had only about 40 knights willing to follow him and tactically he recognized the expediency of supporting Godfrey.

Gaston's appointment, then, as commander of the siege equipment, was a strategic one that suited Godfrey's ambitions. It was a reward for Gaston's presence in the northern camp and it conveyed the message that having a Provençal background was no obstacle to current and future favours from the Duke of Lotharingia. As it happened the appointment was an effective one, Gaston proved himself a scrupulous and dedicated commander. He instituted a division of labour for the various tasks needed in the assembly of siege equipment and carefully accounted for the collection of money and its distribution. For, by contrast to the southern camp where Count Raymond funded the enterprise, there was a public collection in the northern camp in order to pay the artisans of their siege engine. These carpenters did the best they could, but their skills were no match for the sailors and in particular their choice of timber – a type they called *soliva* – for the left side of the great structure was unfortunate as it showed signs of buckling under the huge weight it was supporting.[2]

As the siege towers were raised up, so too was the morale of the Christian army. When the princes appealed to the women, elderly and children to leave the camp in the relatively safe direction of Bethlehem in search of pliant twigs from low bushes and shrubs they met with an enthusiastic response. With an escort of knights and a train of camels and other pack animals, the popular army roused itself from fatigue induced by thirst and set to work. They piled the branches on their animals until it was not possible to carry any more and returned to the camps, there to settle down in a bustle of activity, weaving wickerwork coverings for the siege towers and for the mantlets – large shields – that the soldiers would carry before them into battle to protect themselves from missiles.

Despite all the hardships of the journey, there were still huge numbers of non-combatants in the camps of the Christian army: not only clergy, but thousands of women and children. It was one of the most distinctive features of the crusading army of 1099 that women had gathered in their hundreds to participate, sometimes even leading popular contingents. In the main they had come with their husbands or guardians; this was especially true for the relatives of those farmers who had sold their land and had loaded what possessions they had onto carts. They came as part of extended families, young and old, setting out together join the Holy Journey to Jerusalem. Other women, though, had set out on their own, sometimes disguised as men in order to join the Christian forces as they marched through Europe. As far as the warriors were concerned, such non-combatants had mostly been a burden, although everyone acknowledged the bravery of the women at Dorylaeum who brought water up to the knights under Bohemond's command, helping them survive the long weary day holding fast in the hope of reinforcement.

Accompanying the women were so many children that they were able to form divisions of their own, with leaders named after the famous crusader princes: there was a child 'Bohemond', a 'count of Flanders', a 'Hugh the Great', a 'count of Normandy' and so forth. This emulation was more than the medieval equivalent to a modern child's adoration of a sporting star: it had a practical function. Whenever their gang members were suffering from lack of food, the child leader would go to plead with the prince after whom they were named and invariably he returned with supplies for their needs. The children had fought their own battles too. With long sticks as spears and whatever missiles came to hand, they would challenge the children of the cities that the army had reached and sometimes the melees that developed between the city walls and the Christian camps were so great as to attract the attention of adults and draw them into a more lethal conflict.[3]

At Jerusalem the non-combatants now showed their worth in a massive effort to provide the warriors with all the wickerwork they needed. Hardly a single person was idle. When the soldiers made their next assault there would be no shortage of ladders or equipment. The commoners roamed the land around Jerusalem for miles, gathering any plant sufficiently flexible and sturdy that it could form part of the weave. Hides too, were of the utmost importance. It was explained to the Christian army by their co-religionists who had been expelled from the city that the garrison were preparing quantities of 'Greek Fire'. Made from a closely-guarded recipe involving resin and sulphur, Greek Fire was a highly flammable liquid with the important property that dousing it with water only caused the flames to flare up and burn all the more strongly. Fortunately for the crusaders their local supporters knew how to deal with such attacks. They urged the construction of a layer of hide skins to prevent the fire reaching the timber beneath and that on the day of the attack these skins be soaked in vinegar; with extra casks containing vinegar stored on the siege engine to be thrown over those fires that did break out. All the animals that had either died of thirst or otherwise killed were therefore now skinned and their hides scrapped clean in order to provide the first line of protection against liquid flame.[4]

This new mood of optimism among the non-combatants led them to begin to articulate their own thoughts about the conduct of the siege. Ever since their champion – the colourful visionary Peter Bartholomew – had died as a result of being mobbed after the trial by fire, the poor had lost the main means of expressing their feelings to the nobles. But essentially the same mechanisms of communicating popular sentiment upwards remained in the form of several other visionaries who claimed to be receiving divine messages. On the whole, none of these mystics carried a great deal of authority, but that was beginning to change now as the poor were taking more seriously the prospect of an imminent assault on Jerusalem. They had two major concerns. The first, and one that was shared by many foot soldiers, knights and even princes, was that aristocratic rivalry might cause such division that the army fail to act in a concerted fashion and even be defeated as a result. The second was that once the city was in their hands, the rule that had been observed ever since the failure to loot Nicea should be confirmed and recognized: whosoever first took a property and put their mark upon it would, without question, get to keep it.

In characteristic fashion, the manifestation of these ideas took the form of visions. Back in Antioch, during the outbreak of plague that followed the capture of the city by the Christian army, the most authoritative leader of the expedition and the person who most embodied the need for unity across the diverse geographical contingents, the papal legate, Bishop Adhémar of Le Puy, had died. But curiously, this was not the end of his involvement with the expedition, for several popular voices claimed that he continued to march with the crusade and offer advice. Most of those doing so were in the entourage of Count Raymond of Toulouse and were therefore considered charlatans by all those hostile to the claims of supremacy by the count. The priest, Peter Desiderius, however, was a different case.

Peter Desiderius was chaplain to Isoard I, count of Die, a senior noble in the company of Raymond of Toulouse. Peter had first come to the attention of the wider Provençal clergy at Antioch with a vision concerning the relics of St George. Later, at the trial of Peter Bartholomew, Peter Desiderius had spoken up on behalf of his namesake and fellow visionary, claiming that he had seen a vision of Adhémar and that the papal legate had been burned for three days in hell – although largely protected by a cloak he had once given to a poor person – for doubting the Holy Lance. But, importantly, Desiderius was not trying to ingratiate himself for the sake of patronage from Count Raymond. Indeed outside Tripoli when the count had toyed with the idea of trying to deflect the crusade towards an assault on the city the visionary had spoke out against the count in a very mutinous fashion.

Peter Desiderius, at Tripoli, had claimed that St Andrew had appeared to him with a message for Count Raymond. The count was told to abandon all plans other than a direct march to Jerusalem. The popular enthusiasm at the news of this was such that the crusaders rushed on towards the Holy City without any sensible military formation and were fortunate not to encounter any Fatimid cavalry on the way. Now, at the start of July 1099, this priest who had a great deal of respect among the poor, saw Adhémar once more. In the vision the papal legate urged a fast and that the whole army walk on bare feet around the besieged city. Nine days after this penitential march an all-out assault was to take place that would capture Jerusalem. Rather than bring this news of Adhémar's appearance and the promise of victory to Count Raymond, Peter Desiderius approached his immediate lord, Count Isoard I of Die and Adhémar's brother, William Hugh of Monteil. Back at the siege of 'Arqā, when William Hugh returned from having to fetch the cross with which his brother had been buried, it had been the former followers of Adhémar who had burned their tents in protest at the siege and abandoned the Count Raymond. It was clear that this division amongst the Provençals between those who had travelled with the count and those who had travelled with the bishop had not been resolved even as they camped together before the walls of Jerusalem.[5]

Those of the Provençal clergy who first heard of the new vision had some advice to offer Desiderius. The whole issue of whether Adhémar had truly visited Peter Bartholomew had become too political and many – especially in the northern camp – if they learned that the message about the unifying march had supposedly come from Adhémar would dismiss the idea out of hand. It would be much better to announce that there should be a parade around Jerusalem in a spirit of conciliation, without revealing the source of the initiative. It would also be diplomatic to obtain the support of the Norman bishop Arnulf of Chocques and of the still popular Peter the Hermit. This advice, especially the latter part, was deeply unpalatable for Desiderius. After all it was Arnulf who, at the instigation of the Norman knights, had challenged and brought to trial Peter Bartholomew. In other words, the death of his colleague could be directly attributed to Arnulf. Peter the Hermit, too, was no great friend of Desiderius. While Peter Bartholomew had reigned as the spokesperson of the poor, the Provençal visionaries had eclipsed Peter the Hermit. But now, having quietly sustained himself through the rigours of the journey and without making any claims with regard to seeing dead crusaders or saints, Peter the Hermit's standing had grown again to the point where he was the recognized person to whom alms were given for distribution to the poor.[6]

It was the crowds of poor who urged unity across the two camps and their insistence fed its way through to the lower ranks of the clergy. Peter Desiderius bowed to the prevailing mood and agreed to advocate the proposed strategy. Those Provençal clergy who were the associates of Desiderius extended the hand of friendship to Arnulf and clergy of the northern camp. They called a general meeting of the whole Christian army, one that met on 6 July 1099. The assembly was a great success, at least from the point of view of the poor and the clergy. Enthusiasm for the penitential march was so great that whether they liked the idea or not, no prince could dare defy the public sentiment and dismiss the idea. No one wanted to be castigated as proud and impious when these clerical speakers were raising up a storm of excitement by addressing those very themes. Harmony and modesty were the slogans of the day and all were urged to pray for the intercession of the saints in their endeavours. A fast was begun from the assembly and preparations made for the barefoot march two days later.

The morning of Friday 8 July saw one of the most extraordinary sights of any medieval siege. An enormous crowd of the besieging army, from prince to pauper, was gathered behind a panoply of religious banners, crosses and relics of saints. And everyone was barefooted. While the bishops and priests in their sacred vestments led the procession, the knights and foot soldiers remained vigilant: they were armed and ready for battle should the defenders of the city attempt a sortie. With trumpets blowing, everyone moved out of the southern camp in order to march around the city in a clockwise direction. They passed around in front of the Tower of David, travelled through the northern camp and carefully picked their way over the rugged ground of the Kidron Valley to the Mount of Olives. There, with Jerusalem spread out below, bright and tantalizingly close, the procession stopped and once more heard how it was from this spot that Christ had ascended to heaven and it was from here, also, that the disciples had been taught the Lord's prayer. Peter the Hermit and Arnulf of Chocques both spoke at length about the need to lay to rest the discord that had sprung up among the Christian army. As brothers in Christ they must work closely together in the battle to come.

Such a huge spirit of forgiveness and fraternity was expressed by all that even the fierce enmity between Tancred and Count Raymond was overcome. No one could hold a grudge in the face of the overwhelming desire for unity that was being made manifest by the march and the message of the preachers. A compromise was reached on the payment that Tancred felt was owed him and the two princes were reconciled. With a powerful belief growing throughout the Christian army that they could succeed in the capture of the Holy City they moved towards their final destination, Mount Zion. Here, however, the celebratory and purposeful mood was soured by the response of the Muslim garrison of the city.[7]

Naturally, the defenders of Jerusalem had been incredulous at the sight of their enemies mounting such a parade. Did they really believe they were a Holy People, acting as if God guided their destiny? The Muslim warriors quickly brought out their own standards and pennants and as the Christians slowly made their way around the city, followed them along the walls, screaming, blaring with their own horns, and performing all kinds of acts of mockery to take away the otherworldly spirit of the Christian demonstration. Crowds within the city ran through the streets to get the walls and view the extraordinary spectacle. Up on the battlements, some of the garrison made crosses, only to visibly destroy them, or worse. There were soldiers who delighted in spitting and urinating over crosses that had been hung down from the walls. As they smashed up the Christian symbol they shouted out: 'Franks, how wonderful is this cross?'

All in all the Muslim counter-demonstrations were highly effective at taking the shine off the attempt by the Christians to raise themselves to a new pitch of religious fervour. And when the crusaders reached Mount Zion a new game began. For arrows fired from the city walls could just reach the great throng. While the Christians tried to finish their ceremony with proper dignity, they took casualties from the whistling missiles, including that of an unfortunate cleric struck right through the centre of his forehead. The rage that burned in the hearts of the Christian forces towards their enemies had never been higher, while the defenders of the city had enjoyed themselves and taken heart from the distinctly bizarre and unmilitary behaviour of their enemies. But the new siege towers loomed ominously and there must have been many among the onlookers in Jerusalem who were wondering at the terrible vengeance this ragged and fervent crowd would take if they were to get inside the walls.[8]

At least Iftikhār was doing all he could to ensure that this did not happen. Not only did he order the ceaseless construction of stone-throwing machines, ensuring that they would outnumber those of the attackers several times over, but he took steps to neutralize the threat posed by the siege towers. At the southern gate facing Mount Zion and at the part of the northern wall facing Godfrey's siege engine, masons and carpenters were employed throughout the daylight hours building up the wall and adding wooden hoardings so that the height of the defences at those threatened points was greater than that of the towers.

This was discouraging from the crusaders' perspective, especially those in the southern camp. In the northern camp, however, there were a small circle of princes who were pleased to see Iftikhār putting so much effort in the defences that faced their siege tower. Between themselves, but still a matter of great secrecy to the wider camp, the princes had agreed that despite the effort involved, their actual point of attack would be much further east along northern wall and not the section that their equipment currently faced. They intended to take advantage of the availability of great numbers of willing hands to haul everything during the night before the attack, tower included, around to the more advantageous position.

The night of Saturday 9 July, still glowing with pleasure that the Christian forces had united in their determination to assault the city, the northern army was told of the plan to change the point of attack. The order was eminently sensible and seized upon eagerly, despite the toil that it entailed. While hundreds of crusaders took advantage of the dark, the lack of stone-throwing machines in the sector, and their wicker mantels, to fill in the ditch outside the wall at the point where the attack was now to begin, hundreds more carried the heavy beams and sections of the siege tower across a kilometre of rough ground to its new position. Then all the trebuchets had to be moved and the piles of rocks prepared as their ammunition brought across too. It was backbreaking work, but there were many hands to make it lighter and a grim determination to thwart the preparations of the garrison.

The city awoke to the sounds of hammering as the parts of the siege tower were knocked back into shape at its new location. Only two days had passed since the soldiers on the walls of Jerusalem had enjoyed the sport of mocking the absurd and unmilitary procession around the city, but now they had the unpleasant realization that present in the Christian army alongside the spiritual fervour was a calculating and astute tactical intelligence. Of course Iftikhār at once had all the northern throwing machines moved to guard the new line of approach, as well as all the ammunition, and the bags of chaff for protecting the walls, but the great effort the defenders of the city had put into building up extra height on the walls was wasted and they had lost their first line of defence, the ditch.

The news of the extraordinary efforts made by their northern comrades came as quite a surprise to southern camp. The secret had been well kept. It was pointless for the leaders of the Provençal army to consider copying the manoeuvre; the only flat approach to the city on the south side was the one they were facing. As a result, they had no choice but to contend with the new defensive constructions. For the southern army, however, the most immediate question was not so much the additional height of the wall facing them, but the problem of the ditch. There could be no question of bringing up their tower to the walls of Jerusalem without first filling in that great moat. They had been trying for some time to throw rocks and clods of earth into the ditch and with some success. But even at night it was dangerous work, the defenders of Jerusalem were so close that torchlight could pick out their targets and a deadly game took place between the archers on the walls and those creeping up to the city to toss stones into the ditch.

Given that the northern army was nearly ready to attempt an all-out assault upon Jerusalem, the rate at which the moat on the southern side was being filled was far too slow. Holding their newly constructed mantles before them, the Christians could come within bowshot safely enough, but Iftikhār had placed the majority of his mangonels in this spot and screens woven of branches were no protection against heavy, fast flung, stones. Although the crusaders were eager to make the assault on the city, they were less eager to be the ones who risked their bones by coming up to the ditch. Count Raymond solved the problem by once more resorting to his treasure chest. It was still full of tribute paid to him by Jala-al-Mulk of Tripoli at a time when the emir had greatly feared for his city and his life. Raymond now offered a penny to every person who flung three rocks into the ditch. A penny was a mouthful of water. Suddenly there was no lack of brave souls and if flying rocks shattered bodies and limbs, nevertheless over three days and nights of constant effort the ditch grew less and less formidable, until the crusaders could gaze upon it with great satisfaction. The path for their siege tower was ready.[9]

A meeting of the princes of both camps now took place. Although it was impossible to completely forget the latent rivalry between them, particularly over who should be ruler of Jerusalem, they were pleased with each other's progress. The date of 14 July was agreed for their common assault and in the meantime knights were ordered to construct one ladder or two mantlets between them, while the clergy collected alms for the poor, held vigils, and devoted themselves to prayer.

Throughout all this period of intense activity among the Christian army the hardship of thirst and hunger had not declined. The availability of coin dispensed by Count Raymond – to the garrison of his camp, to the sailors, and to those filling the ditch – meant that supplies obtained from local sympathetic Christians and entrepreneurial crusaders gravitated towards the southern camp. It was in the northern camp therefore that the most striking signs of hunger and dehydration were visible.

Out of concern that the crusaders on their side of the city would be too enfeebled to make a determined assault, Tancred volunteered to ride out on a major raid in search of supplies. With Gaston busy organizing the construction of the siege equipment, it was decided that Count Eustace, Godfrey's brother, should partner Tancred in the enterprise and so, on the morning of Sunday 10 July, about 100 knights rode out of the northern camp. Given that the lands to the east and south had been scoured again and again, while they had heard positive reports from the two Roberts about the region around Nablus, Tancred and Eustace made their way northwards.

For the first day they found nothing but ruined farms and vineyards as all the land as far as Nablus had already been raided by Christian knights. With dawn on the second day, however, as they approached the city, the foraging party caught sight of herdsmen fleeing along a river valley towards the safety of the walls. Galloping after the Muslim farmers, Tancred and Eustace just caught up with them before the city gates and drove the animals aside, where they were able to herd them together. Knowing how great was the hunger back at camp, the two princes were not content with this success and continued the raid further into Muslim held territory, plundering from villages and farms and reaching a major mosque before turning back. Early in the morning on Wednesday 13 July, the fourth day of their expedition, the dust of their troop could be seen from the camp. It was with a huge sense of relief and joy that the herds of animals laden with plunder were welcomed back. There would be no lack of food for those about to assault the walls of Jerusalem.[10]

With the ditch filled in at the key points, the ram and the siege towers ready, and as with many trebuchets and mangonels as they could construct from the remaining wood, the Christian army was ready to attempt the storming of the city. Roast meat filled their bellies and dreams of glory their thoughts. That afternoon they brought the stone throwers into range, and began the attack.

This was not the full charge of the entire crusading army, but a preliminary exchange of fire, to allow those with picks and hammers to work away at the outer wall and to level off the ditch. It was violent enough though. As the sun declined, stones fell through the air like rain, crashed heavily to the ground, and sometimes dealt crushing blows to bone or timber as they found their target. Iftikhār was well prepared for this kind of warfare and for every stone flung towards the city, nine were hurled back at the attackers. Admittedly the hybrid trebuchets were throwing a heavier missile than the defenders' mangonels but the Fatimid soldiers were well prepared. Their own machines were covered with bags filled with chaff to cushion the impact of flying rocks and the same padding was lowered over the wall ensuring that it would not fragment during the bombardment. As night fell and the waning moon, beyond its last quarter, gave only limited light, the exchange of fire dwindled away to a halt.

What were they thinking in their respective positions as they waited for the sun to come around again and bring with its illumination the resumption of battle? The Christians were probably the more confident. When they had first arrived at Jerusalem there had been no miraculous delivery of the city into their hands. As a result they had been downcast and even if thirst had not wrecked their hopes there was the fear that a great army would come up from Egypt and destroy them. Now, however, they were ready to storm the city and had great faith in their siege engines. Inside the city, there was almost certainly an equivalent anxiety. Al-afdal was on the way, but the decisive conflict was upon them before he could possibly arrive. It was astonishing how ominous those towers looked, especially the sturdy one on the south. On both sides of the city nearly all the obstacles between the towers and the city walls had been cleared away. Everything would depend on whether the defenders could batter and burn the Christian towers before they provided a way over the walls. And if this strange and fervent army were to get into the city, what would be the consequence?

Chapter 7

The Storming of Jerusalem

Thursday 14 July 1099. Just beyond arrow shot from the north wall of the city a mass of Christian knights and foot soldiers had formed up in the cool of dawn, their front ranks glittering now that the long shadow of the Mount of Olives had retreated and the rising sun fell upon their chainmail hauberks. Behind the close-packed ranks of professional warriors were thousands of unarmoured crusaders, lean and dangerous looking, with crudely made weapons in their hands. Amongst them were elderly men, young boys and many women. All knew that the decisive day had come and all were ready to risk their lives to make sure the day was theirs. Behind the combatants were the clergy, singing liturgies and calling out to God for aid.

The northern army had formed up in two distinct clusters. Robert of Normandy and Robert of Flanders – as they had so often done before – united their armies in order to fight side by side. Their task was to close to the walls and with an intense barrage of stones flung from machines and a constant hail of arrows try to keep the defenders from gathering at the critical points. To the east of the two Roberts a larger body of crusaders gathered behind a great battering ram. This great mass of troops included Tancred, Gaston and the unaligned northern French knights, now willingly taking their places alongside Duke Godfrey and the Lotharingians. Duke Godfrey's command and fighting position was the top floor of the siege tower itself.

Back at 'Arqā, when Arnulf of Chocques had challenged Peter Bartholomew to prove himself and the Holy Lance through the trial by fire, the relic that so many had looked to as a talisman had been proven discredited, at least in the minds of those unsympathetic to Count Raymond of Toulouse. But there remained in the Christian army a desire to believe in the protective powers of God, as embodied in relics such as the bones of St George, St Cyprian, St Omechios, St Leontius, St John Chrysostom, the cross formerly carried by Adhémar, a ring blessed by Mary and – in the Lotharingian contingent – a large cross covered in gold with a statue of Jesus inside. This shimmering cross had been mounted on the top of the northern siege tower, the most prominent standard for the northern assault.[1]

With the ground floor packed with men and with volunteers ready to push from behind with poles, the plan was to bring the tower close enough to the walls of the city that they could overlook the defences and clear away the defenders while at the base of the wall the ram did its work. Were they to be able to dominate a stretch of the city wall by throwing down stones or their constant firing of arrows, it might even become possible for ladders to be successfully placed against the defences and the walls of the city scaled.

The battering ram was to lead the assault. It was a construction of enormous weight, with the huge iron-headed beam swinging from underneath a sturdy triangular roof protected by wickerwork panels. Those who braved being crushed in the device – comrades of the Lotharingians who had perished with the collapse of the similar siege engine at Nicea – were to also push it in position, but they could count on the assistance of crusaders pulling on ropes ahead of the ram and more pushing with poles from behind.

Ready with heaps of rocks, bundles of arrows and skins of Greek Fire, were the Muslim garrison and their civilian allies looking out from the walls at the grim crusading army. The section of the wall opposite the ram was packed with defenders, for as it was clear no action would be taking place on the west or east walls the Fatimid troops could concentrate their troops in the restricted area that was evidently going to witness the bulk of the fighting. From their point of view it was a shame that the wall was not higher, they had been wrongfooted by the dismantling and reassembly of the siege equipment, but all the same, they outnumbered their enemies in bows and stone throwing machines.

This section of the northern wall formed part of the Jewish quarter and the Fatimid archers and siege crews were assisted by a willing civilian population, ready to bring up water, stones and, indeed, to hurl rocks at the crusaders. Several towers protruding from the city allowed the defenders to shoot arrows right along the face of the wall and the platforms provided by the tops of the towers were perfect for the placement of some of the northern mangonels, whose height advantage ensure they would be in range once the Christians brought their own machines forward. The officers of the Fatimid mangonels had been instructed on which targets were to be their priority. They had enough machines to be able to divide their fire, with some standing by to counter the Christian stone throwers, while five were allocated to the destruction of the siege tower.

The scene at the south side of the city was similar, although the Provençal army had been standing in the bright sunlight of the higher ground of Mount Zion for some time before the shadows retreated from the city below them. Here again behind the armoured warriors were gathered poorer men, women and children ready to cast the lives into the balance. Here also, and in greater numbers, the clergy began the day with chants and prayers. There was no ram on the southern side, but their siege tower was very impressive. Tall and sturdy, it was packed with knights and ahead of it a slight downslope offered to assist those assigned to pushing it towards the walls.

It was this tower that Iftikhār was most concerned about and most determined to halt. Two-thirds of the city's mangonels, including his most powerful machines with the best crews, had been assigned to this position. With the exception of a few riders to act as messengers and a reserve at the citadel, Iftikhār also had his 400 cavalry dismounted and placed on the walls, the majority of them in the south where he personally intended to supervise affairs. Used to firing their recurved bows from horseback, the dismounted warriors would be able to provide deadly and accurate assistance to the rest of the garrison. And there were no shortage of targets about to present themselves.[2]

With the blare of trumpets from the north of the city and their echo from the south the peace of the dawn was destroyed by a mighty roar of 'God wills it!' The crusader assault began. Startled buzzards and vultures flapped into the air from the remains of animals and humans around the city, but there was no safety in a sky that was suddenly full of swift arrows and falling stones, not until they had beaten their way clear to the pure blue air far above human concerns.

Initially all was an indecipherable din, but over time a pattern began to emerge. A tone below the high-pitched whistling flight of arrows were the deep thumping beats of the mangonels, their upflung arms striking their wooden frames and casting out their contents. And for every individual beat of a Christian device, there was a staccato drumming response from within the city as dozens of stones came flying back out at the attacking forces, one moment seeming to hang in the air far above, the next crashing and splintering on the hard ground, sometimes bouncing into human beings, shattering bones and bringing into existence new sounds: screams for aid and screams of pure pain.

The defenders of Jerusalem had prepared bundles of firewood and straw, wrapped in pitch, wax, sulphur and any kinds of rag available, which as well as rocks, they fired in great numbers. These medieval 'Molotov cocktails' burned furiously and left a bright trail as they streaked through the air. The wood was covered in nails, so that on impact with the siege tower or a timber stone-thrower it might stick fast, while the straw bundles were carefully cast ahead of the siege towers to make barriers of flame through which it would be hazardous for the Christians to risk bringing their machines. Soon tall columns of smoke rose north and south of Jerusalem and the inhabitants of the region for miles around knew that fatal events were underway at the Holy City.

With cries of 'heave' a Christian trebuchet crew pulled down the weighted arm of their machine: the other end of the arm shot up, the sling with it, and – with a motion that was quiet and almost elegant – the leather cup swept to the very top of its arc, releasing a heavy stone towards the city, crashing into the walls ahead with a satisfying percussive clap. This was hard work for those hauling time after time at the ropes and as their aching arms began to tire the stones failed to reach quite so high on the walls. It was dangerous work too, because on the top platforms of the nearby towers of Jerusalem there were enemy mangonel crews who were doing their best to inflict harm on their efforts. They were close enough that those working the rival machines could see one another quite distinctly.

Sometimes their trebuchet would shudder from the blows of a hostile rock. Other stones, despite the surrounding protective shield of wicker mantels, crashed into skin and bone, either crushing a limb or instantly killing the crew member by a blow to the skull or torso. Despite the fact that several of the enemy mangonels had clearly been assigned to their destruction, there were many willing hands to take up the work and with regular changes of crew the trebuchet stones flung by the Christian army were generally pitched well up. The reward for an accurate well-delivered cast was, however, lessened by the defenders once again lowering bags fattened out with chaff. Crude and simple, the garrison's tactic was nevertheless very effective because the energy of the stones thrown by the trebuchets available to the crusaders was not so great as to be able to force the missile through the padding. The walls of Jerusalem could absorb the blows from the incoming rocks so long as they were covered in these bags and ropes.

On the north side of the city it was the battering ram that was much more of a danger to the defenders than the continual shower of rocks. Slowly at first, but building up a powerful momentum, the Lotharingians and their allies had pushed the ram up to the outer walls where a few heaves of the swinging beam had demonstrated how effective it could be. They had battered away the remains of the outer defences with ease. Then the ram was pushed right up against the inner wall. This close to the city the ram was safe from attack by mangonel, but it was now vulnerable to rocks of immense weight being dropped directly upon it.

Fortunately for those inside, the steep-sided structure was sturdy enough that these stones were deflected and their thunderous blows echoing within the confined space were made less frightening by the crashing sound that the attackers themselves were generating each time they swung the iron head of ram into the city wall. This was hot work, soon made hotter by a change of tactic by the garrison. From atop the wall the defenders anxiously poured sulphur, pitch and wax onto the machine and set it alight. The cries of alarm from those inside the ram spurred on the entire northern army and all the way back to the camp and the tents there was a great clamour. Soon hundreds of men and women were running up to the ram with skins of water and dousing the flames. They did not mind expending the precious liquid in this fashion, for they hoped to soon be able to satisfy their thirst from the cisterns inside the city.

At great cost in limbs and lives, for the ground around the ram was strewn with the injured and the dead, the ram survived. Again and again the beam was swung hard into the wall before it. And to the excitement of the northern army the news came that the stones were cracking and disintegrating, the ram was forcing a way through! To support the ram the siege tower was pushed forward, close up behind, so close in fact that those on the top floor could throw down rocks at the defenders of the city. It was a brave person who now risked pouring pitch or wax onto the ram. Nevertheless, the city's defenders continued to do so. For a second time the panels on top of the ram caught fire and for a second time, at great cost to their lives, the northern army managed to douse the flames and preserve the ram intact.[3]

The Lotharingian warriors on top of the siege tower were inflicting many casualties on the garrison of the nearby walls, but their position was not safe, the shining cross that had been mounted to reassure the army was a prime target for the five Fatimid mangonel crews assigned to deal with the tower, whose stones battered away at the wicker panels protecting the cross and all those stood near it, including Duke Godfrey.

By the time the sun had risen to its zenith over the Holy City considerable numbers of people had lost their lives, particularly on the Christian side. A steady stream of wounded were being brought to the tents of the northern camp, most of the casualties had been hit by arrows; although there were some who had been fortunate enough to survive having been struck by the heavy rocks fired from the enemy mangonels, even if they were to be disabled for the rest of their lives. The losses among the poor did not undermine the military efficiency of the attack. There were many more people capable of bringing water to the combatants or to assist dousing flames on the ram. Nor was there any lack of personnel for heaving stones into slings or lifting rocks into the back of the siege tower, to be hauled up by rope, so that they could be thrown down at the city. But every single casuality among the knights was a significant loss in military terms; these were warriors who could not be replaced. With around 1,200 knights in total, across both camps, the army could not afford a high rate of attrition. Foot soldiers too, especially the archers, were present in limited numbers. Although they protected themselves as well as they could behind their wicker mantles, the fact was that in the exchange of missile fire the Christian forces were faring worse than the defenders of the city. Their great hope and consolation was the success of the ram.

On the southern side of the city the situation was even worse for the Christians. From his vantage point on Mount Zion, Count Raymond could see that there was a great danger that if he brought his siege tower into action prematurely it would be burnt: for bundles of fiery debris had been strewn between his camp and the city walls, forming a more effective barrier than the great ditch had been. The Provençals had to be patient and endure an uneven exchange of missile fire while the flames died down and the Fatimids began to run short of their carefully prepared combustible missiles. This was immensely fearsome work, without the encouragement of having placed a ram at the city walls.

The Provençal army did have one unexpected source of succour. Back when Count Raymond had been given a massive bribe by the emir of Tripoli to leave the city in peace, he had also been provided with an envoy from the city. This envoy claimed to have prophetic powers and told the Christians that they would indeed succeed in capturing the city on this day. Tripoli had always held a great degree of autonomy from Cairo and the ambassador had been encouraged by his master to make a positive impression on those who might become important princes in the region in case they had to change allegiances. After some discussion as to whether it was 'godly' to believe in pagan magicians, the clergy informed the rest of the Provençal army that just as in the Old Testament there were examples of true prophecies by pagans, so this was another example.[4]

Not that the prophecy seemed to be coming true. Although some members of the southern army came within a few metres of the walls of Jerusalem, protected by mantels, their trebuchets and bow fire simply could not deal anything like the damage that they were receiving in return. Nor was it a great comfort to Count Raymond that the threat of his siege tower was keeping the majority of Iftikhār's troops and mangonels busy at the southern wall, making the assault easier for his fellow Christians on the other side of the city. Clearly, whoever obtained the city first and in particular obtained David's Tower, would be the strongest candidate to rule afterwards and if Iftikhār continued to guard against the motion of Raymond's tower, it would not be the Provençals who broke through.

As the day waned, it seemed that if the Christian army were to gain the city, it would be from the north. There the ram was enduring a constant battering of heavy stones combined with attempts to set it alight, but it was hammering away at a wall that was beginning to crumble. Behind the ram the siege tower too was creaking and groaning with every blow, but so far the panels, covered in skins of animals and soaked in vinegar, were deflecting the rocks and fiery bundles of rags. When the outer panels weakened and slipped, the crusaders did their best to pull them back into shape from inside the tower, Duke Godfrey himself lending a hand.

With joyful cheers from within the frame holding up the ram, the news spread that they had made a hole in the wall. The iron head had broken through completely. Now they needed to move the machine slightly and widen the opening. But at this point the cheering and excitement faded. The ram was stuck. It had been relatively easy to move the whole construction forward, to the efforts of those inside had been added the thrust of crusaders from behind, pushing on long poles. But in the hours that it had been exposed to constant blows, its rollers had broken and the housing of the ram had settled hard in a slight depression now made more difficult to move from due to the rocks piled either side. Although they were exerting themselves to the utmost, the ram would not come away in any direction. Tantalizingly, the soldiers at the wall could thrust the head of the ram right through into the city, but they could not widen the hole. Behind them siege tower was blocking the direct route by which the crusaders could have tried pulling away the machine with ropes.

Before the Christians could improvise some means of shifting the ram it began to disintegrate. Bouts of fire, a constant battering, and now the strain of being forced out of the position into which it had become jammed proved too much, the structure began to crack and the soldiers inside fled. From being on the cusp of victory, the northern army was suddenly thrown into a general dismay. Their ram had become useless and the momentum of the attack had been lost. Worse, the ruined device was in the direct path of the siege tower. If they wanted to move the tower closer to the walls, the Christians had to get their own ram out of the way. A curious about turn in the tactics of the attackers and defenders now took place. It was the crusaders who decided to set fire to the ram and the defenders of the city who when they realized the advantages of the obstacle, began pouring water and vinegar over it to douse the flames.[5]

The battle on the north side of Jerusalem remained centred on the ram, but now the Christian casualties seemed to be in vain. The enthusiasm of the crowd waned. It was one thing to risk your life running with water to assist a ram that was striking a way through the enemy walls, it was another to try to bring fire to the same timber when it was so easily doused from the walls. The commoners began to hang back and the foot soldiers too. Eventually, the more experienced commanders acknowledged that the assault was over. There was no prospect of clearing the walls sufficiently to bring up ladders, and the siege tower was not going to become a means of entering the city while the last few metres between it and the walls was blocked by the ruined ram. They would have to retreat and try to change the angle of the tower during the night, so that it could have a clear path to the walls.

Towards evening the northern army pulled back, with the famous knights of France cursing loudly, striking their hands together in grief and shouting that God had deserted them that day. Robert of Normandy came over to Robert of Flanders and the two of them shared their mutual dismay. To be tearful under the circumstances was not shameful and the princes demonstrated their frustration by their loud laments. Battle was a test of God's will and the Christian army had been judged wanting. They were not worthy to worship at Christ's tomb.[6]

Bitterly, the Lotharingians hauled at their tower, pulling it back a little, until it was out of danger from the stones of the Fatimid mangonels. Eventually too, the exchange of arrows that had darkened the sky throughout the day waned. As the sun descended, shadows crept from the valleys to cover the battle scene and cloak the dead. The northern army had failed.

Had the southern army fared any better? Christian knights rode around the walls of the city to exchange reports on the day's events. But there was no encouragement to be found among the Provençals. In the afternoon Count Raymond had felt the danger from fire was sufficiently reduced that he could bring forward the siege tower. Iftikhār had been waiting for some time for this and all his mangonel crews were focused on the slow moving machine. A barrage of stones struck blow after blow against the tower, eventually causing the upper stories to splinter and fragment, with perforations appearing in the defences as stones shot right through the outer lay of skins. The knights on the top of the tower hastily got down from the machine, just in time too, because the subsequent fire from the Fatimid mangonels was accurate, sending stones ripping through the platform they had just been standing on.

Once the momentum of the siege tower had been halted, all the sacrifice and danger of the missile fire – an exchange that clearly favoured the defenders of the city – was pointless. Furthermore, late in the day a fire had taken hold on the front of the tower. The first priority of the southern army had to be to preserve their siege machine; if they lost the tower, they were left only with ladders and no serious prospect of forcing a way into the city. The attack had therefore petered out entirely while the Provençal army hauled their machine back and successfully fought the flames.[7]

The sun set on a violent and bloody day; a day that had seen the northern army come close to creating an opening in the wall of the city, but which ultimately had been a failure for the Christian army. Many a crusader shed tears of desperation that evening. This was to have been their moment, the day on which they saw their dreams fulfilled and were able to approach the Holy Places in Jerusalem, most importantly, the Holy Sepulchre. Instead God had favoured their enemies. Were they unworthy? Was it not enough that they had starved, fought and marched their way to Jerusalem during the course of the last three years?

There was hardly any moon that night and the Milky Way shone brightly, a wealth of silver stars streaming across the sky. The constellations on the land below were bright too: orange torches and red braziers lined the walls and streets of the city and outlined the camps of the besiegers. Very few people inside or outside of the city could sleep due to anxiety. Could the defenders of Jerusalem dare to hope that the worst was over? They were busy reinforcing their defences, bringing up rocks, water, vinegar and Greek Fire ready for a resumption of battle the next day, with every chance that they could hold off the assault. After all, the southern tower had not proved so sturdy in the face of the fire of a great number of mangonels. Even better, an especially powerful new machine was nearly ready, the missiles from which should be able to reach all the way to the Christian camp.

The garrison also had a plan to deal with the northern siege tower. They had prepared a huge length of timber with iron nails and hooks all over it, covering these with rags soaked and impregnated with pitch, wax, oil and all the kindling they could find. A sturdy chain was attached to the centre of the beam. Once the enemy tower came close enough, the timber would be flung over the wall to the base of the tower and set alight with the assistance of Greek Fire, while the chain would prevent the Christians from being able to pull it away, allowing it to burn up along with the tower. Hard at work throughout the night, the garrison and the non-Christian population of Jerusalem had good reason to hope they might survive the coming assault and therefore be able to hold the crusaders at bay until the arrival of al-Afdal.

On the Christian side an extremely great despondency came over the army, spread by two particular sources of fear. One was a rumour that the Egyptian army was close; the other was that their enemies in the city, buoyant with success, would organize a night-time sortie and burn the siege towers. As regular patrols scoured the darkness around the camps, those who were supposed to be resting lay awake in a turmoil of spirit. What if they could not break into the city, despite the enormous efforts that had gone into preparing the ram, the siege towers and stone throwers? How long did they have before the vizier of Cairo came up with his army? Would they ever see the Holy Places? The same refrains could be heard again and again among the tents, along with heavy sighs. How cruel to be so near the Holy Places yet unable to approach them. They had crossed so many seas and rivers, endured so much poverty, disease and sickness, had fought in so many great battles and yet were kept from seeing Christ's Sepulchre by the fortifications in front of them.

Up on the top of Mount Zion, at the Church of the Virgin, the Provençal clergy were particularly disheartened. They had heard talk among the soldiers about lifting the siege while they still could hope to fight their way to a friendly port. Worse, the men were reminiscing about the sweet embraces of their wives, far from this place of thirst and hardship. The clergy were resolved to pray throughout the night, repeatedly asking God why he was torturing them to the point that they were losing their sanity. An idle question, of course, as they all knew the answer. It was because of the sins of the army that they were suffering. If it risked sounding prideful to plead God on their own account, they prayed that He would assist the crusading army on His own account. For their enemies had humiliated His people, damaged His possessions and were 'polluting' the Holy Sepulchre.[8]

Polluere: a powerful term and a reminder that this was no ordinary army and no ordinary siege. The enemies of the Christians were befouling the Holy Places, simply by their presence. That, at least, was how the crusading clergy looked at the situation and the clergy were a very effective body in shaping the public opinion of the army, especially of the poorer crusaders whom they supported with the distribution of alms. What would it mean for such a force to conquer the city? Was talk of 'pollution' just an exercise in rhetoric? Or had it become a widely held tenet of the crusading army that Jerusalem should cease to be a multi-faith city and become a city for Christians only? And how was this to be achieved? What was to happen to its approximately 40,000 inhabitants? Not that there was any enthusiasm among the crusaders for talk of how they should conduct themselves on the fall of the city; not while they mourned the failure of their attack.

Yet at some point during the hours of darkness a subtle shift took place in the morale of the Christian army. The rumours of an imminent arrival of the Egyptian army were quelled; while as the night hours passed, the dread that the garrison of the city would assault the siege towers abated. It was clear from the constant movement of torches around the city walls that the defenders of the city were more concerned that the Christians might make a night-time attack than they were to attempt a counter-attack. The urgent measures being undertaken by the townspeople made it seem as though they were afraid and that there was no danger they would launching counter-attacks against the towers. As this belief communicated itself through the crusaders' camps, their spirits rose.[9]

In setting his troops and the people of the city to work in preparation for the coming day, Iftikhār had taken a dangerously passive approach. It was clear that no intelligence was reaching him from the Christian camps, or he would have taken advantage of the enormous sense of discouragement that passed through their ranks after their retreat from the walls of the city. The Fatimid general could have sent parties out to try and destroy the siege towers during the night; at the very least these skirmishes would have kept the crusaders in a state of alarm. It was all very well rousing the elderly and the children of the city to help make the rounds, to dig pits and traps around the gates and to bring up rocks to the mangonels. It was sensible too, to have his skilled workers improve the torsion of the ropes of the stone-throwing machines. But the vigorous patrols of the city walls, with vigilant officers appointed to every tower, only served to give the Christians outside the impression that Jerusalem was trembling.

By dawn the crusaders had completely recovered their enthusiasm for the assault. The tops of their siege towers caught the light before the towers of the city walls and the Lotharingian cross of gold glittered brightly. There were even jests and hearty cheers as the crews of the machines took up their stations, with the clergy once standing among them and invoking God's aid. Perhaps they would fare better this day and make the breakthrough that would lead to the fulfilment of their three-year dream.

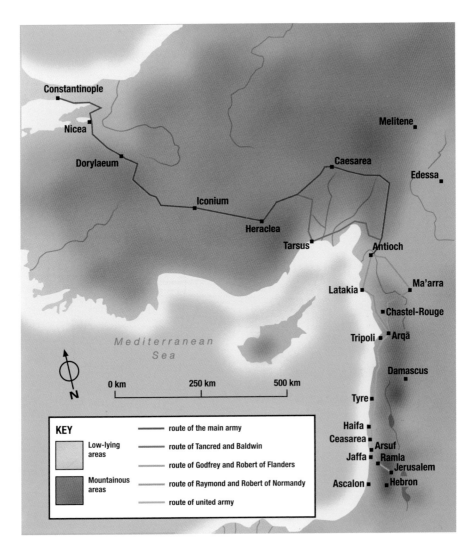

Figure 1 The route taken by the First Crusade

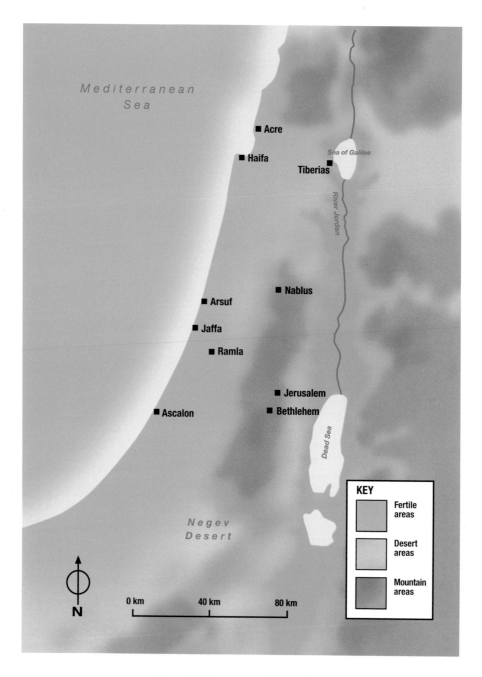

Figure 2 The environs of Jerusalem

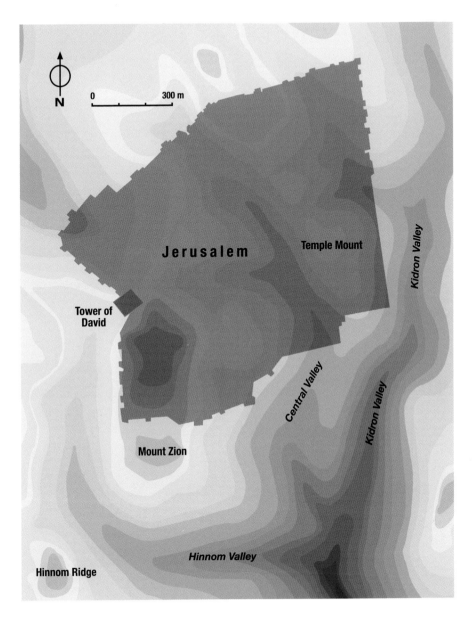

Figure 3 The topography of Jerusalem

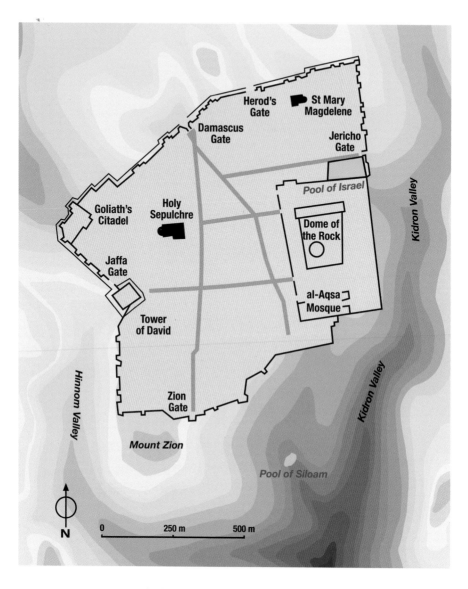

Figure 4 The layout of Jerusalem at the time of the Crusade

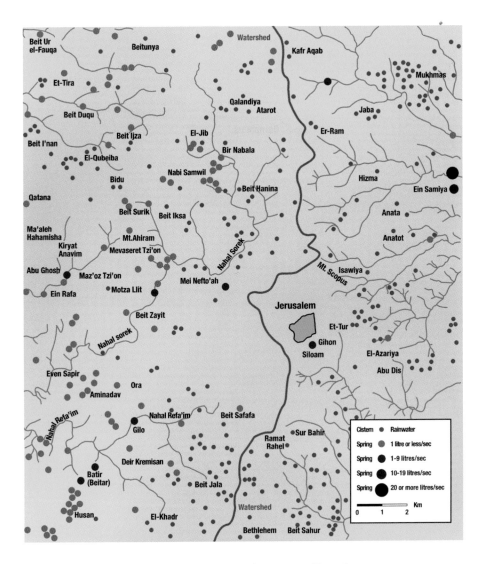

Figure 5 Water sources in the vicinity of Jerusalem

Figure 6 The view from the Pool of Siloam to the walls of Jerusalem, from W. H. Bartlett, *Walks About the City and Environs of Jerusalem* (London, 1845), p. 69

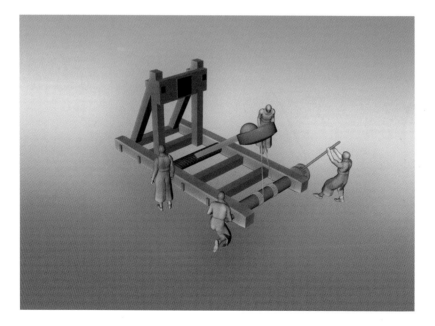

Figure 7 Siege equipment 1: a basic mangonel, used on both sides

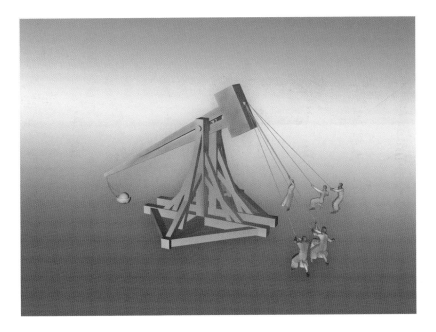

Figure 8 Siege equipment 2: a hybrid trebuchet, used by the crusaders

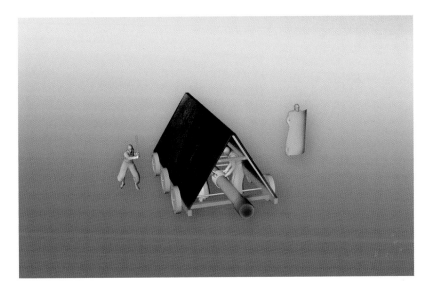

Figure 9 Siege equipment 3: a ram from the front

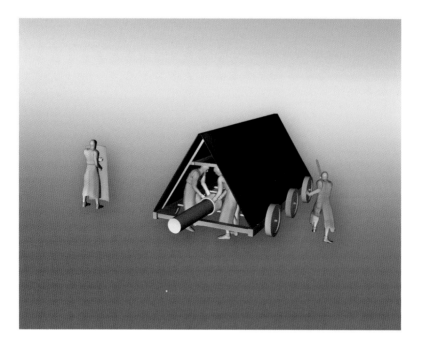

Figure 10 Siege equipment 4: a ram from the back

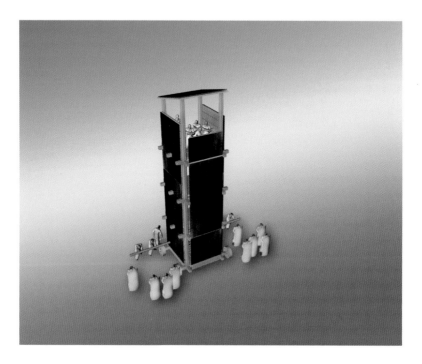

Figure 11 Siege equipment 4: a siege tower from the front

Figure 12 Siege equipment 5: a siege tower from the back

Figure 13 Siege equipment 6: a crow, used by the Provençal army

Key

Raymond's seige tower

Godfrey's seige tower

Godfrey's ram

Mangonel

Large mangonel

Raised wall

Iftikhār's troops

Route of Iftikhār's cavalty

Raymond's troops

Tancred's troops

French knights

Godfrey's troops

Robert of Flanders

Robert of Normandy

Figure 14 The assault on Jerusalem stage 1

Figure 15 The assault on Jerusalem stage 2

Key

- Raymond's seige tower
- Godfrey's seige tower
- Godfrey's ram
- Mangonel
- Large mangonel
- Raised wall
- Iftikhār's troops
- Route of Iftikhār's cavalty
- Raymond's troops
- Tancred's troops
- French knights
- Godfrey's troops
- Robert of Flanders
- Robert of Normandy

Key

Raymond's seige tower

Godfrey's seige tower

Godfrey's ram

Mangonel

Large mangonel

Raised wall

Iftikhar's troops

Route of Iftikhar's cavalty

Raymond's troops

Tancred's troops

French knights

Godfrey's troops

Robert of Flanders

Robert of Normandy

Figure 16 The assault on Jerusalem stage 3

Chapter 8

Friday, 15 July 1099

Friday, 15 July 1099. As soon as the brightening eastern sky allowed the besiegers and defenders of Jerusalem to see one another they resumed the fighting
that had petered out the night before. Yet it was not the Christians who began
the battle. A brand new mangonel was ready on the southern gate that faced
Count Raymond's camp. The garrison of Jerusalem had completed the machine
and hauled it into place during the night and now stood ready to test the
range. With an enormous thump, it cast a rock right up the hillside and sent it
crashing into the palisade of the crusader camp. Greatly encouraged by the
success of their first shot, the Fatimid soldiers next loaded the machine with
carefully prepared bundles. These were giant clumps of coagulated fibres, flax,
resin and pitch. It was too dangerous to light such missiles while they were still
in the cup of the mangonel; instead archers stood ready beside braziers with
arrows whose heads were also covered by a clump of fibre and resin. As soon as
the massive wads of pitch thrown from the mangonel had landed and rolled up
towards the gates of the Christian camp, the archers lit their arrows and sent
them blazing through the dawn air to ignite the bundles.

Iftikhār's preparations had not been in vain. The gateposts of the Provençal
camp soon caught fire and as the heat from the flames grew in force the pitch
holding the fibres of the projectiles together melted, so that very quickly the fire
took hold all along the gate. Before long an enormous blaze was roaring as it
consumed the entrance to the Christian camp. When Count Raymond had set
up his base on Mount Zion he had taken a calculated risk that although he was
too close to the city for comfort, it would be worth the danger to gain the
slightly downhill run for a siege tower. Now, it seemed, his judgement had been
in error, for the gate of his camp was in the process of being completely destroyed
by fire, leaving him defenceless against a sortie from the city. If the siege were
to continue beyond this day, it would probably be necessary to abandon the
position on the hill.

For the moment though, the Provençal army concentrated on dousing the
fires and keeping them from spreading. There was no point expending precious
water on saving the gate, the blaze was too great, but they did have to deal with

the flames licking along the palisade. It was heartbreaking that water, which had either been bought at a great price or else carried to the camp after expeditions involving the labour of thousands of people, now had to be dispensed to quell the unexpected and shocking inferno.

Throughout the crusade there had been a persistent underlying hostility by the clergy towards the women present in the Christian army, but at this moment that feeling was transformed to a belief that God had allowed them to undertake the pilgrimage for a purpose, because the women were indispensable in bringing up water to extinguish the fires. Although it was hard work for women laden with water to come up the hill to the camp gate, all the while exposed to the impact of enemy stones, they did so eagerly. Moreover, once the fires were in hand and the battle focused on the exchange of missile fire, the women took up wood and stones with both hands and ran to fill more of the ditch that obstructed the route of the siege tower.[1]

The efforts by the women of the camp were impressive and their bravery gave great encouragement to the Provençal men. The priority of the soldiers of the southern camp was now that of damaging the new Fatimid machine before it ruined their siege tower and so all the Christian trebuchets were focused on flinging rocks at new mangonel. Once again, however, a layer of leather sacks full of chaff was warding off the missiles of the attackers. The bags were lying on the machine itself and provided enough padding to deflect the incoming blows.

Despite a consistent success in hitting the mangonel, the Christian trebuchet crews realized that they were not going to destroy it so long as the bags remained in place. Some of the artisans in the southern camp therefore began work on a counter-measure. They fastened a powerful iron hook on a long pole, and then they covered the pole in metal plates, so that it could not be easily burnt. This whole device was carried forward while their comrades with wicker mantels protected them. What made the hook effective was a long iron chain fastened to the head of the pole that ran back over a prop. By hauling on the chain the crusaders could lift the sagging hook and then a group of them could manoeuvre the pole back and forth, cutting away at the bags.

They had to come right up in front of the gate to do work this 'crow' and many crusaders fell, pierced by arrows, but the crude implement worked. Once they had the hook caught on a rope they pulled it in and the rope with its bag was torn away. Soon the stones from the Christian trebuchets were able to hit the wooden frame of the mangonel, causing it to crack and shed great splinters. The deadly game continued and despite their losses the crusaders kept up their efforts with the long pole until the enemy machine was inoperative.

Their improvisation was a surprising success. Cheering one another on, the Christians next aimed the crow at a massive beam that had been bound to sacks and chaff and put over the walls of the city to prevent them suffering any damage from stones. Once again the hook caught in the ropes and the Christians began to pull the beam away along with the bags. The Sudanese soldiers lining the walls of the city at this gate looked on at this crude but effective activity with dismay, until one of their number saw an opportunity and without shield or armour climbed over the wall and out onto the beam. While the hook was caught tight he hacked away at the guiding pole until it parted. This was an extraordinary feat and should have cost him his life from the arrows, javelins and stones that were propelled at him. But the hero climbed back unhurt and now the cheering was entirely coming from the top of the walls.[2]

Once more the pattern of the assault became that of an uneven exchange of fire where the defenders of Jerusalem had the upper hand. From Count Raymond's perspective there was nothing for it but for his soldiers to cope as best they could with the losses, while trying to get the siege tower to the walls. The fact that nine or ten stones were flying back against the Christians for every one that they sent towards the city was deeply discouraging but so long as they had their tower and a few working machines, the attackers persisted. And indeed the balance of the day moved slightly towards the crusaders with the outcome of a curious duel. Standing right out on the walls of Jerusalem were two women whose gestures made it seem that they were casting some kind of enchantment at the nearest Christian trebuchet. The captain of this machine took careful aim and the crusaders flung their rock so successfully that it fell upon the women, crushing them instantly along with three girls behind them. This success was greeted with immense delight by the attackers and the clergy sent up prayers and thanks to God.[3]

Overall though, just as on the Wednesday, the assault was failing. One by one the Christian machines were destroyed, burnt or shattered. And their greatest hope, the siege tower, had proven unable to withstand the constant impact of stones and fiery missiles. Partly eaten by flame, partly splintered by rocks and missiles, the upper floor of the tower was in ruins and no knight was willing to stand there. Even the bravest and most eager to win the fame of being the first into Jerusalem saw that it meant death to mount the tower now that it was so damaged and all the protection had been stripped away.

Many of the Provençal army could see that the battle in the south was becoming quite precarious. With the entrance to the camp in ruins, a sortie from the city had the potential to scatter the Christian forces before they could gain assistance from the northern crusaders. Iftikhār was indeed weighing up this possibility and began to mass his troops. His 400 cavalry were all remounted and while some had the duty of riding back and forth across the city to keep him informed of all developments, a great number were kept by the southern exits in case the opportunity arose to turn the faltering assault into a rout.

The Muslim general had successfully stymied the Christian attack at the point he considered to have been the most vulnerable for the city. If the northern assault could be beaten back too there was every chance that Jerusalem would remain in Fatimid hands. Here the conflict had centred around the great beam that the defenders had readied during the night. In the morning Duke Godfrey had once more mounted the siege tower and, in noticeable contrast to Count Raymond who directed affairs on the south side from his headquarters on Mount Zion, led the renewed attack in person. He was joined by Robert of Flanders, Robert of Normandy, Tancred and Gaston who brought their troops up under protection of mantels to resume the bombardment of the battlements of the city with arrows, javelins and the stones cast from the trebuchets allocated to them.

The collapsed ram still remained lodged against the wall as an obstacle, but with the new morning the attackers had the opportunity to run the siege tower up towards the defences on a slightly different angle and squeeze past the ruined machine. Hundreds of eager hands pushed the poles that, along with the efforts of those on the ground floor, moved the siege tower slowly forward.

The Fatimid soldiers and their allies from the city were all focused on the tower, which soon bristled with their arrows. Although the crossbow was not as honourable a weapon as the sword, Duke Godfrey was an expert in all forms of warfare including archery. Despite the deadly rain of missiles he calmly picked out targets from the crews of the enemy mangonels and invariably hit them. That this performance was a genuinely brave and dangerous one was soon proved when a rock crashed through the defences of the tower and into the head of the soldier standing next to Godfrey, breaking his neck and killing him instantly.[4]

The period of greatest risk for those in the tower, however, was soon over, for once the Christian army had pushed the siege machine as close as they could to the walls, the five Fatimid mangonels assigned to this sector could not find a line of fire to it. If their rocks were to clear the city wall they invariably also now flew past the tower, whereas when some mangonel crews attempted to pitch their missiles so that they only just landed past the wall, as often as not the stone landed short of the tower and even among their own defenders at that critical spot. Despite its tendency to lean to the left and despite having shakier joints than the tower of the southern army, the northern tower had done its job and was providing a platform for the crusaders directly above a section of the northern wall of Jerusalem.[5]

If there remained a few feet between the tower and the city wall, it was due to the preparation by Iftikhār of a great tree trunk that was now heaved over the defences and, hanging from a chain, was interposed between the defenders and Godfrey's position. Having first been soaked in Greek Fire the beam was lowered towards the very bottom of the tower, with the defenders having high hopes of it being able to ignite and burn up the siege machine that now represented the Christian army's greatest chance of taking the city. But Tancred had been forewarned by the local Christian population about the method for dealing with this kind of fire. Those in the siege tower were well prepared and they poured out wineskins full of vinegar on to the beam beside them, drenching the tree trunk and quelling the oily flames before they could take hold.

Once the immediate threat of fire had been overcome, the battle turned into a test of physical strength. Abandoning the relative safety of their mantels, Christian soldiers of all ranks ran to the beam and hooking ropes on to the chain, tried to pull it away from the walls. Inside the city the defenders crowded around their end of the chain to keep the tree trunk in place between the tower and the wall. Never was there such a tug of war contest with so much at stake. The Christian leverage proved the more effective and the chain came away from the walls, allowing the huge piece of timber to be dragged clear. Now there was little more than the thickness of the bags of chaff between the tower and the walls of the city. Not that the tower could be moved any further, the left wheels finally gave way leaving the whole construction immobile while tantalizingly close to the city; just too far for a brave warrior to risk the leap.[6]

All this time the knights on the tower had been firing as fast as they could into the throng of enemy soldiers on the wall just below them and for the first time in the siege the casualties in the missile exchange were far greater on the defenders' side. The troops of Robert of Normandy, however, were suffering greatly from the rocks thrown by the nearest enemy mangonels, while for all his efforts, Tancred was getting nowhere in his attempts at hurling rocks at a more distant mangonel. The fighting was grimmer and fiercer than at any previous time in the siege, the air full of missiles and the cries of the wounded.

A sense of frustration was growing on the Christian side. Sensing that the moment was a critical one and that the assault was losing momentum, a priest clad only in his white stole took up a ladder and marched towards the walls.

Those soldiers who had pulled back out of arrow range regained their enthusiasm at this unexpected sight and marched with him, all singing *Kyrie eleison*: 'Lord have mercy'. This surge of crusaders attempting to put ladders up against the walls was beaten back, but fatally for the defenders of the city it coincided with an outbreak of fire among the bags and chaff that faced the siege tower.[7]

One of the unaligned French champions had for some time been systematically attempting to ignite the padding hanging from the walls by devising arrows that had been covered with cotton and set alight before he fired them into the chaff. When at last the flames took hold they sent up plumes of thick black smoke, which seemed to flow up over the walls. The defenders of the city were willing to risk their lives in the unequal battle before the siege tower, suffering great losses for the sake of holding the walls. What they could not do, however, was breathe where there was no oxygen.[8]

As the defenders fell back choking and ducking away from the constant barrage of missiles they left, for a moment, a small section of the walls opposite the siege tower unguarded. Beneath Duke Godfrey's platform, in the middle section of the tower, were a group of French knights, including two brothers from the town of Tournai: Lethold and Engelbert. They were at eye level with the top of the wall and sensing the abatement of activity opposite them, undid some of the protective skins in front of the tower in order to push a plank across and rest it on the top of the wall. Was it foolhardy to cross? Were there soldiers in that dense streaming mass of fumes just waiting for them to try? Holding the plank steady, Engelbert watched his elder brother commit his life to the honour of being the first crusader to stand on the walls of Jerusalem. Lethold crawled across the vertiginous gap into the smoke. As soon as he was across, Engelbert scrambled over, assisted by the eager knights pressing from behind. There were no cheers. This was a moment for silent and determined action. Next across was Bernard, the advocate of the monastery of Saint Valery-sur-Somme. It was midday on 15 July 1099 and three Christian knights were inside the defences of Jerusalem.[9]

The two brothers turned left and, side-by-side with their swords drawn, moved towards those enemy figures who could be made out through the swirling smoke. Bernard turned to the right. As these three knights advanced, the section of wall available to the Christian army lengthened. Horrified at the sight of the crusading knights inside the battlements of the city, the Fatimid soldiers on the nearby walls rushed back, regardless of the smoke, but they were no match for the chainmail-clad knights: the first man to reach the brothers of Tournai had his head cut off by a fierce right handed blow, the body remaining standing while the helmeted head crashed down into the city, before it was booted from the wall walk.[10]

By now there was enormous clamour on all sides. The Fatimids and their civilian allies were hastening to the crisis, but even more swiftly Christian knights were entering the city. As soon as Duke Godfrey had became aware of the possibility of entering the city he had run down from the top level of the tower – Eustace close behind him – and over the planks that now more firmly covered the distance between the siege machine and the walls. Robert of Flanders was also alert to the opportunity created by the enterprise of the first knights to cross and as soon as he had seen Lethold standing on the walls, Robert ordered a full charge with all the ladders his men had to hand. By the time the Fatimid defenders had plunged into the smoke, it was full of Christian knights, swarming over the walls or running up the siege tower and across the makeshift bridge.

Face to face, the more lightly armoured Fatimid soldier was no match for the heavily protected Christian knight and in these confined spaces it was not possible for the defenders of the city to take advantage of their superior numbers or to fire missiles into the melee with any effectiveness. The rallying cries from the crusaders were growing louder and more urgent as they forced their way on and on, hundreds of Christian knights rushing to the bridgehead and thousands more foot soldiers and poor Christians joining the roars as ladders were raised all along the northern wall. Where the ram had collapsed was a narrow hole through the wall and now gangs of men and women eagerly worked their way through the ruined machine to wriggle through it into the city.

By the time Iftikhār had been alerted to this breakthrough on the northern side the invasion had become irresistible. His cavalry had been sent over immediately, only to encounter bewildered and terrified soldiers and citizens streaming away from the savage blades of the Christian knights, who even now could be seen rushing towards them. The riders scattered and with great haste made their way to the last hope of the garrison, David's Tower. But Christian knights were close in pursuit and as the Fatimid riders reached the safety of the ditch and walls of the fortress, they had to dismount and abandon their horses, bridles and saddles to the eager crusaders.[11]

Iftikhār had just retreated from the southern wall in time to reach the citadel safely; while the Provençal army facing his now abandoned position had been very slow to notice the change in pattern of battle. In fact, up at the Church of the Virgin where Count Raymond had his headquarters, his leading knights were proposing that they abandon the assault as a result of the damage to their tower and stone-throwing machines. At that moment a glittering knight on a white horse came riding along the Mount of Olives. By his eager manner and the movements of his hand he indicated that the southern army should renew their efforts. The sun catching his polished shield made this figure look like a divine messenger and the fact that no knight subsequently claimed the credit for having gone to galvanize the southern army leant a great mystery to this gallant figure. Tentatively at first, but with growing confidence, the Provençal forces and their vast contingent of non-combatants moved back towards the city at the urgent gesturing of this knight. They placed ladders against the walls and finding the defenders had fled, surged up into Jerusalem.[12]

There were none among the southern knights now as vigorous as Count Raymond who was running to the city, shouting at those around him to come on: 'Why are you so slow? Look! All the other Franks are in the city already!' The next few minutes could be critical with regard to the future ownership of Jerusalem. Alongside Raymond ran his lieutenants Raymond Pilet and William Sabran; his appointee to the bishopric of Albara, Peter of Narbonne; and Isoard I, count of Die, leader of the 'Adhémar faction'. It was with enormous relief that Raymond and his leading men got to David's Tower to find that while some Lotharingians had reached this strategic spot first, they had simply taken the abandoned horses and gone off in search of battle and booty. There were a great mass of civilians and late arriving soldiers outside the citadel pleading with Iftikhār to lower the drawbridge and let them cross to the safety of the walls. But they were too late and too many to gain asylum. Screaming, they scattered under the onslaught of the Provencal knights, until – with the dead strewn all around – Count Raymond's men took up position around the fortress.[13]

Under a flag of truce, the Provençal count sent a messenger and translator forward to make an offer to Iftikhār. Given the circumstances, Count Raymond's offer was a relatively generous one. The entire Fatimid garrison, along with their wives and children and all their moveable wealth, would be given free exit from the city and a safe conduct to Ascalon in return for surrendering the tower to the Count. With the distant roars of the attacking army in the background and the sight of screaming civilians running for their lives, it was hardly surprising that Iftikhār immediately accepted the offer and cemented it with a generous gift of gold. Count Raymond was by far the best known of the Christian leaders from his negotiations and alliance with the Fatimid emir of Tripoli. Iftikhār therefore had some confidence that the agreement would be honoured. The two parties exchanged hostages and while the Fatimid soldiers kept their drawbridge up, they did open the western gate of the city as a token of their agreement.[14]

An enormous crowd of Christians was now released into the city from the western side and rushed straight into frightened clusters of civilian citizens who had fled there from the north, whom they proceeded to butcher. Meanwhile, at the point of the break-in, having been among the first into the city, Duke Godfrey had quickly mastered the streets of the north-eastern Jewish Quarter in the company of Robert of Flanders, his own followers, and many of the unaligned French knights. A gate facing east, to the Kidron Valley, had been smashed open by some men powerful enough to charge it with their shoulders until the hinge buckled. But it was through the main northern gate that the largest crowds of crusaders entered the city. Once the iron bolts were drawn and the bars were lifted from the gates, the northern commoners rushed in and what little discipline remained in the Christian army was lost. The pressure of the mob at the gate was lethal. Horses, as they were carried along in the press, grew furious and alarmed and began to bite those around them, despite the efforts of their riders. So tight was the crush that 16 men died, falling beneath the feet of mounts, mules and their fellows.[15]

Two years earlier, when Nicea had surrendered to the Byzantine Emperor, there had been extraordinary bitterness in the crusading army, particularly among the foot soldiers and the non-combatants. They had anticipated gaining a share of the booty and were furious with their own princes for allowing Alexius to spare the population of the city and preserve their property. Thereafter the rule was established in the Christian army that whoever captured property could keep it for themselves. In other words, after battle or siege, it was not up to any prince to distribute the booty to their followers, it was 'first come, first served'.

This policy had been manifest after the taking of Antioch, after the defeat of Kerbogha, and at the storming of Ma'arra. It had also been publicly and formally reaffirmed by Arnulf of Chocques, chaplain to Robert of Normandy, at the time of the barefoot procession around Jerusalem before the assault began. As Arnulf put it when he talked about the issue soon after the conquest of the city: 'it was decreed and universally ordained, that with the town having been entered, he who first seized property will be bequeathed it, no matter who he is.' In addition to their thirst, their anger at the defenders for mocking the cross, and their desire to remove pollution from the Holy Places the crowds now entering the city had a powerful material incentive to rush in as fast as they could. This was the end of their journey and their last chance to become rich.[16]

It soon became clear through absolutely pitiful scenes that even by the harsh standards of their day, the sack of Jerusalem was to be a brutal one: the most thoroughgoing and violent known in their times. All the pent-up frustration of the siege, exaggerated by the recent mockery of the defenders, was now released in a horrific fashion. That the male defenders of the city were doomed was almost certain, but the citizens of Jerusalem clung to the hope that perhaps the women and children would be spared, as slaves, or for ransom. Similarly, elderly scholars awaited their fate, hoping that the long tradition of respect for learning across the different faiths in the city would lead to their survival.

Muslim and Jewish women and girls threw themselves at their attackers, grasping their knees, begging and weeping for their lives while their small children looked on. There was no mercy. The women were beheaded or had their brains smashed out with rocks, the screams of their children intensifying the clamour for a moment, before they too were cut to pieces. Babies were grasped by the leg and swung into walls or lintels of doors so that their necks were broken.

Those inhabitants of Jerusalem who simply had their heads struck off with a sharp blade were the lucky ones. Others, chased to the upper floors of buildings and towers, were thrown out to fall to their deaths. Some suffered for a long time, bound and writhing on fires. Heaps of heads, hands and feet could be seen piled up along the rows of houses and streets, where blood was pouring swiftly along the gutters.[17]

Like water flowing through a burst dam, the mob rushed through the streets and doors of the houses of Jerusalem. Whoever came first to a building fixed their sword or weapon on the door as a sign that it had already been seized. All the furniture, corn, barley, wine, oil, money and clothing, whatever was in the building, became the property of the new owner without dispute from their fellow crusaders. All respected the rule of 'first come first served'. Here you could come across a poor crusader proudly leading a newly acquired cow, there a woman carried a bag full of brass candlesticks, mistakenly thinking she had obtained gold. Up and down, through every house in the most obscure parts of the city, through gardens and household plots, over roofs, the excited crowds killed and plundered.

Those who had been on the verge of starvation prioritized food and gathered at ovens to roast newly slaughtered animals. Those desperate for water satiated themselves at the many cisterns in the city, despite the fact that they were becoming tainted by the flow of blood. And those with a taste for beer and wine became thoroughly drunk. All the while the massacre of the citizens of the city continued until it was a common sight to see Christian knights walking through the streets covered from head to foot with the blood of the slain.

Thousands of citizens attempted to hide themselves. But however resourceful they were, it was hard to remain concealed from minds so avid to discover hidden wealth. All over the city a lethal and horrific game of hide and seek was taking place. Everywhere citizens of Jerusalem were being dragged from their cupboards, cellars and attics, murdered and their bodies mutilated. Ears and fingers were cut away for their jewellery, intestines spilled in case bezants or jewels had been swallowed. Some of the more defiant citizens would fly out in a desperate attack on discovery, but the attackers were ready with bows and swords and such efforts were entirely acts of despair.[18]

Meanwhile, in their religious buildings, homes and hostels the Muslim and Jewish scholarly community waited helplessly for their turn. These elderly men, who had written important works of philosophy and theology, had their throats cut by fellow human beings whose concerns were more earthly, namely, whether the scrolls in the buildings and pagan places of worship should be thrown on the flames or whether they might have a value in coin. Many a crusader became wealthy with the ransom paid for such religious and philosophical works: hundreds of dinars were later paid by the Jewish community of Egypt for the return of 28 Torah scrolls.

Here and there, more pragmatically minded leaders of disciplined Christian soldiers attempted to gather prisoners for ransom, particularly from the more well-to-do citizens. A few houses containing Jewish captives survived the invasion of Jerusalem, but whereas the women amongst them were left alone in the north of the city by their Lotharingian captors, in the south they were raped by Provençal soldiers.[19]

Within the chaotic swirling motion of the crowds and the fleeing citizens several distinct currents could be discerned. The more military-minded among the defenders of the city strove to make their way to the 'Sanctuary of David' and although Iftikhār dared not resume fighting in order to assist them, in time a sizeable knot of Fatimid archers and foot soldiers organized themselves in the streets beside the west wall. They were more than capable of fending off the rioting crowds and even though there was no doubt about the final outcome, they put up a very spirited resistance against the Provençal knights who eventually formed up to attack them. These Muslim warriors fought to the very last with no thought of surrender; they fully understood there was no hope of survival and preferred to die with weapon in hand. The fact that the crusaders controlled all the nearby walls and towers meant that this stubborn resistance was eroded away by the rocks and arrows of the Christian soldiers without their being able to inflict many casualties on the attackers, who nevertheless were impressed and sobered by the defiance they encountered long after the city seemed to have been won.

On the opposite side of Jerusalem another pattern was discernable in the movement of those running through the streets. Many of the Jewish citizens hurried to the synagogue in the hope it would be respected as a place of sanctuary. A faint hope. Gathered together in fear and prayer were elderly men and women, mothers with babies and small children. Once the north-eastern gate of the city had been barged open the crowd of crusaders who had rushed in to the Jewish quarter had enveloped the synagogue, cutting it off from those who were arriving too late to gain entry and were slaughtered in the streets. The doors of the synagogue were closed and barricaded, but ominously the roars outside and thuds against the doors did not abate. Soon tendrils of smoke crept in under the door and a great heat could be felt from the entrance. The Christians had piled up wood against the building and set fire to it. Inside, neighbours and friends looked at one another with horror. They were going to be burnt, destroyed along with their place of worship.[20]

Not all the Christian troops were engaged in acts of destruction or participants in the inchoate scramble for plunder. Tancred and Gaston of Béarne, along with their 70 knights, had long planned for this moment. During the siege Tancred had cultivated the sympathy of those Christians who had been expelled from Jerusalem by Iftikhār, they had provided him with valuable information about the state of affairs within the city and – even more valuable – introduced him to two Muslim citizens anxious to ingratiate themselves with the Christian prince for a reward and the safety of their lives. These men had told Tancred of the existence of Jerusalem's greatest treasure: the silver and gold ornamentation of the Dome of the Rock.

Letting only Gaston in on his scheme, as soon as Tancred saw the entry to Jerusalem had been forced he rushed to the siege tower and he and his men forced their way through the press, not to join with those quelling the last pockets of resistance or butchering civilians, but to find this treasure. They ran, scattering the fleeing crowds around them, straight for the Haram es-Sharif complex, the large walled off area that contained the Dome of the Rock and the al-Aqsā mosque, their guides showing them the quickest route.

A double iron gate at the entrance to the Haram, through which refugees were streaming, was hastily closed and locked in the face of the crusaders. But it offered no great resistance to determined blows by Tancred and Gaston's knights, and soon they were through. The vast crowd in the yard fled to the mosque and the Dome, those slow to do so being cut down as they ran. Inside the Dome of the Rock was a sight to satisfy the most avaricious of hearts. Hanging from the roof by silver chains was a vessel made of gold, weighing nearly 50 kilograms. Placed around the interior were 40 silver lamps, each weighing around 10 kilograms. Even better, the interior wall glittered with a band of silver that made its way around the entire circuit. This band was about 45 centimeters wide and as thick as a thumb. When torn from the walls it would amount to a vast weight of silver bullion: over 25,000 kilograms. Decorating the rest of the walls were beautifully ornate designs studded with precious stones and jewels. Plus there were innumerable pieces of costly fabric. It would take six camels to carry the treasure back to the camp, where Tancred – wisely – gave a portion to his nominal overlord, Duke Godfrey and also made a distribution of alms for the poor. Even so, this seizure of such enormous wealth by so few was to lead to a major row among the princes.[21]

Tancred and Gaston were rich, incredibly so. As their men happily obeyed the order to strip the building, the two princes were calculating what this fortune meant in terms of paying off their debts to their knights, re-equipping everyone with new horses, arms and armour and obtaining new followers. Wealth for a medieval Christian prince was hardly ever considered an end in itself, a means for personal ease, rather it was a mechanism through which to raise armies. Tancred's piratical eye was gazing on power, not luxury.

While Count Raymond secured the citadel of Jerusalem and Tancred the most concentrated treasure of the city, Godfrey too had a goal to fulfil once there was no doubt that the Christian army had control of Jerusalem. Although the single largest body of troops was that of the Provençal army, the sum total of all other contingents was greater still. The question of who would be ruler in the Holy City was therefore wide open. By his actions throughout the crusade Godfrey had won the respect of the neutrals. Even over the course of the last two days there had been a clear difference in Godfrey's willingness to brave the bombardment of the siege tower in order to lead from the front and Count Raymond's more distant generalship.

It was almost certain that Robert of Normandy, Robert of Flanders and the unaligned French lords would back Godfrey for the rule of Jerusalem. But what of the non-military crusaders? The clergy and the huge crowds of non-combatants were less impressed by chivalric deeds than devout ones and a greater proportion of them had gathered on the southern side of the city than the north. Given that no one could direct the rampaging Christian crowds, Godfrey put away his sword once the gates of Jerusalem were open and the plundering had begun in earnest.

Keeping only a small bodyguard of his seneschal (steward of his household), Baldric; his chamberlain, Stabelo; and Adelolf, a third knight from his closest followers, Godfrey took off his hauberk and boots. The four knights then left the city through the broken gate facing the Mount of Olives and undertook their own procession, with Godfrey humble and barefoot, giving thanks to God. Having completed the circuit of the city and taken note of the Provençal banners over the Tower of David, they made their way to the Church of the Holy Sepulchre, where Godfrey spent the afternoon in tears, offering prayers and praising God for allowing him to fulfil his greatest desire, the sight of the Holy Places. It was a most astute performance and perhaps as he prayed Godfrey's heart really was filled with a spirit of gratitude to his God. After all, he had survived a very long and hazardous journey to be at this famous place. In any case, the pious and self-abnegating gesture did him no harm in an age where to lust after power was considered a sin.

To the Christians now beginning to gather at the church and those Christian citizens of Jerusalem who had wisely taken refuge in the one building that was guaranteed to be undisturbed by the violent scenes outside, Stabelo explained that the behaviour of the Duke demonstrated the realization of prophecy that had come to the Chamberlain in a dream. Stabelo had seen a golden ladder stretching all the way from heaven to earth, which Duke Godfrey was attempting to climb in the company of a steward, Rothard, who carried a lamp in his hand. But half way up the ladder the lamp was extinguished and the ladder became worn away, obliging Rothard to return to the ground, too afraid to continue. There Stabelo rekindled the lamp and confidently pushed past the unworthy steward to climb with the Duke all the way to the court of heaven, where a table of all sorts of sweet delicious foods awaited them. The Duke and everyone else worthy of being chosen reclined at the table, enjoying the feast at their leisure.[22]

Outside of the oasis of relative calm that was the Church of the Holy Sepulchre, the city was in turmoil. While the rampaging Christian army was hacking apart Muslim and Jewish citizens all over the city, it was the Haram complex that became the focus of a last stand by the defenders of Jerusalem. Despite the fact that Tancred's men had earlier broken down the gates, hundreds of refugees streamed inside the walls of the holy site in the hope of finding sanctuary, invading Christians hard on their heels.

Those who ran in to the Dome of the Rock found the Normans desecrating the walls, prising away silver and jewels, but they also found respite from the mob. Human wealth too was a factor in Tancred's calculations. Provided they surrendered themselves for ransom, Muslims were allowed up to the roof where

300 of them gathered on the ledge that surrounded the great dome. There they held Tancred and Gaston's banners as a sign that they were prisoners of these knights. By contrast, those who turned left, northwards, after entering the Haram found only death. Some were hunted down inside the complex; others ran through the exit in the northern wall that led down some steep stairs to a great cistern. There the first to gather were pushed into the water as more and more panicked citizens ran down in the hope of escape. The marble pillars of the cistern supported an arched roof that was at ground level. There were many openings in this roof and now as those below were cut down or drowned in the cistern, others who had attempted to run across the roof but had fallen through one of the openings fell on top of them. Some Christian pursuers were so eager that they too could not avoid plunging down the shafts and, if they did not break their necks or tear their guts open on masonry, they too drowned in the bloody lake.[23]

It was at the al-Aqsā mosque, to the south of the Haram site, that the city's Muslim civilians rallied themselves and led counter-attacks, taking advantage of the fact that there was almost no leadership at all among the nearest crusaders. By late afternoon a crowd of Muslim fighters had gathered what weapons they could and had formed improvised militia that struck back with some success. The doors of the mosque had been shattered by the early Christians arrivals, who were now caught searching inside the building for treasure by the reorganized Muslim crowd. The eagerness of these crusaders for booty became their doom as they were hunted down and killed. In turn the crusaders in the vicinity rallied and abandoning the search for plunder, fought back so savagely that the militia retreated. But they were not broken and as word of their resistance spread, more citizens and remnants of the Fatimid garrison joined with them. The balance of the battle around the mosque once more moved in favour of the defenders of Jerusalem and the Christians withdrew.

The conflict at the mosque raged back and forth as the crowds rushed one another in a massive disorganized melee, both sides lacking direction and commanders. In time, however, a particular group of Christian knights, with a great deal of practice in the sacking of towns and killing of civilians arrived at the scene. These warriors were uninterested in the scramble for housing for they intended to return to their castles and manors as soon as they could: all that mattered to them was the fame they were acquiring as the conquerors of Jerusalem. These knights were the unaligned French champions formerly grouped around Hugh the Great, a band that included Drogo of Nesle, Everard of Le Puiset, Thomas of Marle and their wounded hero Raimbold Crotton. Now in their element, staying together as a cohesive party, they were systematically butchering the entire non-Christian population of the city. It was these knights and, in particular, Everard of Le Puiset who dealt with the increasingly dangerous counter-attack. Covered in blood, Everard strode through the disputed terrain, protected from arrows by his long chainmail hauberk and a great shield.

When he encountered hundreds of fighters from the militia bearing down upon him with their spears raised, Everard did not flinch but called out to his companions not to run. They had faced more dangerous blows in tournaments; indeed, even boys and girls could stand against this crowd who were no more dangerous than a flock of sheep. Everard's shouts served their purpose, encouraging the Christian forces by drawing their attention to the lack of military training of the opposing crowd and reminding the knights that although they were considerably outnumbered, it would be shameful for experienced warriors to give ground to an improvised army consisting mostly of civilians.

Taking the offensive the French knights ran into the cluster of spears and clubs. Surprised and hindered by their own press of numbers, the citizens of Jerusalem fought poorly. While the blows of the Muslim weapons were impeded and those that landed were rarely lethal – the knights being protected by iron hauberks – the sharp blades of the Christian soldiers were deadly. Hacking all about them, the swords of the knights cut through ribs and necks, stabbed through groins, backs and stomachs, forcing a path right in among the crowd. Despite their determination to sell their lives dearly, the Muslim militia could not hold together in the face of such a tightly organized and well-equipped troop. They scattered and the last opposition to the conquerors of the city was at an end. For the rest of the evening until nightfall, all the subsequent violence was simply butchery.

So many Muslims had fled into the mosque that the scene there was hellish. Blood was splashed all up the walls, over doors, seats, tables, columns. It was impossible to move through the building without walking through streams of blood and those who did so were soaked in gore up to their knees. Even after the massacre was finished, when some of the Provençal clergy made their way to the famous building, which they mistakenly believed to be the Temple of Solomon, they could not believe how much blood was sloshing around the floor. Those familiar with the classical authors considered the sacking of Jerusalem bloodier than Caesar's victory over Pompey; than the battlefields of Troy; or the civil war between Marius and Sulla.[24]

Despite the shocking scene, the clergy felt like rejoicing. For them it seemed only proper that the pagans who had blasphemed in this spot for so many years should now purify it with their blood. Full of cheer and enthusiasm, the Christian clergy then gathered at the Church of the Holy Sepulchre where, as night fell, they joined together in celebration, clapping their hands and – in addition to chanting well known Offices, such as that of the Resurrection – singing a newly created song to the Lord for the occasion. Whether Lotharing-ian, Provençal, French, English, Italian, all the clergy were united in a cathartic moment. God's will had been done and they, who smiled at one another with tearful eyes, were fortunate enough to have been his instrument. Everyone present felt the historic importance of the moment and they knew that this day, 15 July 1099, would be famous thereafter. Like Easter and Christmas, this would surely become one of the great celebratory dates of the Christian calendar. The clergy whose arduous journey was at a triumphant end, gave thanks that they had lived to see such an important event.[25]

In fact this sense of completion, of having been chosen to do God's will, was not to become an event as celebrated in the Christian world as those singing in the church that night were anticipating. It was hard for later generations to be quite so celebratory about the destruction in a matter of hours of some 40,000 people. The massacre in Jerusalem at the end of the crusade was grim even by medieval standards. Within two generations even Christians living in Jerusalem would describe events at the Temple on 15 July with a sense of horror rather than pride, while the Muslim and Jewish world naturally came to mark the date with an indelible sense of appalling tragedy.

Chapter 9

The Aftermath

When the tumult of the ransacking of Jerusalem had quietened down, the princes of the Christian army made their way to the Church of the Holy Sepulchre. There, despite the celebratory activities of the clergy, they shared a sense of unease at the dispersed and disorganized state of their troops. It was just possible that the rumoured Egyptian army was close and as matters stood the city was no state for a defensive battle. One by one they listed the towers and gates of the city and assigned guards to each of them. This arrangement, it was made clear, was only an ad hoc precautionary defence and was only to last until one of them became ruler of Jerusalem. Thereafter, the disposition of the city's defences would be entirely at the command of whoever took power. To be assigned a tower for the night ahead was not become its owner. The significance of this reservation lay in Count Raymond's insistence that he watch over the most important military fortification in the city: David's Tower.[1]

Weary knights took up their stations around the walls of the city before cleaning and sheathing their swords. Their duty to their lords kept them from joining with the crowds below and participating in the tumult of feasting and drinking. In the meantime the princes bathed, dressed themselves in fresh clothes, and with bare feet gathered once more to undertake a pious tour of the Holy City, guided by the local Christian clergy. Under the cool evening sky, the procession was in strange contrast to the fervour of the day's fighting and subsequent massacre. It was as though the torsos and human parts littering the streets were invisible. As the revered sites were approached, these hardened crusaders fell to their knees and, full of emotion, kissed the ground. They were particularly humble as they returned to the Church of the Holy Sepulchre, for the Christian citizens of Jerusalem now emerged from the churches they had sheltered in to surround the victors, bearing crosses and relics of saints.

A spirit of devotion and contrition swelled up among even the most iron-hearted of the crusaders: many confessed their sins and took vows never to repeat them. The more devout believed that through this walk and the completion of their pilgrimage they were guaranteed entry to heaven. Many knights gave generously in alms so that the old and sick of the city were catered for.

Then the bishops and priests celebrated mass and in giving thanks to God they conveyed their belief that all those who had died during the course of the pilgrimage were temporarily called from their enjoyment of eternal blessedness to join the survivors in the fulfilment of their vows. In particular, Adhémar, the papal legate, was thought to be present among them. There were those who swore they saw the bishop of Le Puy on the walls of Jerusalem leading the critical breakthrough. With the comforting notion that all their fallen comrades were sharing in the sense of completion and heavenly reward, the ceremonies continued late into the night, with great shouts of praise and collective rejoicing.[2]

There was one surprising feature of the scene – surprising as far as the princely leaders of the crusade were concerned – and that was the veneration in which the local Christians held Peter the Hermit. After God, it was to Peter that they gave thanks for the restoration of Jerusalem to Christian rule. The Christian citizens of Jerusalem constantly thronged around the hermit, showering him with gifts and treated him like a living saint, someone through whom the Lord had demonstrably made His will known. Ever since the catastrophic defeat of the People's Crusade at Civitot Peter's role as a leading figure on the crusade had been eclipsed by the more disciplined princely armies. He had maintained a residual influence with the non-combatants, but had nothing like the status that was now being accorded to him.

As the knights glanced at each other with some bemusement, the explanation for this enthusiasm became clearer. Several years before the beginning of the crusade Peter had been in Jerusalem and, distressed by the hardship suffered by visiting pilgrims, had promised local Christian clergy that he would take a letter from the Patriarch back to the west and arouse their co-religionists to come and redress the injustices that were being inflicted upon them. After a meeting with the Patriarch, Peter had vowed to use all his eloquence on behalf of the Christians of Jerusalem. From their perspective it seemed that he had succeeded spectacularly. They knew nothing of the failure of Peter's army and little of the decisive role of Pope Urban II in organizing the more effective contingents of the crusade. In the eyes of the local Christians now gathered to welcome the warriors and pilgrims from the west it was the diminutive, somewhat embarrassed preacher, who was prime mover in this miracle.[3]

After the celebratory prayers and singing had finally died away, the conquerors of Jerusalem made their way to their new homes, where their servants had obtained all they needed by way of food, drink and luxurious furnishings. During the night, as the revelry in the west of the city diminished, Count Raymond fulfilled his agreement with Iftikhār. The Provençal army allowed the Muslim general to slip out of the city safely with a sizeable number of his soldiers and their families as well as a few citizens who had escaped the slaughter; an escort of Christian knights having been assigned to protect them on the journey as far as Ascalon. In return, the count occupied David's Tower with a tremendous feeling of satisfaction. So long as these defences were in his hands, it would be hard for any other prince to become ruler of the city.

With dawn came a renewed bout of looting as those who had missed out from the day before scoured every possible hiding place. It was not long before the news of Iftikhār's escape spread through the city. Incensed with a sense of betrayal a Christian crowd gathered at the Dome of the Rock, where it was known that a group of pagans remained captive. In fact, 300 terrified Muslim citizens had spent the night there, hoping that the banners of Tancred and Gaston would protect them. Perhaps they might have, but made furious by the fact their chief opponent had escaped them, the Christian mob were not to be restrained by the banners, even if they did belong to two of their more popular heroes. Grimly, the crusaders entered the building and set about the task of slaughter, decapitating men and women with their swords. The surge of citizens away from the stairs caused some to fall over the edge of the building and it was not long before other Muslims deliberately threw themselves to their deaths to avoid the blades of the implacable crowd.[4]

As soon as Tancred learned that his prisoners were under attack he rushed to the Dome. But it was too late. Every single one of them was dead and blood coated the walls of the building. A ransom of three persons per 100 dinars was the conventional exchange in the region at this time; Tancred and Gaston had just lost a small fortune and it was no consolation that they already controlled a great wealth in silver and gems: when it came to booty there was no such thing as having too much. But storm as he might, Tancred found no sympathy from those responsible for the bloodshed, many of whom envied and resented his seizure of the wealth in the Dome.[5]

While gangs of crusaders roamed the streets, the princes and the senior nobles of the crusade met at the al-Aqsā mosque – together with the Dome of the Rock considered by the Christians to be the Temple of Solomon – later that day with a view to deciding who should rule the city. A discordant note was immediately present among them in Tancred's outrage at the disrespect shown to his banner and in the shouts of his critics in reply that Tancred had stolen wealth that rightfully belonged to the Church. In any case, before the leading warriors of the crusade could settle down to their political manoeuvring, the clergy intervened. As far as the crusading clergy were concerned, the rule of Jerusalem should be a matter for the church, not the laity. But rather than risk a direct rebuff from the knights by proposing that a Patriarch govern Jerusalem, the clergy postponed the issue by pointing out that they could not hold serious talks on the future while so many corpses and human remains lying in the streets and buildings threatened to bring plague down upon them all.

Already there was a distinct stench in the air and while corpses lay in piles throughout the whole city, the Temple in front of them was filled with a particularly large number of cadavers. A few Muslim or Jewish citizens had survived the massacre, having been captured in a house whose new occupant had shown them mercy. These survivors were now set to work hauling the bodies out of the gates, tying them together in mounds as big as houses, and setting fire to them. There were pitifully few prisoners to do the work though and it was clearly going to take far too long if it was left to them. The clergy therefore decreed that as a penance for having committed murder, the Christian army was to move the bodies of the slain. There was precedence for this kind of thinking. After the battle of Hastings, the victors were enjoined to perform (or pay for) a year's penance for every person they had slain. But at Hastings Christian had fought Christian. At Jerusalem no one felt particularly penitent for having killed pagans.

In a manner that was ominous for those clergy who hoped that the new ruler of Jerusalem would be one of their own number, the lay members of the Christian army simply disregarded the imposition of this penance. Instead the princes, by making funds available for the payment of a wage, solved the problem in their own fashion and recruited labourers from the poor. The issue of cleaning up the city drew attention to a peculiar feature of the crusading army. During the course of the pilgrimage, even the lowliest member of the Christian forces had the status of a free person. No lord could simply command them to work, as though they were serfs back in Europe.[6]

While the work of removing the corpses proceeded efficiently enough under the stimulus of pay, the conquerors all enjoyed an unlimited supply of clean water and a great abundance of food. In the newly cleaned streets crowds of crusaders would gather to talk, enjoy their sense of achievement, and listen to the songs that were already being composed to celebrate their achievements. An impromptu market came into being, where those who had been quick enough to claim well supplied houses brought their excess goods to swap with one another or sell. There was such a quantity of grain that even those who had missed out on plunder and had to rely on alms or the stipend for moving bodies could afford to refresh themselves with all the food they could eat. The humour of the Christian occupiers of Jerusalem rose as they filled their bellies and strolled around the sites of the famous city.

That this feeling of happiness could simultaneously coincide with a willingness to murder fellow human beings was evident after a meeting among the
princes on the third day after the conquest of the city. There they decided that
given the prospect of a massive army coming up to the city from Egypt, they
could not risk having any enemies within the city. Even though there were few
enough Muslim and Jewish survivors, there were still too many for safety and
the leaders of the Christian army decided a further bout of bloodshed would be
necessary. A pitiful afternoon's work saw those being held for ransom or for
work as slaves butchered helplessly. By now the only Muslim or Jewish survivors of the sack of Jerusalem were those who had departed with Iftikhār, those
who had managed to escape the walls of the city in the confusion of events on
the fifteenth of July, or those very fortunate indeed, in encountering a crusader
willing to hide or disguise them. That some Jewish civilians were later sold as
slaves by Tancred and ended up in Norman Italy, while others were ransomed
by their co-religionists in Egypt, shows that there were some such prisoners in
closely guarded houses, protected not by charitable feelings but a drive for
wealth. Later, when it seemed that insufficient ransoms would be paid for these
captives, Tancred had the least valuable of them beheaded.[7]

In his desire to raise himself up a rank in power, Tancred had earned a
great deal of resentment, especially with regard to his appropriation of such an
enormous hoard of silver. A row broke out as Arnulf of Chocques launched
an unexpected and vigorous attack on Tancred's plundering of the Dome of
the Rock (part of the Temple complex as the Christians saw it). The case presented by Arnulf to the leaders of the crusade was that although everyone was
entitled to keep whatever property they had seized from non-Christians, the
Temple was not to be included in the law of conquest because it was a venerated
Christian site. Would they have tolerated the robbery of the Church of the Holy
Sepulchre and the other Christian churches during the storming of the city?

This was a dark moment for the Norman prince, who had already spent
most of the fortune he had gained in rewarding his followers, paying off all his
debts and recruiting another 40 knights: a major step forward in the pursuit of
lordly power. It was an attack from an unexpected direction, because Arnulf
of Chocques was a fellow Norman (chaplain to Robert of Normandy) and a
good friend of the man Tancred had backed for the bishopric of Bethlehem:
another Arnulf, bishop of Matera. Tancred and Arnulf of Matera had journeyed
together on the crusade and this Arnulf had benefited from their relationship
as a result of Tancred arriving first at Bethlehem and offering protection to the
local Christians. Even though Arnulf of Matera could hardly read and was not

much better educated than the commoners, he was offered the Episcopal rule of the church of Bethlehem. But despite this alliance with Tancred, the two Arnulfs now had their own agenda based on the possibility of Arnulf of Chocques becoming patriarch of Jerusalem and therefore being able to give greater legitimacy to his friend as the bishop of Bethlehem than could any secular prince. One of the main obstacles to that glorious prospect was the hostility of the non-Norman clergy to Arnulf of Chocques and their belief that he was simply a creature of the Normans, particularly because he had led the faction that brought down the Provençal visionary Peter Bartholomew. By attacking Tancred, Arnulf of Chocques was displaying his willingness to put the needs of the Church before all factions. If this was not likely to overcome the deep antagonism between him and the Provençal clergy, it would at least make a very favourable impression on the important new constituency, the Christians of Jerusalem and its environs.

Taking on the Norman prince, however, was no easy prospect. As he had shown in matching words with the Byzantine Emperor, Tancred was capable of holding his own in highly tense verbal exchanges. He began his response skilfully, appealing to his fellow warriors with the point that he was no student of rhetoric, but rather his talents lay with sword and spear. From that perspective, the military one, his actions had been exemplary, for now silver, gold and gems that had lain idle were being put to use in raising an army. The overall result of taking the silver from the Temple was a gain for the public good of the Christian cause and that was not to mention the alms given to the poor. All that was taken was now put in motion so that its productivity could grow, when the treasure had been stuck in the building it did not increase.[8]

Tancred's line of appeal could not use the argument that the Temple was a Muslim sacred place and not a Christian one. It was universally accepted that the building marked a location previously sacred to Christians. Perhaps affected by the knowledge that Muslims claimed Mohammed's night time journey to heaven had begun at the now contested spot, Arnulf claimed it was the site at which the patriarch Jacob had seen a ladder touching the heavens with angels climbing up and down; a site at which the infant Christ had spoken; and at which the adolescent Christ had driven out the money changers.

From the perspective of Godfrey, this was a very unfortunate crisis and a difficult one to resolve. Tancred was a popular figure and to find against him would be to risk alienating the Normans at a time when their support was essential if Godfrey were to become ruler of the city. Moreover, Godfrey, as Tancred's nominal overlord, had benefited from a share of the treasure. On the other hand, Godfrey could not risk the accusation of impiety by openly siding with Tancred in this debate. Military expediency was not grounds for despoiling the Church of wealth. A compromise would have to be reached.

Fortunately for those who wanted harmony in the Christian ranks, there was room for a compromise: Tancred would give back to the Church a tenth of the wealth he had obtained. Having proved himself as a militant champion of the rights of the Church and having been seen to make stirring speeches in that cause, Arnulf had achieved a great deal of his purpose simply by raising the issue. A tithe of Tancred's plunder, 700 marks, was a handsome accretion of ready cash under the circumstances. For Tancred's part, he was only too pleased to legitimize his retention of the rest of the silver, having been alarmed that he might lose very much more. Despite all his recent expenditure he was still able to donate such a sum to the Temple. To the great approval of all sides – except those jealous of the growing power of the two figures concerned – the patriarch and the prince were publicly, and indeed personally, reconciled.[9]

On 22 July 1099, a week after the capture of Jerusalem, the princes and senior nobles finally met to resolve the question of who should rule the city. This had been a well-advertised meeting, the subject of much of the discussion in the streets by the lower social orders. But before the negotiations could begin, their meeting was interrupted by a delegation of the crusading clergy who insisted that it was wrong for the princes to dispose of the city as though it were their property. This group of bishops and priests was not as impressive as it might have been. For one thing it did not include Arnulf of Chocques and his friend Arnulf, bishop of Matera, who disassociated themselves from the current initiative. They were betting on the secular powers and having recently reached an accord with the princes did not want to damage relations with the future ruler of the city.

The papal legate, Adhémar, had commanded a great deal of respect among all the princely leaders of the crusade, not least because of his effective command of an important group of Provençal knights as well as his even-handedness in church matters. After Adhémar had died, a victim of the plague that broke out in Antioch in the summer of 1098, there were few remaining clerical leaders with anything like his authority over the Christian army. There was at least one long-established bishop present among them, one with an illustrious lineage – a member of the Staufen family and brother to Frederick I of Swabia – and considerable experience: Otto, who had been bishop of Strasburg since 1082. But Otto was an 'imperialist' in the sense that he had taken the side of the Emperor Henry IV in a famous dispute with Pope Gregory VII that had raged through Europe, leading to civil wars and schism within the church. Otto had come on the pilgrimage as an act of penitence and reconciliation, but he was certainly not going to fight for a theocratic style of rulership at Jerusalem. Indeed, on his return to Strasburg, the church reform party found him little changed. One of them wrote an obituary for Otto, who died in 1100: 'the schismatic Otto of Strasburg, having returned from the journey to Jerusalem, but, it was believed, still with his schism uncorrected, reached the end of his life.'[10]

Among the more credible advocates of the rights of the church and one who might well have been willing to stand up to the princes at Jerusalem, was William, bishop of Orange. William had stepped into Adhémar's role as best as he could, although he was eclipsed by the agitation of the popular visionary Peter Bartholomew. William certainly had the potential to become an important leader of the clergy, but he died in December 1098 at Ma'arra, leaving Peter of Narbonne, the recently created bishop of Albara, as the head of those who believed in the primacy of church authority over the Holy City. A priest at the outset of the pilgrimage, Peter had only been appointed to his bishopric during the course of the crusade by the influence of Count Raymond and had lost Albara, the base of his temporal power, when the Raymond had ordered Peter to bring his garrison and accompany the expedition on the march to Jerusalem.

Despite his lack of experience and followers, Peter of Narbonne tried his best to act as an advocate of the reform minded clergy, who were, after all, the largest faction of those churchmen who had undertaken the pilgrimage. Peter interrupted the discussion of the princes saying that 'since spiritual matters proceed temporal ones, righteous and proper procedure demands that you first elect a spiritual leader and after that elect a secular ruler; and if you do not we shall not recognize your choice.' The princes were not impressed, meeting this intervention with shouts of anger and replied that it had made them all the more determined to reach a decision about the rule of Jerusalem straight away. The clergy were ushered out and the secular nobles of the Christian army returned to their deliberations. For all the spiritual goals of the expedition, the secular princes were not going to be swayed from establishing a political structure they were used to, one with a liege lord at the head of society.[11]

Who were the main candidates for the lordship of Jerusalem? Of those who commanded sizeable numbers of knights, there were only really two prospective rulers: Count Raymond of Toulouse and Godfrey of Lotharingia. Count Robert of Flanders and Duke Robert of Normandy had a great number of followers; they had a distinguished lineage and – with the exception of Robert of Normandy's propensity to prefer the good life to arduous sieges – had also proven themselves as worthy leaders during the sieges and battles of the crusade.

If either of them had been interested in remaining in the Holy Land, they would certainly have been in contention to take power at Jerusalem. Behind the scenes, the more senior Norman nobles and clergy suggested to the duke that he should consider vying for the position. But neither Robert of Normandy nor the Robert of Flanders were interested. As soon as they could, the duke and the count intended to return home, where they planned to resume their rule over substantial and wealthy lands.

Duke Godfrey, on the other hand, had nothing to go back for. Before setting out from Bouillon, Godfrey had come to terms with his local enemies and abandoned a prolonged struggle to defend his inheritance. Richer, the bishop of Verdun, obtained the county of Verdun and the towns of Stenay and Mouzay for a great sum of coin. This agreement also included a clause that Godfrey destroy his castle at Montfaucon. The abbey of St Gertrude at Nivelles bought Godfrey's personal lands at Baisy and Genappe while Bishop Otbert of Liége got the core territories of Rheims and the castle of Bouillon itself. Godfrey had no intention of returning to Lotharingia: he had staked his future on this expedition. The large funds Godfrey had garnered from the sale of his lands at least guaranteed that he came on the crusade with a sizeable army and the resources to support them. Indeed, as the demands of the march had sapped the wealth and supplies of other Lotharingian nobles, they became more and more dependent on Godfrey. Henry of Esch and Hartmann, count of Dillingen and Kyburg each had had considerable resources, enough to finance the build-ing of a siege engine at Nicea at their own expense. They were so destitute by the siege of Antioch, however, that they survived on a stipend of bread, meat and fish from Duke Godfrey. Hartmann was obliged to enter battle against Kerbogha on a donkey, holding only a Turkish round shield and sword, having sold all his arms and weapons a long time earlier.[12]

As far as the neutrals were concerned, the Lotharingian Duke had won a great deal of respect by his conduct throughout the expedition. Godfrey's feat in cleaving a Muslim rider entirely into two parts was one of the most famous episodes of the whole crusade. It had been noted too that during the assault on Jerusalem, and at great personal risk, Godfrey had directed his troops from the top of the siege tower and had been among the very first of the conquerors to enter the city. He was famous, furthermore, for one other incident.

On the journey towards Antioch, after the army had survived the hardship of the terrain of the high Anatolian plains, they had come to a fertile region with great woods full of game. Having made camp in a pleasant meadow, the Christian nobles rushed out to enjoy their favourite pastime: the hunt. Young hounds bounded along forest paths and as they followed the scent of a variety of beasts, Godfrey's knights became dispersed. Somewhat apart from his men, the duke heard screams and rode towards a thicket where he discovered a lowly member of the Christian army running for his life from an enormous bear. At once Godfrey spurred on his horse and drew his sword. The bear turned to this new threat with equal energy and met the duke at full height, bounding into horse and rider with claws raised and jaw opened wide. A huge roaring bellow resounded through the forest. The bear threw Godfrey from his mount with a blow of its arm at the same time as it tore open the horse's throat with its teeth. Later Godfrey was to say that he was convinced his death was upon him and an ignoble one too. But his luck was in, the bear's attention was on the horse and Godfrey was able to spring to his feet.

The duke now received the worst wound he was to obtain on the whole expedition and a near fatal one at that. It was self-inflicted. His sword had become entangled in with his legs and in his panic Godfrey pulled it free at the cost of a deep wound to his calf. Blood began to spurt from his leg as he stabbed at the bear, his life ebbing away. Fortunately one of Godfrey's knights, Husechin, had been riding as fast as he could towards the source of the great roaring noises and – instantly appraising the situation – he jumped from his horse to run in to pierce the bear through its liver and ribs. Between them, the two knights finally overcame the ferocious beast, before Godfrey sank to the ground, pale with loss of blood. Almost disastrous at the time, ultimately this encounter between Godfrey and the bear was to do the duke no harm. Long after his wound had healed the story was being told of how the duke had come to the aid of a poor Christian and slain a monster. The fact that he had nearly died as a result of slicing open his own leg was forgotten.[13]

For all Godfrey's personal achievements, he fell short of his main rival in one crucial respect. Count Raymond had the single largest following of knights and a great deal of wealth. Looked at from a purely military perspective it was the Provençal count who would make the better ruler of Jerusalem because he would be the more able to defend the city. Like Godfrey, Raymond had retired from political life in his home territories before setting out on the crusade. He had assigned his holdings in Rouergue, Viviers, Digne and Avignon to his son, Bertrand, who in 1095 had made a valuable political marriage to Helen of Burgundy and appeared to be in a secure position to govern in his own right. Taking with him his third wife, Elvira, daughter of Alfonso VI, king of Leon and Castille, the elderly count had no strong motive for returning to Toulouse when the prospect of a glorious career in the Holy Land was available to him.

From the very beginning of Pope Urban II's efforts to raise a Christian army to go east, Count Raymond had seen himself as the person to lead it.

That ambition had been checked by fact that so many princes and knights had taken up the idea of crusade that it was impossible to control. Who, indeed, could command a fiercely independent figure like Bohemond, or the famous Robert of Normandy? But as soon as Bohemond had abandoned the expedition in favour of becoming ruler of Antioch and the other princes showed signs of faltering in their desire to reach Jerusalem, Count Raymond had tried to assert himself as overall commander. At a council of the princes willing to march south at Chastel-Rouge on 4 January 1099, part way between Antioch and the recently captured town of Ma'arra, Count Raymond offered Duke Godfrey and Robert of Normandy 10,000 solidi each to join his following; Robert of Flanders 6,000; Tancred 5,000; and smaller amounts proportionate to the strength of other leaders. The offer was rejected, but the authority of the count was not lost on the emir of Tripoli, who favoured Raymond above all others with lucrative payments in the hope of deflecting the Christian army away from his territories and, if possible, against his enemies.[14]

Raymond did not have a reputation for bravery. In fact rather the opposite was the case: due to a protracted illness at the siege of Antioch, the belief spread that the count's behaviour fell far short of that expected of him. But there was no doubting the piety of the count. Nor could it be denied that Raymond had the favour of Adhémar, with whom he had travelled and fought from the very beginning. After the death of the legate, Raymond had obtained the support of all of Adhémar's followers and it was this accretion of strength in particular that now made him the strongest candidate for the rule of Jerusalem. In recognition of this, the princes offered Raymond the crown.[15]

This was not the generous offer it appeared to be. While the princes had faced down the clergy and disabused them of the notion that a Patriarch would govern Jerusalem, they could not carry the army with them in the notion that the new secular ruler would be 'king' of the city. The popular feeling and one that had to be taken into account, was that it would insult Christ, who had been obliged to wear a crown of thorns in this place, for one of his followers to proudly don a crown of gold. Had Raymond accepted the initial offer and attempted to set himself up as a king, there would have been roars of outrage and his already mutinous Provençal army might have deserted him; particularly those who had set off under the leadership of Adhémar.

Not only did Raymond have to deal with the problem of the title, but also the whole nature of elections at this time were fraught with subtle manoeuvres. The most important feature of an election – whether of pope, bishop, abbot or king – was that it was considered a religious experience. The will of God was made manifest by the result. In this spiritual context, for a candidate to be too eager for the position was to fail to show the virtues of humility and worse, to veer towards the sin of lust. Candidates were expected to have the title thrust upon them, against their own resistance. The most famous reforming pope of the era, Gregory VII, described his election to the papacy in 1073 as follows: 'suddenly . . . there arouse a great tumult and noise among the people and they threw themselves upon me like madmen.' Much as he felt himself unworthy, the inspired crowds raised him to the papal throne in a model of how divine will was coupled to popular enthusiasm.[16]

This ethos also worked to prevent Raymond from being able to accept the first offer put to him. He had to publicly demonstrate his lack of pride and be compelled by popular demand to overcome his modesty and humbly take up the responsibility. Therefore Raymond had to pass in the first round, relying on his supporters to stir up a wave of enthusiasm that could safely bring him to power at a later stage of the discussions. In a very humble speech declining the offer, Raymond confessed that he shuddered at the thought of anyone taking the name of 'king' in Jerusalem but perhaps it was more palatable to another.[17]

If Raymond was relying on a popular movement to move matters in his favour, he was bitterly disappointed. While the senior nobles were deliberating in council, Raymond's candidacy had been undermined, not by the Lotharingians or Normans, but soldiers from among his own Provençal forces, anxious to return to Languedoc. Throughout the streets of the city – where popular gatherings discussed the happenings of the princes – these soldiers had spread malicious rumours about Raymond's character and raised the temperature of public feeling to such a pitch that far from being able to take control of the city, Raymond was constrained by the threat of widespread opposition to his candidacy to demur at the initial offer.[18]

Naturally, Duke Godfrey was next offered the title and Godfrey was in a much more favourable position to accept than Raymond. First, the crowds held him in much higher esteem than they did the Provençal count; secondly, since Godfrey had not expressed any opposition to the title being first offered to Raymond, he could not be accused of being greedy for the crown; and thirdly – and quite decisively – Godfrey accepted the role of ruler of the city, but astutely declined the contentious title of king. Instead he would be prince and defender of Jerusalem. The elderly count was defeated by his own unpopularity and a quite brilliant accommodation by the Lotharingians to the sensibility of the Christian army; one that conceded the symbolism of the crown but retained the substance of political power.

No sooner had Godfrey been proclaimed as 'Prince of Jerusalem' than he moved swiftly to consolidate his position: all displays of reluctance now abandoned in favour of decisive measures to ensure military control of the city. Rallying the Roberts, Gaston, Tancred and several other princes to his side, Godfrey insisted that the Tower of David be surrendered to him. Raymond, already furious with the having the rulership of Jerusalem slip through his fingers, absolutely refused to concede the strategically important fortification. A spiritual excuse was offered by way of explanation for this stubbornness, with the count saying that he needed the tower to ensure that he and his men were treated properly while they waited at the Holy City for Easter, that most celebrated day of the medieval Christian calendar. But this pretext did nothing to hide the fact that the Christian victors were rapidly falling apart.[19]

Once more those Provençals anxious to leave the Holy Land abandoned the count and undermined his attempt to portray the Lotharingians as a threat to their ability to stay in Jerusalem safely until Easter. They obliged Raymond to put the issue of the Tower of David before the Bishop of Albara for judgement. Despite the fact that Peter of Narbonne had been Raymond's appointee to the see, Peter promptly gave the citadel over to Godfrey, now undisputed ruler of the city. It later transpired that it was the dissident Provençal knights who came to Peter with their weapons drawn and insisted he hand over the keys to the tower.[20]

Once the city was secured against his rival – on 25 July 1099 – Godfrey dispatched Tancred and Eustace to Nablus. The relationship between Tancred and Godfrey was becoming a firm one. When he first left his uncle, Bohemond, at Antioch, Tancred had brought his 40 knights to the following of Count Raymond for a payment of 5,000 solidi and two fine horses. Soon chaffing at his relationship with Count Raymond and claiming that he had not been paid, Tancred abandoned Raymond for the less imposing authority of Duke Godfrey, whilst clearly keeping an eye on his own prospects. The fact that Godfrey was now ruler of Jerusalem and had tactfully supported the young prince – both in his acquisition of a great treasure and in gaining the lordship of Bethlehem – earned him Tancred's loyalty. And a valuable loyalty it was too, 80 knights willing to stay and campaign in the vicinity of Jerusalem were very precious given the certainty that in time the other princes would leave the region.

When Tancred and Eustace had conducted their raid on Nablus, in the days before the final assault on Jerusalem began, they had noticed how poorly defended the city was. No garrison of Muslim cavalry had come to contest them for the herds they had stolen. So on the 25 July they rode out with their knights and a sizeable body of foot soldiers to demand its surrender in the name of the new ruler at Jerusalem. The town offered no resistance and the

Christian lords were quickly and comfortably accommodated in Nablus with their troops.

Back in Jerusalem, feeling abandoned and betrayed, Count Raymond stormed off from the city on the 28 July, declaring himself dishonoured. Ignoring the threat posed by the long-awaited Egyptian army, Count Raymond, with those personally loyal to him as well as the crowds who had believed in the popular visionary Peter Bartholomew, took themselves to the Jordan and having gathered palms undertook a strange ritual. Peter Bartholomew had given instruction to Count Raymond that his desires would be met by God if he were rowed across the river on a raft of branches, clad only in his shirt and trousers, there to be prayed for by the crowd. The significance of the ritual was unknown to those present, but Count Raymond underwent it all the same. It acted as a salve for his hurt and as a demonstration that some crusaders, at least, still believed in his special relationship to God.[21]

Inside the walls of Jerusalem, however, Godfrey was presented with an even greater sign of God's favour. As it had become more and more likely that the Christian army would reach Jerusalem and besiege of the city, one of the Christian clergy living in Jerusalem had taken their most venerated relic and hidden it. A fragment of the cross on which Christ was crucified had been made into a gold clad cross about 20 centimetres high. Fearing that this, the Lord's Cross, would either be stripped of its gold by Iftikhār's men or damaged in the turmoil of the siege, the cleric had hidden it in a run-down and dusty house, one that had been long abandoned. Now that there was a rightful Christian ruler in the city, the cleric felt it safe to bring the cross to light again. On Friday 29 July 1099 – a day that co-incidentally saw the death of Pope Urban II, shortly before the news arrived in Rome of the success of his crusade – a great procession was held through the streets of Jerusalem, where the clergy led the people to the hiding place of the relic. Then, with great veneration for the cross, all returned to the Church of the Holy Sepulchre. It was a very auspicious start for the new prince.[22]

The other keystone of Christian control of Jerusalem was the election of a patriarch to head the clergy. If the patriarch was not to be the head of a theocratic system of government over the city, he still was a powerful figure, in charge of greater revenues than were available to the king and with a great deal of autonomy. Clearly it was of great importance to Godfrey that the chosen patriarch was someone whom he could co-operate with. It did not trouble the Latin Christian army that the clergy of Jerusalem already had a head. Their patriarch, Simeon II, had fled to Cyprus in anticipation of the siege. From the island he had done his best to ingratiate himself with the crusading princes, sending them gifts of pomegranates, fruits, fat bacons and fine wines. This counted for little in the aftermath of the conquest, for the Latin Christians wanted one of their own, even if that meant the risk of producing a schism between the recently arrived clergy and those loyal to their former patriarch.

The difficulty for the Christian clergy was in finding a suitable candidate from among their own ranks. There were very few survivors with anything like the education expected for someone holding such an exalted position. Otto of Strasbourg would have been an attractive candidate from Godfrey's point of view, not least in his respect for secular authority. But his past association with the enemies of the reform papacy counted against him, as did his desire to return to Germany. It was the Norman, Arnulf of Chocques, who – as he had long hoped – therefore emerged as the leading candidate.

Arnulf of Chocques was skilled at logic and had taught the subject to Cecilia, daughter of William the Conqueror, at the Holy Trinity convent in Caen. In grammatical learning too, Arnulf was qualified for a high position in the church. On the death of the crusading bishop Odo of Bayeux at Palermo, early in 1097, Arnulf inherited control of a great deal of the bishop's funds and valuable possessions. With this came a higher profile among the Christian army and Arnulf proved to be a very capable speaker and leader of Christian services.[23]

Above all because of his education, Arnulf was a clear contender for the position of patriarch. But his authority was undermined by the fact that the former supporters of Peter Bartholomew – who included some of the more fervent and popular preachers – hated him as being responsible for the visionary's death. To some extent Arnulf had tried to conciliate the neutrals and the local Christians by gaining a share of the silver from the Dome of the Rock for the Church. But Arnulf's enemies drew attention to the fact that he was an illegitimate child: worse, the child of a clergyman. Moreover, during the course of the crusade his enjoyment of the company of women had earned Arnulf such a notorious reputation that the versemakers of the expedition were inspired to compose salacious tales about him.[24]

What might have tipped the balance with the neutrals and secured Arnulf's appointment was his active leadership during the course of the crusade and a willingness to share the risks of the soldiers. At Nicea he had stood among the throwing machines, urging the soldiers on in the hard and dangerous work of flinging stone after stone at the city. At Dorylaeum Arnulf had been among those in the vanguard of the army who – under the leadership of Bohemond – had weathered half a day of attack while waiting for the rest of the army to come up; there he had kept his composure and helped organize the initial scattered army into a coherent defensive force. Most noted of all his deeds was the fact that in the spring of 1099 Arnulf had volunteered to leave the siege of 'Arqā, go to the coast and sail north, skirting the Arab cities, to find Godfrey and Robert of Normandy and remonstrate with them on the need to rejoin the rest of the army, given the rumoured approach of a Turkish force.[25]

On 1 August 1099 Arnulf won the acclaim of the majority of the assembled clergy. As with Godfrey's title a certain amount of tact was required in consolidating his position. Given the sensitivity of the position and the significant level of opposition, Arnulf took the title of Chancellor of the Holy Church of Jerusalem, Procurator of the Holy Relics and Custodian of the Alms of the Faithful. In effect he was the patriarch and it was only a matter of days before he was using the term in his letters, but Arnulf awaited papal confirmation of his extraordinary promotion with a certain anxiety and caution. As leader of the Church of Jerusalem, Arnulf's first act was to agree with a proposal by Godfrey that 20 brothers should be assigned to keep the divine offices, singing praises and hymns to Christ every hour, and offering mass. They would be paid for out of the offerings that came to the Church. To let the Christian population of the city know when psalms were being sung and mass was underway, they commissioned bronze bells, for under Muslim rule no Christian church had bells that sounded, nor had any other signal been made from a church that service had begun.[26]

In the two weeks since the Jerusalem had fallen, while the Christians were manoeuvring against one another in order to shape their structures for governing the city, al-Afdal had finally brought his great army out of Cairo. The vizier was a methodical man and fully aware of the importance of effective logistical support for a major military undertaking. He had led an army to capture Jerusalem in August 1098 and had done so very efficiently by bringing with him a great number of mangonels and plenty of supplies for the construction of more. Despite the advantages of catching the Christian army outside the walls of the city, al-Afdal could not accelerate the motions of the Fatimid bureaucracy in time to achieve this: it took around two months to fully mobilize the army.

The mustering of the Fatimid army was always a cumbersome process, with civil administrators having to be part of the process as they were responsible for the soldiers' pay. In 1099 the mobilization was hampered by the fact that Egypt had experienced a serious plague on and off for the previous five years, as well as the fact that the army had marched north only the previous year, bringing with it much of the equipment stored in the three great storehouses of Cairo. The state armoury and arsenal, including a workshop employing

3,000 craftsmen, had been labouring hard to replenish the necessary arms and armour. When it did finally get underway, however, the Fatimid army was an impressive sight. Berbers and Arabs provided the light cavalry that were so important to the pattern of warfare in the region, but a more heavily armoured component was present in the form of Armenian horsemen and Sudanese foot soldiers. The latter formed about a third of the armed forces available to al-Afdal and were distinctive to Christian eyes, due to the darkness of their skin and the fact they were armed with unusual weaponry. As well as bows, which they fired from bended knee, they had iron-tipped whips that when wielded skilfully could strike with such force that they splintered shields and even cut through the links of chain mail. These whips could be used to lash at the faces of approaching horses, deterring the all-important charge of the Christian cavalry and had the additional psychological advantage that their use in large numbers created an intimidating wave of noise.[27]

All in all, the Fatimid army assembling at Ascalon was around 20,000 strong, many of them troops of the highest calibre. If al-Afdal, who was personally leading the army, was a little complacent, that was understandable. His general Iftikhār was in Ascalon with the garrison from the citadel of Jerusalem and with an accurate assessment of the strength of the Christian army. The Muslim troops could expect to face about 1,200 knights and 10,000 foot soldiers and should have a considerable advantage in siege equipment. The odds therefore favoured the Egyptians by some two to one. Still, there was no reason to take any chances and al-Afdal waited at Ascalon for the fleet to bring the supplies that would be needed for the siege and for reinforcements from the coastal cities.

News of the growing size of the Fatimid camp outside of Ascalon reached Jerusalem on 4 August. Godfrey's response was to send a messenger to Nablus, to set Tancred and Eustace's troop in motion with orders to scout for accurate intelligence. The Christian ruler of Jerusalem set the rendezvous for Ramla and while Tancred rode west to the coast, Godfrey acted with great energy to get the maximum possible number of soldiers in the field. Already he had decided not to be penned up within the walls of the city but to go out and meet the enemy in the field.

The scouting manoeuvre by Tancred and Eustace was successful. Riding southwards from Caesarea with the sea on their right hand side, their presence in the area was entirely unexpected and the Christian princes surprised a group of riders from the vanguard of the Fatimid army that they encountered on 7 August. The Christian knights scattered their opponents and took several captive. These prisoners confirmed that al-Afdal was at Ascalon with the core of the Egyptian army just awaiting the arrival of the final batch of supplies and reinforcements before setting out. A courier was sent at once to Jerusalem confirming that the rumours were correct, while Tancred and Eustace continued on to Ramla.[28]

Leaving only a small garrison for the Tower of David and the city, Godfrey rode out for Ramla on 9 August in the company of Robert of Flanders, the Patriarch and his clerical ally Arnulf, bishop-elect of Bethlehem. Before their departure a barefoot procession had been held before the Church of the Holy Sepulchre and the Temple of the Lord, praying to God not to allow the sacred places so recently purified to be profaned once more. Peter the Hermit – the talisman of the poor – and the Patriarch took up the Holy Cross and carried it with the departing knights.[29]

Whereas Robert of Flanders accepted the need to accompany Godfrey without demur, for once his close friendship with Robert of Normandy broke down. The Norman duke and Raymond of Toulouse were doubtful. Was this all simply an exaggerated alarm so that Godfrey could set a precedent in wielding power over them all? Rather than leave with the others, they simply sent ahead a few trustworthy knights. Only after these knights had raced back with the news that the prospect of battle was indeed a genuine one did Robert of Normandy and Count Raymond ride out of Jerusalem, leaving the city almost bare of defenders and the remaining population praying fervently and incessantly that the Christian warriors would not be overcome.

In the meantime, Arnulf, the bishop-elect of Bethlehem could not be found, nor was he ever seen again by the Christian army. Duke Godfrey had given the bishop the responsibility of returning to Jerusalem to encourage the stragglers to hurry if they wanted to participate in the coming battle. Arnulf's alliance with his namesake, Arnulf of Chocques, now patriarch, had advanced his prospects for a successful career in the Holy City and its environs. That career was abruptly terminated by his capture en route between Ramla and Jerusalem. Given that no subsequent effort was made to ransom the bishop or exchange him for a senior Muslim prisoner, it is likely that Arnulf was killed on the spot.

On 11 August, with their full force of knights, about 1,200, and with 9,000 foot soldiers, the crusading army set out for Ascalon. It was almost reckless in ambition, to march so deep into enemy territory with such a modest force. But to take the offensive had the critical advantage that the majority of the army wished to return to Europe and might not have united in order to conduct a potentially long and difficult defence of Jerusalem. Furthermore, they had the example of Bohemond's daring march to intercept the much greater force of Ridwan of Aleppo at the siege of Antioch. All the senior knights, except those with Count Raymond and Robert of Normandy had fought in that famous victory.

All the same, it was a terrible gamble, to march nearly 40 kilometres into hostile territory to give battle. The consequences of defeat would be disastrous. Not only would Jerusalem be lost, but it would be unlikely that many of the knights, let alone the foot soldiers, would escape all the way back to Antioch and safety. This really was an 'all or nothing' encounter and the Christian princes knew it. No longer bickering for position, everyone accepted Godfrey's command. The ruler of Jerusalem was careful not to antagonize anyone and included all the prominent leaders in his councils. Their first decree was to emphasize that the coming battle was about the security of their lives and of Christian Jerusalem and not about booty. Any crusader who began looting before the battle was concluded would have their ears and nose cut off. They also agreed a marching order that took into account the danger of being surrounded and the typical tactics of the Muslim armies they had fought thus far. Assuming that a simple formation of vanguard and rearguard would find itself enveloped, the Christians spaced out their order of march into three sections based on their regional affiliation, front, middle and back, each of which in turn was organized with three distinct sections:

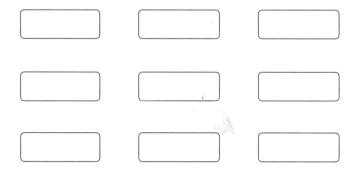

The idea, potentially a very effective one, was that no matter which direction an attack came from, the commander of a section could turn to face the enemy without creating major weaknesses for the army as a whole. Duke Godfrey in the centre was available to bolster the ranks that most needed assistance. In the event, the careful planning of their marching order proved to be unnecessary, the Egyptian army was still in camp.[30]

Towards sunset, about 25 kilometres north of Ascalon, the crusaders encountered enormous herds of cattle, camels, oxen, sheep and goats. These animals were being brought to feed the huge numbers of soldiers at Ascalon and provide them with milk and meat for the coming siege. The herdsmen fled at the approach of the Christian army, although as they numbered in the thousands they might have put up sufficient resistance to save a sizeable part of the herd from capture. But their shock at the unexpectedly large force marching towards them was too great to think of anything but escape. In keeping with their new rule concerning booty, there was no dispersal of the crusading army in pursuit of these animals, nor any attempt to rope them off as personal property. To meet the needs of feeding the Christian army, a certain number of the sheep were butchered, but the rest of the animals were ignored.

That night around their camp fires the crusaders spent a wretched time, without tents or wine and with very little bread, grain or salt. Meat, at least, was in abundance, with mutton being substituted for bread. A strange and disconcerting rumour spread that al-Afdal intended to massacre all those in Jerusalem over 20 years of age, but that the younger Franks would be held in captivity to mate with Egyptian women to breed a warrior race from Frankish stock. Meanwhile, the fleeing herdsmen arrived at the camp of al-Afdal. Their reports were, however, somewhat garbled. It was a serious blow that a Christian raiding party had stolen the herds intended for the siege of Jerusalem, but the Egyptian vizier had no idea that the full force of the crusade was nearly upon him. Rather, he assumed that the knights would be returning in the direction of Jerusalem with their spoils. There was no need for hasty measures; instead he planned to set out in a few more days, when the auguries were propitious.[31]

The arrival of dawn on 12 August 1099 found the crusader army stirring. A cacophony of trumpets and horns sounded out, drowning the chorus of birds that fled into the sky. The fanfare was hardly necessary for few had slept well under the open sky, knowing that their fate and that of everyone waiting in Jerusalem was to be decided in the day ahead. Again the leaders of the army impressed upon everyone the need to refrain from looting until the battle was won. This time the message was reinforced by Arnulf and Peter, who as they took confession and blessed the army with the Holy Cross, made it clear that anyone who took plunder prematurely would be excommunicated.[32]

Once more the Christian army assembled in their three-by-three formation and resumed the march to Ascalon. As they did so, an extraordinary response came from the herds milling around the soldiers. The animals pricked up their ears and as the army marched forward, the domesticated creatures did the same. When the army paused or accelerated, the herds kept pace. This proved to be more than just a curious pattern of behaviour; it meant that when the Egyptians saw the clouds of dust in the sky that indicated a large force was approaching, the size of the Christian army appeared to be massively exaggerated.[33]

From al-Afdal's perspective, the morning had brought the greatest shock of his political and military career. That the Christians would dare abandon their walls and come to fight the mighty Egyptian army at Ascalon could hardly have been anticipated. Nor that they would pass up the chance of taking a great deal of plunder back to Jerusalem in order to risk their lives in battle. There was little time for preparation. While trumpets and drums sounded the mobilization, it was the Sudanese infantry who could most quickly be sent to interpose themselves before the advancing crusaders. The rest of the army, especially the heavily armoured Armenian knights needed time to prepare themselves. From the walls of Ascalon, the citizens stared with alarm at the great clouds of dust that marked the rapid advance of a Christian force that seemed to match the numbers of Fatimid troops in the camps below, now the scene of urgent activity and the source of blaring calls to arms.

As the crusaders closed upon their enemy, they redeployed, forming a longer front and sending foot soldiers with archers ahead to protect the cavalry until they were close enough to charge. The herds of animals that had followed them this far now fell away as the pace of the army quickened. Duke Godfrey and his men took the critical left flank of the line, critical because as they were advancing with the sea on their right, it was the more exposed left wing of the Christian army that had the best view of the Jaffa and Jerusalem gates of Ascalon. Godfrey's plan was, if possible, to avoid committing his troops until the last, so that he could monitor developments from the direction of the city and respond if additional Muslim troops issued forth.

On the right, riding through orchards that reached nearly all the way to the sandy shoreline, was Count Raymond and the Provençal army. Their task was also to hold back in case of Muslim reinforcements or a faltering in the momentum of the overall attack. In the centre, Robert of Normandy and Robert of Flanders, once more side by side, were to lead the main assault with Tancred and many other less prominent leaders supporting them. As the Christian centre came into contact with the Sudanese infantry arrows began to fly, soon the knights spurred their horses and lowered their lances and as they charged the formation of the army looked like a flattened V, the wings moving less swiftly than the centre, ensuring that the line would not be enveloped.

For a while the fighting was fierce and the whips of the Sudanese troops offered some protection against the advancing cavalry. But there was no core to the Fatamid army, no heavy cavalry to come to the assistance of their infantry. Instead all was confusion among the tents. As the fighting became fiercer it favoured the mail-clad knights, to the point that the losses of the Muslim infantry were intolerable. They scattered and the way was open to the weak and disorganized heart of al-Afdal's army.

Seizing the opportunity, Godfrey signalled for the whole army to join the assault and right across the line, from Raymond's forces at the coast through to the Lotharingians on the left, the banners of the Christian army moved deep into the Fatamid camp. He may not have enjoyed the grind of sieges, but when Robert of Normandy was given the opportunity to fight he rode into battle as courageously as any knight. Having spotted al-Afdal's standard, a golden apple on the top of a pole covered with silver, Robert and his followers charged at the knot of Muslim warriors around it and Robert himself struck down the standard bearer. Nearby Robert of Flanders had ridden with equal determination through the Fatimid army; while Tancred, unsurprisingly, was raging through the heart of the camp.[34]

Faced with this onslaught, without adequate organization and equipment, the Fatimid army broke apart. Some ran towards Ascalon in the hope of reaching the gates before the Christian knights, others ran towards the sea in the hope of swimming out to Egyptian ships. Still more just stood, helpless and bewildered to find their enemies all around them. An immense slaughter began. Like butchers killing beasts in an abattoir, the knights struck out left and right with clinical efficiency, piling up the corpses. A miserable fate overtook many of those who had run for the gates of the city. Crowded together in their panic, the fleeing army created such a press that hundreds suffocated. Hundreds more were doomed by the hurried closure of the gates. Those who had chosen to seek safety towards the sea were no better off as they ran into Count Raymond's army and their deaths. Pitiful scenes were played out as men ran back and forth on the sand until caught and stabbed. Seeing the battle was lost, the ships of the Egyptian navy hoisted their sails and stood out to sea.

Many of the Muslim soldiers had climbed palm trees or into the branches of olive and fig trees, hoping to be concealed among the leaves. Once discovered, those within reach were speared and slaughtered, while those higher up in the branches provided targets for archers, until, wounded, they fell to the ground and the blades that awaited them. Although the beginning of looting among the tents of the Egyptian army gave some Muslim soldiers the confidence to attempt a rally, Duke Godfrey had his own men well in hand. Berating the Christians who had paused in their destruction of enemy soldiers, Godfrey scattered the remaining pocket of resistance and the massacre continued throughout the afternoon.[35]

At last the Christian army regrouped and the army was given permission to gather booty. It was an immense haul. Not only were there thousands of camels, cattle, donkeys, sheep, goats and oxen, there were tents full of military equipment. Singing praises to God and looking forward to the celebrations on their return, the greater part of the army set out for Jerusalem, triumphant and happy. Proud of his role in the battle, Robert of Normandy paid 20 marks for the banner of al-Afdal, which he donated to the Church of the Holy Sepulchre, where it was displayed until recaptured by Saladin in 1187. The might of Egypt was shattered. By this victory the crusaders had ensured that Jerusalem, the city for which they had endured so much suffering, would remain in Christian hands for the foreseeable future.

Chapter 10

Legacy

In its own terms, the First Crusade was an extraordinary success. Having set out in 1096 with only the most vague idea of the political situation in the Levant, three years later the crusaders had established a new Christian principality at Antioch, a new kingdom at Jerusalem, and had taken over the Armenian lordship of Edessa. Moreover, they had defeated the powerful army of Kerbogha, general for the Seljuk caliphate based in Baghdad, and that of al-Afdal, the vizier of the Fatimid caliphate of Cairo. These achievements more than fulfilled the vows the pilgrims had taken back in Europe, for they had not only placed the Holy City in the hands of a Christian ruler but their military victories against much larger armies had ensured that the fledgling Christian states were secured, at least for the short term.

The princes and the leading knights of the army were almost instantly considered heroes by the Latin Christian world. Very soon after 1099 lords were being entertained in their halls by verses composed to honour the venture, verses which were careful to celebrate the deeds of any relative of the host might who was on the crusade. While the travels of singers and performers spread tales of the conquest of the Holy City right across Europe, more sedentary monastic scholars accomplished the same popularization of the crusade through their writings. There seemed to be no more worthy subject matter than the story of the Holy Journey and by 1110 several accounts of the crusade, refined and polished and with edifying examples of praiseworthy behaviour, were circulating throughout the literate circles of Western Europe.

The knight whose reputation was most celebrated was Godfrey, the tall, fair-haired, conqueror of Jerusalem. All sorts of legends sprang up about him, with a variety of popular tales presenting the Lotharingian warrior as a near saint. Godfrey gained the power to heal the blind; his election to the rule of the city came after a lightning bolt lit a candle he was holding; he fought famous trials of individual combat against Muslim princes; and so forth. Later composers of romantic verses found Godfrey an attractive figure for their chivalric tales and in some he was made the grandson of the Swan Knight, one of six brothers who were said to turn into swans when the golden necklaces that they were born with were removed.[1]

One of the reasons that such legends could spring up in regard to Godfrey is that he did not live long after obtaining his new domain. Therefore no distasteful incidents of political alliance with local Muslim rulers or examples of military setback existed to cloud the purity of his story. Godfrey died on 18 July 1100 and with his death came a short political struggle for control of the new kingdom. The Normans and Lotharingians, who had co-operated at the siege of Jerusalem, now fell out. Tancred, in alliance with Diambert, archbishop of Pisa and papal legate, who had recently arrived in the region and who had managed to obtain the patriarchate of Jerusalem, urged his uncle, Bohemond, to come south and take the city. In the meantime the Lotharingian entourage of Godfrey seized the all-important citadel of Jerusalem and sent their messengers to Edessa to appeal to Baldwin, Godfrey's brother, to take over.

The race was won by Baldwin and by Christmas 1100 his position was secure enough that he could hold a ceremony in Bethlehem in which he was reconciled to Diambert, with the patriarch crowning Baldwin king of Jerusalem. The reign of Baldwin I was a modestly successful one from the perspective of the Christian nobility of the kingdom and while he suffered the occasional severe military check, by his death in 1118 Baldwin had gradually expanded the territory under Christian control, notably by the capture of the Fatimid coastal cities of Acre in 1104, Tripoli in 1109, and Beirut the following year.

Not all the prominent leaders of the First Crusade enjoyed as much success in later life as the Lotharingian brothers. Robert of Flanders did well enough, returning to his country with great fame and a number of relics, relics that won him the enthusiasm of the local clergy and the nickname Robert of Jerusalem. Manoeuvring with some success between the German, English and French kings, Robert was able to govern Flanders with near complete autonomy until his death on 5 October 1111, drowning after a fall from his horse while on an expedition with the French king, Louis VI, 'the fat'. His close comrade on the First Crusade, Robert of Normandy, lived a great deal longer, but would have swapped all those extra years for the freedom of his crusading companion.[2]

On his return to Normandy, Duke Robert was immediately embroiled in a struggle for control of England. With his older brother, William II, dying in a hunting accident in the New Forest on 2 August 1100, the duke was in a position to claim the English crown, but only if he could unseat his younger brother, Henry, who had benefited from William's death and Robert's absence to move quickly to consolidate himself as king. Successfully landing in Portsmouth in 1101 thanks to the corruption of the admiral of Henry's defensive fleet, an invasion by Robert's army began well; only to peter out as the church intervened to prevent a bloody civil war between the brothers and their respective supporters. Robert was never again to have such an opportunity to defeat his younger brother.

Over the next four years, while Henry slowly but surely consolidated his position in England and undermined the strength of those knights who had opposed him, Robert's domain grew weaker and weaker as – at the cost of his political authority – the duke's energies were spent on living a pleasant and dissolute life. In 1105 Henry felt confident enough to launch a major invasion of Normandy and by September 1106 Robert, having seen the loyalty of his followers disintegrate, decided to risk everything with a desperate attack on Henry's army at Tinchebray. Defeat meant that the rest of Robert's long life was one of captivity, for the first 20 years at Devizes Castle, before his removal to Cardiff Castle where he died in 1134. The Latin writers of the Christian world were universal in their pity for the former crusader.

By contrast with the downward trajectory of Robert, the young Italian Norman, Tancred, went on from the conquest of Jerusalem to become a famous prince in the Near East. Back in 1096, Tancred and his uncle, Bohemond, had made a pact to go on crusade together. Tancred had agreed to set out on crusade with Bohemond as his lord, while Bohemond swore that Tancred would be his second in command. This arrangement was adhered to throughout their lives.

In August 1100, Bohemond was imprisoned after being surrounded by the Damishend emir Malik Ghazi Gumushtakin and captured near Melitene. Tancred, who had been building up his own small principality of Galilee, hurried north to act as regent of Antioch. With Bohemond's release in 1103, however, Tancred was in a difficult position; having lost his estates in Galilee to King Baldwin I due to his absence at Antioch, he was back to being the lord of only very minor territories. Whatever tension may have arisen between the two relatives as a result in this diminution of Tancred's status they did not fall out but rather co-operated in order to extend the authority of Antioch against their many enemies.

After a year campaigning together to strengthen the principality of Antioch, Bohemond once more left Tancred in charge of the principality. Because he had an ambition to rid Antioch of its greatest threat, the Byzantine attempts to regain the city, Bohemond left for Italy and France in 1105 to recruit an army with which he intended to best Alexius, the Byzantine Emperor. Bohemond's tour through France was a triumphant one, culminating in him marrying Constance, the daughter of King Phillip and obtaining the hand of Cecilia, her half sister, for Tancred.

In the autumn of 1107 Bohemond invaded Greece, setting up a siege at Dyrrhachium. But Alexius moved swiftly too, settling his affairs in Anatolia so that he could be free to bring up his army and navy in reply. Soon it was Bohemond who was on the defensive and in September 1108 the Norman prince was obliged to recognize he had been defeated with a treaty that surrendered the autonomy of Antioch by making its ruler a vassal of the Byzantine Empire. Rather than implement the Treaty of Devol, Bohemond retired to Apulia, where he died in 1111, a celebrated figure but one whose final place in the political hierarchy of the times was far more modest than the empire he had dreamed of.

While Bohemond's star had declined, Tancred's had risen. After Bohemond's defeat at Dyrrhachium in 1108, Tancred took charge of Antioch once more, holding it in the name of Bohemond's young son. As ruler of Antioch, Tancred very effectively sustained the autonomy of the principality, with success in battle against rival Christian lords and also against Ridwan, the powerful ruler of Aleppo. Having skilfully arranged alliances with Latin Christian, Muslim and Armenian rulers in the region Tancred looked to be a position to increase his authority and fame even further, when he fell ill and died on 12 December 1112, only 36 years old. His had been an extraordinarily vigorous life of warfare, even by the standards of the day, and a striking example of how military success and strategic acumen could take a young knight with just 40 followers to the heights of fame and power.

The rivalry between Tancred and Count Raymond of Toulouse, that had been so evident at the siege of Jerusalem, was also continued throughout their lives, for Count Raymond remained in the region as an ally of the Byzantine emperor. Early in 1101, a new wave of crusaders began to arrive at Constantinople, inspired by the success of those who had embarked on the expedition of 1096. Raymond of Toulouse was in Constantinople at the time and at the urging of Alexius joined the crusade. Whereas Raymond and the Byzantine forces wanted to campaign in western Anatolia, the news of Bohemond's capture by Malik Ghazi excited the newly arrived knights, causing them to ride off eastwards with the intention of rescuing their hero. The adventure ended catastrophically for the Christian army when it ran into a united Muslim army: Malik Ghazi and the Seljuk sultan of Rum, Qilij Arslan, were supported by troops from as far afield as Aleppo. Count Raymond barely escaped alive (loosing his precious relic, the Holy Lance in the process) and made his way back to Constantinople.

Sailing towards Latakia, where a great many of his troops were based, Count Raymond was unfortunate in becoming separated from his fleet and having landed at Tarsus, he was immediately arrested by a knight called Bernard the

Stranger and sent to Antioch. It must have been painful for the Provençal veteran to be a prisoner of the young Norman prince, but Tancred could hardly justify holding Raymond for any length of time. The count was released after vowing that he would not campaign in the region of Antioch.

From this low point of military defeat at the hands of a Muslim army and capture by a fellow Christian, Raymond's fortunes improved dramatically. Reunited with those Provençal troops remaining in the Near East – some 300 knights – Raymond conquered for himself a new principality at the expense of the Muslim rulers of the cities and towns around Tripoli. From a base at Tortosa, Raymond conducted raids and by the spring of 1104 he had constructed a major new castle overlooking Tripoli itself. Raymond died at this castle, Mount Pilgrim (or the castle of Saint-Gilles as the Muslim world called it) on 28 February 1105, shortly after the emir of Tripoli had resigned the suburbs of his city to Christian control.

Of the other prominent Christian figures involved with the siege of Jerusalem, Peter the Hermit returned to Europe and founded an Augustinian monastery at Neufmoutier, Flanders (in modern day Belgium). He died in 1115 as prior of his monastery, a celebrated figure. Arnulf of Chocques, on the other hand, had a more troubled career. Having won the position of Patriarch of Jerusalem in the aftermath of the siege, he lost it in December 1100 with the arrival of the genuine papal heavyweight, Daimbert, legate and archbishop of Pisa. Hanging on in the position of archdeacon of Jerusalem, Arnulf made a comeback to the Patriarchate in 1112, only to once again be deposed by a papal legate in 1115. On appeal to Pope Paschal II, Arnulf regained his high position in 1116, which he kept until his death in 1118.

Eustace, the older brother of Godfrey, returned to Europe after the crusade to rule the very important and wealthy county of Boulogne. Even so, the kingdom of Jerusalem was sufficiently attractive that Eustace set out to take the crown when, in 1118, he heard of the death of his younger brother Baldwin I. Having reached Apulia, Eustace learned that another former crusader, Baldwin of Bourcq had managed to obtain the throne ahead of him, so he turned back and remained lord of Boulogne until his death around 1125.

Of the less senior figures involved in the crusade, a great deal is known about the French knight Thomas of Marle, because he returned to a life of notoriety in the vicinity of Reims. There he outraged the church by his constant depredations and sadistic tortures of those who resisted him and his men. Eventually Thomas drew upon himself the wrath of Louis the Fat, and died, on 9 November 1130, as a result of injuries sustained when Raoul, count of Vermandois, acting on behalf of the king, ambushed him.

A close friend of Thomas on the crusade followed a similarly errant path on return to Chartres. Raimbold Croton came home a hero, celebrated in verse for being the first to place his hand on the walls of Jerusalem in the premature assault of 13 June. But the positive reputation Raimbold had earned with the population and the clergy of Chartres was dissipated as he used violence against non-combatants to resolve a dispute with Bonneval Abbey. Raimbold had one of the monks whom opposed him castrated. As a result, the crusader was given 14 years' penance by Bishop Ivo of Chartres.[3]

Aside from the famous, or notorious, figures in the Christian army at the siege of Jerusalem, can anything be said about what happened to the former serf, the female servant, the farmer and the other categories termed *pauperes* by contemporaries? The scant evidence that exists for the lowly crusaders suggests that providing they managed to avoid death or captivity as a result of a Muslim raid, they did very well. No one in the newly founded Latin Kingdom of Jerusalem was a serf, with all the onerous obligations and restrictions that lay upon that class back in Europe, rather, those who settled down as farmers had what for the times was a relatively large degree of freedom. This can be seen from the charters of the kingdom.

At Beit-Jibrin, for example, built in 1136 and whose charters were renewed in 1158 and 1177, the settlers had the right to leave the land if such was their choice. Instead of field use being subject to the decision of the lord, tenures in Beit-Jibrin were hereditary and could even be sold by the farming family who owned one. The farmers did have to pay rent to the lord, but this was not a fixed one base on the amount of land cultivated, rather it was *terraticum*, a portion of the crops. This gave the farmer some security against years of natural hardship or years where warfare led to the loss of the crop.

A similar picture is evident from Castle Imbert, now Akhzib, where a colony was established by royal initiative during 1146–1153. To attract settlers, those who came to the town received houses as hereditary possessions without rent or duty. Each farmer obtained a plot of land for tillage and a further allocation of land in order to cultivate vines or a garden. The obligation that came with these holdings was simply to pay the king a quarter of the crop. The king also obtained revenues from his control of baking and bathing, but on the whole was drawing less wealth from the Christian peasantry of his realm than was a French, German or English lord of the same era.[4]

Another example also suggests that life for the Christian poor in the Near East could be relatively favourable. Writing in 1184 the historian and chancellor, William of Tyre, described a settlement where 'certain cultivators of the fields from the neighbouring places had gathered together and . . . they had built there a church and a suburb near the fortress of Daron, where the men of less substance could prosper more easily than in the city.' The fact that the colonists were described as coming together in order to erect a church and dwellings on their own initiative suggests a great deal more autonomy existed for them than would have done in, say, France at the time. These poor Christians seem to have been free from lordship and indeed prospering as a result.[5]

If the serfs and farmers who had given up everything and left for the Promised Land had hoped to find a better life at the end of the road, then it seems that their aim was achieved. The small minority of them, that is, who survived the hardship of the journey. Although he was exaggerating for the sake of encouraging more Christians to come settle around Jerusalem, Fulcher of Chartres, while living in the Holy City wrote a famous passage, which expresses this idea:

For we who were Occidentals have now become Orientals. He who was a Roman or a Frank has in this land been made into a Galilean or a Palestinian. He who was of Reims or Chartres has now become a citizen of Tyre or Antioch. We have already forgotten the places of our birth; already these are unknown to many of us or not mentioned any more. Some already possess homes or households by inheritance. Some have taken wives not only of their own people but Syrians or Armenians or even Saracens who have obtained the grace of baptism. One has his father-in-law as well as his daughter-in-law living with him, or his own child if now his step-son or step-father. Out here there are grandchildren and great-grandchildren. Some tend vineyards, others till fields. People use the eloquence and idioms of diverse languages in conversing back and forth. Words of different languages have become common property known to each nationality, and mutual faith unites those who are ignorant of their descent. Indeed it is written 'The lion and the ox shall eat straw together' [Isai. 62.25]. He who was born a stranger is now as one born here; he who was born an alien has become as a native. Our relatives and parents join us from time to time, sacrificing, even though reluctantly, all that they formerly possessed. Those who were poor in the Occident, God makes rich in this land. Those who had little money there have countless bezants here, and those who did not have a villa possess here by the gift of God a city.[6]

As well as emphasizing the prospect of prosperity for those who settled in the kingdom, Fulcher's description here, some 25 years after the massacre in Jerusalem, reveals that a certain amount of integration was taking place between Christians and Muslims. Christians, who had married converts, were living with their Muslim relations. Moreover, the religious affiliations of the people of the region were not permanently fixed. Whilst on an expedition with

King Baldwin I, Fulcher was able to converse first hand with local inhabitants of the kingdom who had recently converted.[7] Similarly the Muslim histories have very many examples of Christians converting to Islam.[8]

In fact, despite the horror of the slaughter on 15 July 1099, the Muslim world was slow to respond to the crusade and the establishment of a Latin Kingdom based at Jerusalem. Bitter rivalry between the great centres of Cairo, Baghdad, Damascus, Mosul and Aleppo meant that although the military forces available to the Christian lords were always very slender – except, temporarily, when a host of military pilgrims arrived at Jerusalem – for nearly three generations no Islamic ruler proved able to inflict a decisive blow upon the Christian kingdom.

Soon after the conquest of Jerusalem, however, there were some notable Muslim victories over Christian armies, which shattered the self-belief of the Christian knights and restored confidence to Muslim princes in their military prowess. At Ramla in 1102 the Fatimids revenged themselves for Ascalon with a significant victory over Baldwin I: the Christian ruler barely managed to escape with his life. At Harran in 1104 Jokermish, the governor of Mosul, and Suqmān, one of the Seljuk brothers who had ruled Jerusalem before it was captured by the Fatimids, outmanoeuvred a powerful Christian army that included Bohemond as one of its leaders. While the Norman ruler of Antioch escaped, Baldwin of Bourcq, lord of Edessa and future king of Jerusalem was captured. An even greater victory of Muslim forces over the Antiochene Christian army took place at Field of Blood in 1119, when Īlgāhzī, brother of Suqmān and now ruler of Aleppo, crushed the troops of Roger of Antioch, who was run through by a sword under his standard.

These victories were important psychologically and transformed the morale of the Muslim world with regard to their Christian enemies, but they did not lead to an overthrow of the Christian lordships due to the closely guarded autonomy of the major Muslim cities, which several times led Muslim princes to prefer alliances with Christian knights rather than let a ruler of their own religion become too powerful. The fractures in the Muslim political world were exacerbated by the growth of a new Islamic religious movement, the Bātinīds, more commonly known in the Western world as the assassins. This sect had broken away from the Sunni Caliph in 1094 and used the tactic to which their name has become attached, that of murdering prominent political and religious enemies, to create political instability among their opponents. Hasan ibn Sabbah, the Bātinīd leader based in Alamūt in north-western Iran sent missionaries throughout Syria in the early part of the twelfth century. Although their numbers were small they found a base of support, particularly in towns and among the lower social orders. The Bātinī seized a number of mountain strongholds and entrenched themselves against their enemies. More than one Muslim leader who had been successfully fighting against the Franks died at the hands of the Bātinīds.

From early on, however, there had been a current across the entire Muslim world in favour of taking the threat posed by the crusaders very seriously. Islamic theologians, such as al-Sulami who preached in Damascus, called for the Muslim world to rally against the Christian invaders and lamented the fact that the secular nobility no longer pursued *jihad*, the duty to wage holy war. Al-Sulami wrote his *Book of Holy War* in the years that followed the fall of Jerusalem, but outside of intellectual circles obtained little support for his proposal that the caliphs should conduct at least one expedition a year against the infidel. The first prince to speak the same language and harness the idea of a counter-crusade against the infidel to his own political ambition was Zankī, atabeg of Mosul.

In 1144, Zankī delivered the first really serious blow to the Christian cause, one from which they never fully recovered. He besieged and took Edessa from its absent lord, Joscelin II. For this deed Zankī became famous throughout the Muslim world and just as the Christian knights who fought at the siege of Jerusalem thought that they had thereby earned the right to enter Heaven, it was said of Zankī that he appeared in the dreams of pious men, telling them that because of the conquest of Edessa God had forgiven all his sins. There was a lot to forgive; Zankī was a prince who preferred to rule by fear rather than consent and his movements were accompanied by public executions of those whom he determined to be guilty of even slight misdemeanours. This harshness was his own undoing, for less than two years after his famous conquest Zankī was killed at night in his tent by his own troops.

While the Muslim world was slowly developing the notion of *jihad* and directing it against the Christians of the Near East, in Western Europe the concept of crusading was evolving also. The most innovatory feature of the notion that it could be holy to take up arms for Christ was the appearance of the military orders: fraternities of monks who retained their arms and military function. Living like monks with no personal wealth and with a great devotion to Christian ritual, the military orders nevertheless provided regular military service for the Kingdom of Jerusalem, initially by protecting the pilgrim routes.

Some clergy found the idea that it was possible to be both a knight and a monk monstrous. But with the support of the papacy and especially of the influential leader of the Cistercians, Bernard of Clairvaux, the military orders went from strength to strength. The two largest orders were the Knights of the

Temple of Solomon of Jerusalem, the Templars – whose name derived from the fact they were based in the complex that had been the al-Aqsā Mosque but which the Christians mistakenly thought of as the Temple of the Lord – and the Order of Saint John of Jerusalem, the Hospitallers.

In the West the orders quickly obtained several major bequeathments of land and income and uncountable minor ones. Donations took the form of estates, buildings, dependent populations as well as financial concessions. The most spectacular endowment of this sort was that of Alfonso I of Aragon who left his entire kingdom to the Hospitallers, the Templars and the Church of the Holy Sepulchre in equal parts. Not that the Aragonese aristocracy allowed the inheritance to be disbursed in such a way, but in their settlement with the orders they left them with huge revenues and property.

The other great evolution of the crusade was its acceptance at the highest levels of Christian society. Crusading became the pursuit of kings and, as a consequence, to go on crusade was to earn the approval of all of aristocratic society. On 1 December 1145, in response to the news that Edessa had fallen to Zankī, Pope Eugenius III issued a papal bull, now known from its opening words, *Quantum Praedecessores*, in which he urged King Louis VII of France and his princes to go on a great expedition to the Holy Land. The original appeal of the pope had been made to Louis VII, but Germany too was galvanized to participate and on Christmas Day 1146, at Speyer, Conrad III agreed to lead a German contingent to the east. This was called the 'second' such expedition by contemporaries, who passed over the smaller and more sporadic adventures that had taken place since 1099 and the fall of Jerusalem.

Despite the fact that kings rather than lesser lords led the Second Crusade, it was an abject failure. In the winter of 1147/8 both French and German armies came to grief in Anatolia. Short of supplies and harassed by the attacks of Turkish and nomadic armies, the Christian forces disintegrated, thousands of foot soldiers and poor crusaders being killed or led off to captivity. Only a small core fighting force of knights made their way to Jerusalem, where they were well received by Queen Melisende in the spring of 1148.

A great assembly was held at Acre on 24 June 1148 with all the senior nobles of the kingdom of Jerusalem as well as the leaders of the Templars and Hospitallers meeting with the newly arrived crusaders. After some debate the decision was taken to attack Damascus. Theoretically it was a bold idea that had the potential to counter the growing strength of Mosul and Aleppo. But it was a high-risk strategy. The rulers of Damascus had proven themselves willing to ally with the Christian princes rather than submit to control from the East. A treaty from 1139 had been the most recent formal expression of this. To attack

Damascus, but to fail, would be to destroy that alliance and to throw Damascus into the hands of more powerful Muslim rulers to the east. And so it proved.

Yet at first the decision, taken against considerable opposition, seemed justified. On Saturday 24 July 1148 the impressive Christian army fought their way to the gardens and orchards south of Damascus and set up position with good control of water and pushed their advance troops right up to the walls of the city. Something that, as Ibn al-Qalansi the Damascene eyewitness noted, had never been before achieved by an attacking army.[9]

Two days later, however, with the Christian army having failed to follow up its advantage with a serious attempt to storm the city, the situation began to improve for the inhabitants. Light cavalry reinforcements had arrived and the Muslim forces could now mount raids to harass the crusaders. At the same time, the Damascenes embarked on a frenzied burst of diplomatic activity. They appealed to Nur ad-Dīn, the ruler of Mosul, but they also seem to have offered lands and territory to Christian leaders, including the Templars, if they would halt the attack. This, at least, was the view of William of Tyre, the future chancellor of the Kingdom of Jerusalem, and it is supported also by a Muslim source, Abu Shama, albeit writing a century later.

It did not help the Christian princes directing the siege that they had already begun to squabble over who should be ruler of the captured city. The barons of the kingdom of Jerusalem and the Queen agreed that its lord should be Guy Brisebarre, lord of Beirut and that it should be a fief of the kingdom. Thierry, count of Flanders, however, put himself forward, with the support of Conrad and Louis, proposing to govern Damascus as a semi-independent principality.

On 27 July 1148 the whole army was persuaded to move to the plains east of the city in order to assault what they had been told were the weaker walls. The move was a major mistake, as it cut the army off from water supply and the walls of the city were in fact sturdier at this section. Disheartened and concerned by rumours of the imminent arrival of Nur ad-Dīn, the Christian army broke off the siege and returned to Jerusalem, humiliated. Conrad departed soon after for Constantinople, writing to Germany the following bitter letter:

> Let us now speak of our troops. When following the advice of the common council we had gone to Damascus and after a great deal of trouble had pitched our camps before the gates of the city, it was certainly near being taken. But certain ones, whom we least suspected, treasonably asserted that the city was impregnable on that side and hastily led us to another position where no water could be supplied for the troops and where access was impossible to anyone. And thus all, equally indignant and

grieved, returned, leaving the undertaking uncompleted. Nevertheless, they all promised unanimously that they would make an expedition against Ascalon, and they set the place and time. Having arrived there according to the agreement, we found scarcely any one. In vain we waited eight days for the troops. Deceived a second time, we turned to our own affairs.[10]

The enormous effort at rousing Europe to crusade in response to the fall of Edessa had come to nothing.

One of the most important consequences of the failure of the Second Crusade to take Damascus was that the population of the city changed their attitude towards the strongest Muslim prince of the region. Nur al-Dīn was the second son of Zankī the Turkish atabeg of Aleppo and Mosul, who had conquered Edessa in 1144. After the assassination of his father, Nur al-Dīn and his older brother Saif al-Dīn Ghazi divided the kingdom amongst themselves, with Nur al-Dīn governing Aleppo and Saif al-Dīn establishing himself in Mosul.

Nur al-Dīn had sought to make alliances with his Muslim neighbours in northern Iraq and Syria in order to strengthen the Muslim front against their Christian enemies. In 1147 he had signed a bilateral treaty with Mu'in al-Dīn Unur, governor of Damascus; as part of this agreement, he also married Mu'in al-Dīn's daughter. His aspiration to become ruler of Damascus was no secret and while the military elite of the city remained determined to preserve their autonomy from the ruler of Aleppo, the broader population, suffering from several years of famine and the shock of nearly having been victims of a Christian sack, considered having Nur al-Dīn as overlord a price worth paying for prosperity and security.

On 18 April 1154 Nur al-Dīn brought his full army to Damascus. He advanced upon the city from the east and a sizeable force from Damascus opposed them, with some fighting, but no committed battle. The next day the troops of Nur al-Dīn pressed harder and were close enough that a woman from the Jewish section of the town could lower a rope for a foot soldier to climb in. No sooner was one of Nur al-Dīn's banners above a section of the walls of the city than it surrendered and the new ruler of the city was careful to ensure peace, while abolishing unpopular taxes on foodstuffs. By the Friday prayers, the farmers, women and artisans of the city were openly calling out Nur al-Dīn's name, wishing him long life and victories. As far as the Christian Kingdom of Jerusalem went, this was a disaster, so wrote William of Tyre, lamenting that a formidable adversary arose, where previously had been a weak ruler willing to pay regular tribute to Jerusalem.[11]

Severe illness, however, brought Nur al-Dīn's campaigning to an end and for several years the pressure of Muslim forces on Christian territories eased, until the emergence of the man who was to successfully unite all the major Muslim cities and restore Jerusalem to Muslim rule: Saladin. Salāh al-Dīn Yūsu ibn Ayyūb had come to prominence in the company of his uncle Shirkuh, one of Nur al-Dīn's generals. Shirkuh had been given the important mission of answering the request of the Fatimids for aid against the Christians, who at the urging of the Grand Master of the Hospital had broken a peace treaty and in October 1168 had attempted to besiege Cairo under the leadership of king Amalric of Jerusalem.

Shirkuh had managed to interpose the Sunni army between the Christians and the Shia capital and once Amalric had been beaten back, entered Cairo himself. There it was only a matter of time before Shawar the Fatimid vizier was overthrown in favour of Nur al-Dīn's officers. On 18 January 1169 Shawar was ambushed, decapitated and, to deflect any possible rioting against the new rulers, his palace was given over to the public for pillage.

The attack on Cairo by the Christians had proven to be a profoundly mistaken initiative, perhaps an even more disastrous one than the attempt to take Damascus. William of Tyre, writing at a time when the consequences of Shirkuh's victory had become clear stated:

> O blind cupidity of men, worse than all other crimes! O wicked madness of an insatiable and greedy heart! From a quiet state of peace into what a turbulent and anxious condition has an immoderate desire for possessions plunged us! All the resources of Egypt and its immense wealth served our needs; the frontiers of our realm were safe on that side; there was no enemy to be feared in the south. The sea afforded a safe and peaceful passage to those wishing to come to us. Our people could enter the territories of Egypt without fear and carry on commerce and trade under advantageous conditions. On their part, the Egyptians brought to the realm foreign riches and strange commodities hitherto unknown to us and, as long as they visited us, were at once and advantage and an honour to us. Moreover, the large sums spent by them every year among us enriched the fiscal treasury and increased the private wealth of individuals. But now, on the contrary all things have been changed for the worse. The sea refuses to give us a peaceful passage, all the regions round about are subject to the enemy, and the neighbouring kingdoms are making preparations to destroy us.[12]

Shirkuh took the title of vizier and king, but did not live long to enjoy it, dying of overeating on 23 March 1169. His successor was Saladin. Not all of the other Sunni generals present agreed with the appointment and some of them returned to their overlord Nur al-Dīn. Those who remained, however, proved sufficient to crush a revolt by the Egyptian army and drive it in to Upper Egypt. Nur al-Dīn's main instruction to Saladin was that the new ruler proclaim the Sunni religion. This was obeyed without great disturbance and upon the death of the Shi'ite Caliphe, al-Adid in 1171, the remaining members of the Fatimid elite were placed in honourable captivity so that the dynasty died out over time.

From Nur al-Dīn's perspective, the new Sunni control of Egypt meant vast resources that could be used to assist the main conflicts, which for him were in Syria. Saladin had a different political outlook, believing that rather than drain the new realm of resources it should be strengthened as a base of operations. Throughout his subsequent career Saladin showed a constant concern for the defence of Egypt. Saladin also encouraged Italian cities to trade directly with Cairo, which they increasingly did.

This independent policy led to fears among Saladin's supporters that Nur al-Dīn might seek to depose him as ruler of Egypt. A potential military confrontation between the two leading Sunni princes was avoided by the death of Nur al-Dīn, on 15 May 1174. Saladin promptly came north with an army to Damascus, which he occupied on 28 October 1174. He reinforced his legitimacy there, and indicated his ambition to reunite the Muslim world, by marrying Nur al-Dīn's widow. It is testimony to Nur al-Dīn's political skill in building a base of support at Damascus that Saladin was not faced with a renewed attempt by the city to become free from external control; he was faced with very little resistance to his own takeover. Leaving his brother Tughtagīn as governor, Saladin then pressed on to Aleppo.

Here the mood of the population, and especially of the ruling elite, was more hostile. Saladin's ambitions seemed nothing more than those of an aggressive proponent of his own dynasty, attempting to usurp that of Zankī. Nur al-Dīn's young son, Malik as-Salih appealed to the population of Aleppo to protect him from Saladin, and, interestingly, the Zankīd faction urged the Christian ruler, Raymond III of Tripoli to assist them. They also hired assassins and appealed to Mosul for assistance. Saladin survived the assassination attempts and retreated to Hims to ward off the attack from Raymond. The arrival of troops from Mosul led to the Zankīds going on the offensive, but they were decisively beaten in battle at the Horns of Hamah (1175), partly because Saladin had obtained reinforcements from Egypt but also because some of the Mosul officers were sympathetic to him as someone with the potential to unite the Muslim world.

At the end of April 1175, envoys came from the Sunni caliph, formally investing Saladin with the government of Syria and Egypt. He now had hegemony, if not direct power, over the entirety of the Muslim Near East.

It is hard, and perhaps unnecessary, to separate Saladin's personal piety from his political strategy. Certainly there are no shortage of anecdotes about him to build up a picture of a person who was very diligent in prayer and attentive to the imams and the views of renowned theologians. But the fact that Saladin abolished all taxes determined to be contrary to Islamic law, as was his first act at Damascus, helped consolidate his support, particularly among merchants and intellectuals whose loyalty lay outside of any one particular city. He was breaking down local restrictions and helping create a more unified Muslim state, while emphasizing that this was being done out of zeal for the love of God.

In his personal conduct Saladin set an example for his administrators, in particular by having no interest in accumulating riches. Ibn Shaddād described how his staff would have to conceal the amount of cash they had at their disposal because if Saladin believed he had reserves, they would be distributed to petitioners. On his death Saladin was found to own almost no personal wealth.[13]

Saladin's careful attention to his responsibilities as leader of Islam reflected his concern to establish legitimacy, particularly with regard to Aleppo and Mosul. Being a Kurd, his dynasty represented a break from the Seljuk Turks, whose cadres formed the core of the ruling elites north of Baghdad. The Seljuks were sceptical, if not openly hostile, and exemplary conduct by Saladin was essential to reconcile them to his rule. Even at the end of his career, after his successes in defeating the Christians, it was considered remarkable that he could count on support from the Seljuk elite. On one occasion, in 1191, when Saladin was departing Mosul, a descendent of the atabeg Zankī, whose position at the top of Syrian society had been overthrown by Saladin, helped him get into his saddle and arranged his garments. A companion of this Seljuk lord was surprised at the sight and commented that Saladin need not worry for his life while he had a Seljuk prince help him mount.[14]

Having establishing a stable peace in Syria and appointing his relatives to many of the key castles and cities, Saladin returned to Egypt, where he reorganized the fleet and rebuilt the walls of Cairo. At the same time he promoted colleges for the fostering of a layer of Sunni intellectuals and administrators, indicating, as Nur al-Dīn had done, an appreciation of the importance of such a social layer for the long-term cohesion of a large realm.

While the major Muslim cities of the region were being drawn together under Saladin, the Christian Kingdom of Jerusalem and the adjacent Christian principalities were fragmenting disastrously. With Baldwin IV suffering from leprosy, to the point where no one could look at him without feeling sick, the key question was that of finding a husband for his elder sister Sybil, someone who would be able to lead the realm in the event of Baldwin's incapacity or death.

Two factions emerged. Baldwin of Ibelin was a prominent local noble who had the support of the lords of the northern Christian principalities, Raymond III of Tripoli and Bohemond III of Antioch. Against them were the senior office holders of Jerusalem, including Joscelin III of Courtenay, the seneschal of Jerusalem and Raynald of Châtillon, lord of the lands east of the Jordan. It was this faction who in 1180 managed to have Sybil married to their candidate, Guy of Lusignan. The Lusignans were a noble family from Poitou and vassals of Henry II of England. Four generations of family members had participated in crusades. The northern faction struck back against Sybil and her new husband by placing their hopes in Sybil's son by her first marriage, the infant Baldwin, whom they had crowned as Baldwin V, co-king of the realm in 1183, even though he was just five years old and had to be carried on the shoulders of Prince Raymond for the ceremony.

Despite his illness, Baldwin IV was able to defeat Saladin's invasion of 1182. He also proved to be extremely capable in lifting a siege in August that year and again obliging Saladin to withdraw. But with his death in the spring of 1185 and young Baldwin V's death in the summer of 1186, the kingdom was once more thrown into crisis. Understanding the dangers they faced, the High Council of the kingdom proposed a compromise between the rival factions, Sybil would be recognized as queen by all, providing she repudiated Guy of Lusignan. All parties agreed to this decision, including Sybil, who added the important proviso that she should be free to choose her next husband. The point of this qualification was shown immediately after Sybil was recognized as queen, when she outwitted the High Council by choosing Guy as her husband once more. This was a skilful tactical move for her supporters, but strategically disastrous for the kingdom. The rivalry between Guy and those who refused him homage, such as Baldwin of Ibelin and Raymond III of Tripoli, was so deep that in face of the prospect of civil war Raymond even sought and obtained troops from Saladin in defence of his lands at Tiberias.

In 1187 Saladin once more invaded the Christian kingdom, this time with an army drawn from all over his realm: some 20,000 troops. Bohemond III was busy dealing with a Turkmen invasion of his Antiochene principality. Raymond III was willing to make peace with Guy, but was mistrusted. The Frankish forces, created by denuding all the cities and castles of their garrison, numbered some 60–70 per cent of Saladin's. Raymond III advised the king not to fight a pitched battle but to shadow Saladin until the Muslim ruler was obliged by lack of resources to dismantle his army, Gerard of Ridefort, master of the Templars, took exactly the opposite view, insisting on battle as soon as possible. With Guy needing a victory to secure his position as king, he welcomed Gerard's viewpoint. The new ruler of Jerusalem therefore gambled nearly all the military resources of the kingdom on an all-out assault against the larger Muslim army; leading his forces to a crushing defeat at Hattin on 4 July 1187. There, in a matter of hours, the core fighting force of the Kingdom of Jerusalem was destroyed.

On 2 October 1187 Jerusalem surrendered to Saladin, whose soldiers entered the city under a very tight discipline. A faction of the Muslim army urged Saladin to take revenge for 1099,[15] but the sultan overruled them. Two fully armoured warriors and ten foot soldiers from Saladin's army were placed as guards in each street of the city and not one incident of revenge against the Christian population was reported.[16] There was neither violence nor plunder, instead, as had been agreed between Balian of Ibelin the last commander of Christian forces in Jerusalem and the sultan, the Christian population were given the chance to ransom themselves to avoid captivity. The wealthy Christian property owners were not dispossessed; in fact they were able to sell their houses and furnishings before leaving the city. The poor gathered at the gates of the city, begging for the coins that would allow them to leave and avoid a life of slavery.

Heraclius, the patriarch of Jerusalem, rode out of the city at the head of a train with all the wealth of the Holy Sepulchre and other churches. It was put to Saladin that this gold and silver should be seized, but the sultan refused to act treacherously and only took ten dinars from Heraclius, the patriarch's personal ransom.[17] Similarly, once the Hospitallers and Templars realized that they would be allowed to leave with their goods, their enthusiasm for ransoming the 40,000 Christians too poor to save themselves from slavery waned. After securing the release of some, the military orders departed the city with their remaining wealth.[18] Seeing the plight of the Christian poor, Saif al-Dīn, Saladin's brother, asked for 1,000 slaves as a reward for his role in the conquest of Jerusalem. This was agreed to, whereupon Saif al-Dīn let them all go as an act of charity in the name of God.[19]

Another group who benefited from Saladin's sense of honour and mercy were the women of those knights who had fought with Guy at Hattin. Wives and daughters now without guardians came to the sultan in a body and begged him to aid them. When Saladin saw their weeping, he felt pity for their plight and had his scribes take a note of the missing men. Those still in captivity were released, while the women of those who had died in the battle were given a payment so generous that they praised the kindness of their conqueror.[20]

All this testimony to Saladin's merciful behaviour is not simply contemporary Muslim propaganda designed to enhance his reputation, as it comes to us from a Christian source, the history known as *The Old French Continuation of William of Tyre*. The Muslim sources for Saladin's conquest of Jerusalem support the same view, that the sultan was exceedingly humane, escorted the ransomed Christians to safety, allowed the non-Latin Christians to continue to live in the city and kept none of the money that the Muslim army had gained for himself.[21]

Less than 100 years after its foundation, the Kingdom of Jerusalem was effectively at an end, although it lingered on in name even after 1291, when Acre, the last Latin ruled city of the region was conquered.

The victors of the siege of Jerusalem in 1099 thought that their deeds would be remembered forever. In a way they were right, but not at all in the sense that they would have imagined. For the Christian conquerors, especially the clergy, the victory on 15 July was an event whose only parallels could be found in biblical descriptions of God's people overcoming mighty enemies. Even more impressive than the deeds of Moses or Judas Macabeus, the Christians at Jerusalem had endured a journey whose length and hardship was without precedent. That they had succeeded in regaining the Holy City from the infidel was an extraordinary triumph and surely a display of God's power. When they put their achievements in perspective, the crusaders were so moved by the evidence of divine favour that they felt certain the anniversary of the capture of Jerusalem would became a day of major celebration in the Christian calendar.

The events of 15 July are remembered, but as an atrocity rather than as a cause for exultation. Naturally, in the Muslim world, the conquest of Jerusalem is the archetype example of Western barbarity. But even in the Christian world the memory of the massacres that took place when the city fell soon began to taint the glorious image of success promoted in the aftermath of 1099 by song and chronicle. As early as 1184, William of Tyre was sounding a sombre, rather than celebratory note, in his account of events.

Despite the loss of Jerusalem to Saladin in 1187, the concept of crusading continued to form an important aspect of the medieval world. But with the emergence of first reforming and then anti-clerical, secular, values in Europe, the whole idea of crusading -- of waging war under papal direction -- became discredited. One of the criticisms that Europe's sixteenth-century reformers directed towards the papacy was against the involvement of the church in warfare. As Martin Luther expressed it: 'if in my turn I were a soldier and saw in the battlefield a priest's banner or cross, even if it were the very crucifix, I should want to run away as though the devil were chasing me!'[22] The bloody scenes that took place on the fall of Jerusalem in 1099 were not celebrated for long in the Christian world – far from it – they became a source of shame.

To look back at the fall of Jerusalem with modern eyes is to feel a sense of revulsion. Yet, without sympathizing at all with the crusaders, it is possible to understand them and understand the frenzy with which the slaughter of the citizens took place. Long held religious desires meshed with material ambition and an accumulation of rage and frustration to produce an explosion. The crusader running through the streets of Jerusalem that day was gaining glory for God, property for themselves, and venting the fear and wrath that their enemies had created in them.

All warfare requires humans to look upon one another without empathy. In the context of the religious beliefs of the besiegers, their insecurities, their ambitions, and the distinctly alien culture that faced them, such lack of empathy for the Muslim and Jewish population of the city by the crusaders was inevitable. Under the circumstances, none of the crusading princes could have restrained the army, even if they had wanted to.

While it is the massacre of the citizens of Jerusalem that the siege of 1099 is remembered for, the violence has overshadowed other extraordinary features of the conflict. That the besiegers were split into two antagonistic camps was remarkable; that they not only had to cope with deep rivalries between the secular princes, but also between the lords and the clergy too, meant the conduct of the crusading army was very untypical for the era. Again, the presence of such a huge number of non-combatants was rare in a medieval besieging army. But perhaps the most distinctive feature of the siege of Jerusalem was in the mentality of the besieging force. Here was a geographically and socially disparate army that had come together across thousands of miles to capture the city that stood at the heart of their theology. The journey itself was worthy of an epic. They were camped outside Jerusalem for 39 days, the resistance of the garrison and the citizens a final obstacle to the achievement of their longed-for goal. Theirs was a unique experience and a unique story, one that despite the horror of their deeds deserves to be told and to be understood.

Appendix

The Sources

Writing a narrative of historical events means having to make choices at almost every point. It is not possible to even begin a book like this without making a number of major decisions. When some sources say, for example, that Peter the Hermit was the originator of the crusade, while others refer only to Pope Urban II, how can they be reconciled? Perhaps the pope and the preacher reached the conclusion that a military expedition to the Holy Land was called for at more or less the same time and independently of each other? Perhaps Peter the Hermit's communications on return from his pilgrimage to Jerusalem influenced the thinking of the pope? Or perhaps there should be no reconciliation: Peter the Hermit's role in initiating the movement could have been pure invention by poets wishing to give a coherent and personalized framework for their song of the crusade.

Modern historians tend to favour the reader with a discussion of the sources alongside each controversial point and on the whole readers appreciate this kind of history. If a conclusion is reached, it comes after a presentation of the evidence that draws attention to the circumstances in which the source text was written, the readership it was intended for, and therefore its biases. Very often it is not possible to reach firm conclusions and therefore, quite properly, academic historical works are filled with sentences beginning, 'perhaps', 'possibly', 'it is likely that' and so forth. This is a healthy corrective to history writing of an earlier era where the sequence of events is depicted as though no doubts at all existed as to what actually happened, or as though the particular way in which the historian assembled their material was the only possible one.

It might seem that this book belongs to the earlier tradition of historical writing. This is because I have striven in the writing to impart a sense of dynamism and coherence to the account that would have been lost if at every difficulty or at every attempt to assess the character of the persons under discussion I had paused to explain my reasoning and introduce the qualifications that strictly speaking should have appeared in most sentences. One of the key tests of the validity of the choices made by a historian writing narrative history is how convincing their account is as a whole. The benefit of leaving a discussion of the sources to the appendix is that the main body of the text therefore is focused entirely on a reconstruction of events and the 'bigger picture'. But, unlike those earlier authors who were so confident in the authority of their assertions, I fully acknowledge that this account of events reflects my choices and that other historians might make from the same material a different pattern. Not an entirely different pattern, certain undisputable events took place at very definite times. But the meaning of the events, the dynamics that led to them, the assessment of the characters involved, in a word, the 'colouration' of the narrative, very much depends on the historian.

Take the example of Count Raymond of Toulouse. There is complete agreement among historians about such matters as: where the Provençal army was deployed; that on the fall of Jerusalem the count made haste to secure the Tower of David; that he failed to obtain control of the city and took himself off to the Jordan to bathe in its waters. It is possible to write about these events and portray the count as farsighted, magnanimous, self-sacrificing and noble.[1] I have taken a rather different view based on my interpretation of the material that suggests a faction of the former followers of the papal legate, Bishop Adhémar of Le Puy, emerged to hamper Raymond's ambition from within the Provençal forces. Here Raymond is depicted as a relatively cautious military commander, a clumsy politician, and a man who became frustrated in his desire to have the reputation and responsibilities of a figure like Moses. One of these assessments is closer to the historical count than the other, but it would be a daring, if not rash, person who could be confident that 900 years after the man was alive, their interpretation was right in all respects. Most likely there are elements in both views that touch on the actual character of Count Raymond.

It is absolutely certain that if I were given the opportunity to travel back in time and the language skills to understand what I was seeing, I'd find many divergences between the actual events and this account. Nevertheless, I'm not a 'relativist' in that I do not believe all historical narratives are equally valid. Some capture the sense of events more accurately than others. In aspiring to come as close possible to depicting the actual course of events of the medieval past it is necessary to work with source material that is at times contradictory, to make informed choices that fill in the gaps where crucial information is missing, and to draw on what modern scholarship can tell us about the less obvious meanings and contexts of the documents under discussion to understand as precisely as possible what our medieval authors, whether consciously or unconsciously, are telling us.

For the reader interested in the technical aspects of understanding medieval history, much of the academic reasoning and analysis that lies behind the narrative arrived at here can be found in my earlier book, *The Social Structure of the First Crusade* (Leiden, 2008). Furthermore, I was enormously helped in formulating this account by the considerable scholarship that now exists in regard to the First Crusade and two works in particular stand out: Joshua Prawer's article 'The Jerusalem the Crusaders Captured: A Contribution to the Medieval Topography of the City' in P. W. Edbury ed., *Crusade and Settlement* (Cardiff, 1985) and John France's magisterial book *Victory in the East. A Military History of the First Crusade* (Cambridge, 1994).

But it is not necessary to be an academic specialist to appreciate the relative value of the information given in this book. Moreover, the reader will want assurance that all the specific incidents described in the text, no matter how outlandish, appeared in contemporary or near contemporary accounts. I therefore offer my assessment of the value of the sources for the First Crusade in this appendix with the intention of giving some transparency to how I arrived at the choices I made.

Although not necessarily the most informative, the key account of the First Crusade is the *Gesta Francorum et aliorum Hierosolimitanorum*. At the time of writing, a new edition of this history is in preparation by Marcus Bull, but in the meantime the most recent version of the text is that of Rosalind Hill (1962), which was issued with an accompanying English translation and which was used for this book (GF in the footnotes).[2] The anonymous author of the *Gesta Francorum* was a crusader who travelled from Italy as far as Antioch in the contingent of Bohemond. It was completed shortly after the last event that it described, the victory of the Christian forces near Ascalon against al-Afdal, on 12 August 1099. But much of the history was probably written up earlier, after the siege of Antioch, with the historian resuming his account having returned to Jerusalem after participating in the battle against the vizier of Egypt.

There is quite a considerable debate about whether the author was a knight or a cleric. I favour the view that sees him as a knight.[3] But irrespective of this debate, the *Gesta Francorum* has to be considered a first class source due to the fact it is the work of an eyewitness, set down very soon after the events it described. Any historian departing from this account has to have very good reasons for doing so.

There is a history of the First Crusade by a Poitevin priest called Peter Tudebode, which is almost identical to that of the *Gesta Francorum*: the *Historia de Hierosolymitano Itinere*. Again, a lively debate exists among crusading historians about this text. Namely what is the relationship between the work of Peter and the work of the anonymous author? The problem is that while there are certain features of the account that make it look like Peter took the *Gesta Francorum* and made a few amendments to it, from time to time Peter seems to have access to a version of the *Gesta Francorum* that is slightly fuller than we have in any manuscript that survives today. In any case, the new information Peter adds is always of interest and since he was a crusader and an eyewitness a great deal of confidence can be given to the information derived from him. The edition used here is that printed in the *Recueil des historiens des croisades, Historiens occidentaux* series (PT in the footnotes). J. H. Hill and L. L. Hill provided an English translation of the work.[4]

Another eyewitness account and one that has just as good a claim to authority as the *Gesta Francorum* and the *Historia de Hierosolymitano Itinere* is Raymond of Aguilers's *Historia Francorum qui ceperunt Iherusalem*. The edition of this text that I prefer, as it is based upon a careful reading of all the known manuscripts, is that provided by John France for his 1967 Ph.D. thesis (RA in the footnotes); unfortunately this thesis has not been published, perhaps because of the publication of an edition in 1969 by J. H. Hill and L. L. Hill. Because it is not easy to access France's edition, I have also given references in brackets to the more readily viewable edition in the *Recueil des historiens des croisades*.[5] The Hills have provided a rather free and not entirely satisfactory English translation of the *Historia Francorum*.[6]

Raymond of Aguilers was a canon of the cathedral church of St Mary of Le Puy, in the Auvergne region of France. He participated on the expedition with the Provençal contingent, probably that of Bishop Adhémar of Le Puy, the papal legate, to judge by the bias of his detail. Having earlier been raised to the priesthood during the course of the expedition, Raymond of Aguilers subsequently joined the chaplaincy of Count Raymond IV of Toulouse.[7]

As with the two sources mentioned above, the *Historia Francorum* was written very soon after the end of the First Crusade: shortly after the battle of Ascalon. The final version of the history was based on notes or longer extracts that Raymond wrote during the course of the expedition. In contrast to the terse narrative of events in the *Gesta Francorum*, Raymond was given to filling out his core account with additional colourful incidents, especially those that supported the idea that there was a divine will supporting the crusaders. The miracles and visions that fill the *Historia Francorum* have led some later historians to treat Raymond as someone who invented such incidents to convince readers of his viewpoint. But there is an important difference in faithfully reporting what he believed to have happened and making up material.

What gives the modern historian confidence in Raymond's account is the fact that although Raymond desired to believe in the miraculous powers of the Holy Lance, he reported his own doubts in the relic in a confessional and candid passage. The particular strength of Raymond's history is that it gives an insight into the political dynamics within the Provençal army and more than any other source it pays attention to the thoughts and actions of the poor crusader.

Slightly less valuable, both because it is rather brief in its account of the siege of Jerusalem and also because it is not the work of an eyewitness is Fulcher of Chartres's *Historia Hierosolymitana*, the definitive edition of which is that by Heinrich Hagenmeyer in 1913 (FC in the footnotes).[8] Fulcher was born in 1058 or 1059 in Chartres and was a participant in the First Crusade. His description of the departure of the various contingents makes it clear that he set out with Duke Robert II of Normandy and Count Stephen of Blois. When, on 17 September 1097, Baldwin of Boulogne detached his forces from the main body of the Christian army and marched towards Tarsus, Fulcher was with him. Fulcher stayed with Baldwin after the Lotharingian prince became ruler of Edessa, on 10 March 1097, and therefore missed the siege of Jerusalem. He did, however, accompany Baldwin, now count of Edessa, when he journeyed to Jerusalem late in 1099 to worship at the Holy Sepulchre and was also present when Baldwin came to Jerusalem, on 9 November 1100, to obtain the title of king.[9]

Since Fulcher made his home in Jerusalem and began the first draft of his history around 1101 – with the first redaction of the *Historia Hierosolymitana* being completed around 1105 – he was therefore writing whilst living among crusaders who had captured the city in 1099. This, along with the accuracy of his observations, makes Fulcher only marginally less valuable than the direct eyewitnesses and it is a shame that he did not devote more of his history to the siege.

Another very important non-eyewitness account is that of Albert, a monk of Aachen. That the *Historia Iherosolimitana* of Albert of Aachen is now considered a crucial source for the First Crusade, is in large part due to a wonderful new edition and translation by Susan B. Edgington (AA in the footnotes).[10] The strength of Albert's history is that it is rich with vivid descriptions, supplying a great amount of detail that makes the other sources appear sparse in comparison. Earlier historians thought that it was a relatively late work as it continues to describe events all the way up to 1119. But Peter Knoch and Susan Edgington have demonstrated that the section dealing with the siege of Jerusalem was set down in 1102 or soon after.[11]

Albert longed to go on the crusade with the departing contingents mustered by Duke Godfrey of Lotharingia, but various obstacles were put in his path.

Instead, he eagerly sought returning crusaders and was filled with enthusiasm to tell their story. As Albert based his history primarily on oral sources, 'the narration of those who were present' and newly composed epic songs, his is a very valuable work.[12] What makes it particularly important here is that it has a strong interest in the activities of the Lotharingians and gives their perspective on events. There are many incidents concerning the crusade that are only known because Albert wrote about them and while he was not always free from errors I have tended to take a great deal from Albert's history. Only in a few instances where it has not proved possible to synthesize the eyewitness accounts with the information provided by Albert have I declined to follow him.

Far shorter, just some 5,000 words, is a partial account of the siege of Jerusalem in a manuscript that once belonged to the abbey of Ripoll in Catalonia, now lodged as Bibliothèque Nationale (Latin) 5132, Folios 15 v. 23–19 v. 25. John France discovered the text and published an edition of it in the *English Historical Review* (RF in footnotes).[13] This is a work that ends in a long celebratory praise poem, but before the verses begin, the author wrote about the siege with such vivid detail that John France's description of it as the work of an eyewitness seems correct. Although short, the text gives unique and fascinating descriptions of the attempts by the Provençal army to overcome the defences of Jerusalem facing them.

To have six works of such merit is a relative luxury for a historian of the late eleventh century. Although there remain gaps that have to be filled with conjectures and contradictions that require the historian to come down on one side or another, these accounts are really excellent sources and the material derived from them makes up the core of this narrative. There are several other important medieval accounts of the siege of Jerusalem, but due to the fact that they were set down a little after the events of 1099 and because they depended less upon evidence from eyewitnesses, they form a second tier of sources, still useful, occasionally providing new information, but not to be counted upon if they diverge from the six sources described above.

Baldric, archbishop of Dol, wrote his version of events around the year 1108. He was a scholar with a high level of education and extensive knowledge of the classics, which he put to good use in his poetry, for which he was much better known than for his *Historia Hierosolymitana*.[14] At the time of writing there is no modern edition of Baldric's history. The edition in the 1898 fourth volume of the *Recueil des Historiens des Croisades*, while not ideal by modern standards, did at least avoid the mistake of earlier editors who took a rather untypical manuscript tradition as the foundation of their editions. It is therefore the *RHC* edition that is the one used by this study (BD in the footnotes).[15] A research project has been created under Marcus Bull to produce a new edition, which will hopefully appear in due course.

Inspired by the events of the crusade and by his reading of the *Gesta Francorum*, Baldric decided that the anonymous author, through his clumsy writing style, had made worthless a subject that deserved to be treated far more eloquently.[16] By rewriting of the *Gesta Francorum* Baldric arrived at a work that was more dramatic, richer in details and theological observations. Baldric was also, unfortunately, inclined to constantly adjust the information in his source to make the Christian army glitter as an illustration of divine approval, charity and harmony. Although some of Baldric's additional descriptions are attractive, they can only be used with a great deal of caution. Not that all the additional information in the *Historia Hierosolymitana* can be dismissed as imaginative; Baldric himself drew attention in his prologue to the fact that the work as a whole did include new information from returning veterans, but on the whole, despite its colour, this history is much less reliable for information on the siege of Jerusalem than the earlier works.[17]

In the twelfth century the most popular account of the First Crusade was another reworking of the *Gesta Francorum*, that by Robert the Monk, writing around the same time as Baldric of Dol. Around 100 manuscripts of Robert's *Historia Iherosolimitana* survive today, a very substantial number, but there is no modern edition; the most recent being that published in the *RHC* series in 1866.[18] This edition is not ideal, as it was based on just 24 of the surviving manuscripts; nevertheless it is used here (RM in the footnotes).

The *Historia Iherosolimitana* was written by a monk, Robert, who was present at the Council of Clermont, 18–28 November 1095, but thereafter was not an eyewitness to the events he described.[19] He worked from a monastery in the episcopate of Reims. Robert was heavily dependent on the *Gesta Francorum* for the basic form of his history and for most of its content. His reworking of the *Gesta Francorum*, however, introduced new material and significant elaborations. There is a certain amount of historical information in the text that is original to Robert. This might well be valuable eyewitness testimony from returning crusaders, but – like with Baldric's work – any such genuine material has to be reconstructed to free it from the distorting effect of Robert's belief that the historian who embarked on writing about the journey to Jerusalem must be pleasing to God, for this, with the exception of the martyrdom of Christ, was the most miraculous undertaking since the creation of the world.[20]

There is a poetic history, the *Historia Vie Hierosolimitane* of Gilo of Paris, which has almost the same material and ordering as the narrative history of

Robert the Monk. Whether one influenced the other has proved to be difficult to establish, but the current view is that they share a now missing common source.[21] Gilo was a Cluniac monk from Toucy in Auxerre who subsequently became cardinal-bishop of Tusculum.[22] His metrical history was certainly written at some point before 1120, most probably towards the end of the first decade of the century. On occasion Gilo offers a small amount of information that is not to be found in Robert's history and he is cited from the modern edition, with accompanying English translation, provided by C. W. Grocock and J. E. Siberry (GP in the footnotes).[23]

Another cleric to be inspired by the *Gesta Francorum* to want to write his own history of the crusade was Guibert, abbot of Nogent. Guibert's work has many commentaries, observations, reports of visions and miracles, which means that – unlike the histories by Robert and Baldric – it diverges considerably in structure and in content from the *Gesta Francorum*. Guibert also incorporated more historical material into his work than either of the other two northern French historians, both concerning the departure of the expedition, to which he was an eyewitness, and from the testimony of those who had returned from the expedition.

There are five editions of the *Gesta Dei per Francos*, the most recent being the exemplary modern edition by R. B. C. Huygens, 1976, which is used here (GN in the footnotes).[24] Huygens convincingly argued that the date of composition of the history was probably 1109.[25] The fact that Guibert held strong opinions and enjoyed polemics makes him a more valuable source for this book than his counterparts. Guibert interrupted his narrative to engage in theological debate and commentary more than any other early source for the First Crusade and therefore, while he was sympathetic to the nobles and scathing towards the poor crusader, Guibert provides flashes of illumination into the social relations that prevailed on the crusade.

Another slightly later but still useful source for the siege of Jerusalem and in particular for the part played by Tancred is the *Gesta Tancredi in expeditione Jerosolymitana* of Ralph of Caen. When Bohemond came to France and Normandy in 1106, he recruited a number of followers amongst whom as Ralph, a priest of Caen. Ralph was in Bohemond's chaplaincy until journeying to Antioch, where, before 1111, he joined the following of Tancred until the death of the prince, 12 December 1112.

Ralph's history is essentially a panegyric to Tancred. What makes it an important text for the crusade is that Ralph seems to have been free from the influence of the *Gesta Francorum* tradition. His sources seem to have been veterans of the crusade, especially Bohemond and Tancred. For all its enthusiasm and exaggeration of events that favoured Tancred, Ralph's history cannot have strayed too far from the memory of crusading participants, as it was edited by Arnulf, the chaplain to Robert II, duke of Normandy who became patriarch of Jerusalem in 1099.[26]

We are lucky to have this source and only one manuscript of the work exists, which survived a fire in 1716 that destroyed the library of the monastery of Gembloux where it was kept. The edition of the *Gesta Tancredi in expeditione Jerosolymitana* printed in the *RHC* series is the one used here (RC in the footnotes). B. S. Bachrach and D. S. Bachrach provided an English translation in 2005.[27]

Although many later Latin authors wrote about the capture of Jerusalem in 1099, very few added any details that could be used to supplement these sources. Orderic Vitalis wrote a section on the First Crusade in his extraordinary *Historia Ecclesiastica* (1123–41), but inserted the work of his friend Baldric of Dol, almost word for word. The small number of changes that Orderic made to *Historia Hierosolymitana* are worth noting though, as they were often reference to knights with land in England whom Orderic would have known about.

Much later, 1167–84, William of Tyre composed his *Chronicon*, an extremely sophisticated history of the Latin Kingdom of Jerusalem. This history is set down by someone too far from events to count as a major source for the siege but it has some unique details that can be considered reliable given William's background. William was born in Jerusalem around 1130 and lived in the city for some 16 years before leaving to obtain an education in Europe. On his return, he became Chancellor of the Kingdom of Jerusalem from 1174 and Archbishop of Tyre from 1175 to his death c.1185.

Given that William had access to an oral tradition concerning the city of Jerusalem and was extremely thorough in his use of written sources, including some now lost to us, it is with some confidence that I have taken up one or two points from his account, mainly to do with the experiences of the local Christian population who remained within the walls of the city during the siege. In 1986 R. B. C. Huygens provided a modern, scholarly, edition of the *Chronicon* of William of Tyre for the *Corpus Christianorum* series, which is used here (WT in the footnotes).[28]

Turning away from the Latin sources, it is with great disappointment that the historian searches almost in vain for Jewish and Muslim perspectives on the siege. There were Jewish accounts of the passage of the First Crusade through the Rhineland and these are harrowing to read, for they are detailed laments in honour of those from the Jewish community who were slaughtered by Christians associated with the People's Crusade.[29] Surprisingly, however, no major literary Jewish source exists for the much more devastating massacre in Jerusalem in 1099. Important fragments have, however, been found among the massive collection of Jewish manuscripts found in Old Cairo in the mid-nineteenth century, a collection known as the 'Genzia documents'. An English translation of a key letter, along with a valuable discussion as to the implications of its contents, can be found in an article by S. D. Goitein and further commentary on the relevant Genzia fragments is provided in Moshe Gil's *A History of Palestine, 634–1099*.[30]

The Muslim sources for the siege of Jerusalem are equally fragmentary, at least as we have them today. There was an early history of the crusade written by Hamdan b. 'Abd al-Rahim, called *History of the Franks who Invaded the Islamic Lands,* but very unfortunately no copy has survived to modern times. As the poems and polemics of the day said nothing about the actual events of 1099, historians have to turn to later works for the Muslim perspectives of the siege. Even then, the information available is very patchy. The Syrian writer al-'Azimi, for example, writing in 1160 says only this for 1099: 'then they turned to Jerusalem and conquered it from the hands of the Egyptians. Godfrey took it. They burned the Church of the Jews.'[31] Al-Qalānisī, based in Damascus and also writing around the year 1160, offered a little more on the subject. His *Continuation of the Chronicle of Damascus* is an impressive work and an important one for the events of the region in the early twelfth century; H. A. R. Gibb translated it in full into English. But for the siege of Jerusalem the information in the Damascus Chronicle disappointingly scant. Al-Qalānisī wrote that it was the news that al-Afdal was on his way with a large army that prompted the Franks to renew their efforts to take the city. Again, unlike any of the Latin sources, the Damascene historian reported that the Franks had burned a major synagogue. 'The Franks stormed the town and gained possession of it. A number of the townsfolk fled to the sanctuary and a great host were killed. The Jews assembled in the synagogue, and the Franks burnt it over their heads. The sanctuary was surrendered to them on guarantee of safety on 22 Sha'ban [14 July] of this year, and they destroyed the shrines and the tomb of Abraham.'[32]

Considerably later, around 1200, Ibn al-Jawzī, writing in Baghdad gave details of the looting of the Dome of the Rock. 'Among the events in this year was the taking of Jerusalem by the Franks on 13 Sha'ban [5 July]. They killed more than 70,000 Muslims there. They took forty-odd silver candelabra from the Dome of the Rock, each one worth 360,000 *dirhams*. They took a silver lamp weighting forty Syrian *ratls*. They took twenty-odd gold lamps, innumerable clothing and other things.'[33]

Writing around the same time, from near Mosul, Ibn al-Athīr is more valuable in that, as was generally the case with this scholarly historian, many of the details he provided in his chronicle, *The Complete History* match what we know from the Latin sources. Ibn al-Athīr has the correct date for the capture of the city, 15 July, and correctly states that while the Muslims countered the attack on the south side of the city, it was taken from the north. He reported that the siege tower on the Mount Zion side was completely destroyed by fire and all inside were killed. Also correct was his statement that the Muslims in the Tower of David survived to obtain a safe escort to Ascalon during the night. The figure of 40 trebuchets that al-Athīr claims were built by the crusaders is a significant exaggeration and this casts doubt on another more important figure in the account, that of the numbers of Muslims killed in the massacre, which he puts at 70,000. Al-Athīr's account emphasizes the fact that at the Aqsā Mosque a great number of scholars and religious men were killed. He also offered similar details to Ibn al-Jawzī on the booty taken from the Dome of the Rock.[34] A modern English translation has been provided by D. S. Richards.

Carole Hillenbrand's discussion of these sources has pointed out that none of them portray the Christians as fighters for their religion.[35] For the first 100 years or so of the Muslim historiographical tradition concerning the capture of Jerusalem, the Christian army was portrayed as an unexpected arrival into the Muslim political world, but not as a military force with a very distinct religious agenda. It was left to the theologians and poets to draw out the religious issues at stake arising from the crusading movement and some Muslim writers, such as al-Sulami (1105) were very swift to grasp that 'Jerusalem was the goal of their desires.'[36] Such polemical works are very important for tracing the evolution of *jihad* into a Muslim counter-crusade against the Latin Kingdom of Jerusalem, but as they contain no historical information about the siege of Jerusalem it is impossible to use them except perhaps as a source for the state of mind of some of the Islamic clergy in the aftermath of the crusade. It can be argued that some scholars, at least, felt that there was a need to unite the Islamic world against the newly arrived unbelievers.[37]

Abbreviations

AA	Albert of Aachen, *Historia Iherosolimitana,* ed. S. B. Edgington (Oxford, 2007).
AC	Anna Comnena, *The Alexiad*, trans. E. R. A. Sewter (Middlesex, 1979).
BD	Baldric of Dol, *Historia Hierosolymitana, RHC Oc.* 4, 1–111.
CA	*La Chanson d'Antioche*, ed. S. Duparc-Quioc, 2 (Paris, 1977).
CC	*Corpus Christianorum, Continuatio Mediaevalis.*
EA	Ekkehard of Aura, 'Chronica', *Frutolfs und Ekkehards Chroniken und die Anonyme Kaiserchronik*, ed. F-J Schmale and I. Schmale-Ott (Darmstadt, 1972).
FC	Fulcher of Chartres, *Historia Hierosolymitana (1095–1127)*, ed. H. Hagenmeyer (Heidelberg, 1913).
GF	*Gesta Francorum et aliorum Hierosolimitanorum*, ed. R. Hill (London, 1962).
GN	Guibert of Nogent, *Gesta Dei per Francos*, ed. R. B. C. Huygens, *CC* LXXVIIa (Turnhout, 1996).
GP	Gilo of Paris and a second, anonymous author, *Historia Vie Hierosolimitane*, ed. C. W. Grocock and J. E. Siberry (Oxford, 1997).
MGH **SS**	Monumenta Germaniae Historica Scriptores, Scriptores in Folio, 32 (1826–1934).
OV	Orderic Vitalis, *The Ecclesiastical History*, ed. and trans. M. Chibnall, 6 (Oxford, 1969–79).
PL	*Patrologiae cursus completus*, ed. J. P. Migne, Series Latina (1844–66).
PT	Peter Tudebode, *Historia de Hierosolymitano Itinere, RHC Oc.* 3, 3-117.
RA	Raymond of Aguilers, *Historia Francorum qui ceperunt Iherusalem*, ed. John France (unpublished Ph.D. thesis: University of Nottingham, 1967).
RC	Ralf of Caen, *Gesta Tancredi, RHC Oc.* 3, 587–716.

RHC Oc.   *Recueil des historiens des croisades, Historiens occidentaux* 1–5
             (Académie des inscriptions et belles-lettres: Paris 1841–95).

RF   Anonymous, J. France ed., 'The text of the account of the
             capture of Jerusalem in the Ripoll Manuscript, Bibliothèque
             Nationale (Latin) 5132', *The English Historical Review* 103, 408
             (July 1988), pp. 640–57.

RM   Robert the Monk, *Historia Iherosolimitana, RHC Oc.* 3,
             717–882.

SSFC   C. Kostick, *The Social Structure of the First Crusade* (Leiden,
             2008).

WT   William of Tyre, *Chronicon*, ed. R. B. C. Huygens, *CC* 63
             (Turnhout, 1986).

Notes

CHAPTER 1

1   BD 16.
2   BD 17; GN 331.
3   AA 2–6; GN 121.
4   AA 38, 254.
5   EA 140; GN 118–20.
6   EA 144.
7   AA 50–2.
8   RC 607; GF 7.
9   GF 3.
10   AA 23–7.
11   AA 45–9.
12   J. R. Jewett, 'Arabic proverbs and proverbial phrases', *Journal of the American Oriental Society* 15 (1893), 28–120, 91.
13   AA 34–6.
14   AA 14, 38.
15   AA 38–44.
16   GN 131; see also *SSFC* pp. 211–12.
17   AA 86.
18   AC 327–8.
19   Dudo of Saint-Quentin, *Libri III de moribus et actis primorum Normanniae ducum*, *PL* 141, [Col.0651A].
20   AC 325–6.
21   GF 13.
22   FC 203.
23   AA 104.
24   AA 108.
25   AA 110.
26   AA 112.
27   RA 21 (239); AA 112–14.
28   AA 118.
29   AA 118–20.
30   GN 204; AA 120–4.
31   AC 337–8; AA 124.

CHAPTER 2

1   AA 126–8.
2   RC 619; AC 340.
3   GF 18–19.
4   RC 622; GF 19; CA 2144–52.
5   RC 623–4; AA 130; GF 21.
6   FC 195–7, AA 130.
7   GF 23; AA 138.
8   RA 28 (241).
9   RC 630–1.
10 AA 156–64.
11 AA 170–6; WT 236.
12 GN 135; CA 4050–118.
13 GF 30–1; RA 41–3 (244–5); AA 216–20.
14 RC 649; GN 254.
15 GF 35–8; AA 232–8; RC 648.
16 AA 242.
17 AA 244.
18 GF 41.
19 GF 46; RM 800; AA 268, 356.
20 GF 46–7.
21 FC 234–5.
22 AA 300.
23 GF 33–4, 56–7, 63; FC 228; PT 74; RA 236 (282); AA 306, 308; GN 217.
24 RA 236 (282); GF 57–8; PT 68–9.
25 RA 89–100 (253–5), 229–30 (280–1), 254 (284).
26 RA 203 (276), 257 (285); GF 65,;RM 823.
27 AA 316–18.
28 FC 253; RC 667; AA 334.
29 RA 263 (286).
30 RA 270 (287).
31 GF 80, BD 86, CA 4050–118.
32 RA 270–1 (287).
33 RA 282 (289).
34 RA 283 (289).
35 RA 289 (290).
36 RA 289 (290).

CHAPTER 3

1   Ibn al-Athir, *al-Kamil fi'l-Ta'rikh*, trans. D.S. Richards, 2 (Aldershot, 2006), 1. 13–14.
2   *Historia Belli Sacri, RHC* III, p. 181.
3   RM 791.
4   Ibn al- Qalānisī, *The Damascus Chronicle of the Crusades*, trans. H. A. R. Gibb (New York, 2002), p. 149.

5 RC 651.
6 RC 662.
7 R. Ellenblum, 'Frankish castles, Muslim castles, and the medieval citadel of Jerusalem', in *In Laudem Hierosolymitani*, ed. I. Shabrir, R. Ellenblum and J. Riley-Smith (Ashgate, 2007), pp. 93–110.
8 RA 306 (293).
9 RC 684–5.
10 RA 306 (293).
11 RC 689; CA 3815–84; OV III 606–7. J. Regnier, *Bulletin du Bibliophile et du Bibliothecaire* (Paris, 1862), p. 1067.
12 Ivo of Chartres, Letter 135, to Paschal II, *PL* 162 col. 144D; OV IV 287.
13 PT 103.

CHAPTER 4

1 RA 301 (292).
2 WT 8.4; GF 88.
3 RA 308 (293).
4 RA 311 (294); AA 410–12.
5 GF 89.
6 RA 312 (294); PT 27.
7 AA 412, 452; GN 274.
8 RC 691.
9 RM 865–6.
10 AA 430.
11 GF 89; RA 311 (294); WT 8.7.
12 WT 8.7
13 RA 317 (294); AA 408.
14 A. Bernard and A. Bruel (eds.), *Recueil des Chartes de l'Abbaye de Cluny* 6 (Paris: Imprimerie nationale, 1876–1903), 5. 51; L. M. Paterson and C. E. Sweetenham, *The Canso d'Antioca. An Occitan epic of the First Crusade* (Aldershot, 2003), pp. 41–2.
15 Guibert of Nogent, *Monodiae*, ed. E.–R. Labande (Paris, 1981), 3.11.
16 AA 408.
17 RA 321 (295).
18 AA 410.
19 RA 322 (295).

CHAPTER 5

1 WT 8.6.
2 RA 333 (297).
3 RA 181 (271).
4 AA 406.
5 AA 134.
6 Guibert of Nogent, *Monodiae*, 3.5.

7 AA 406; WT 8.6.
8 RC 690.
9 RC 689–90.
10 AA 420–2; PT 107.
11 *Josephi historiographi Tractatus de exordio sacrae domus Hospitalis Jerosolimitano, RHC Oc.* 5, 405–421, here 409; W. Dugdale, *Monasticon Anglicanum* 3 (London, 1718), 2, 171–3.
12 WT 8.8.
13 S. D. Goitein, 'Contemporary letters on the capture of Jerusalem by the Crusaders', *The Journal Of Jewish Studies* 3, 4 (1952), pp. 162–77, here p. 162.
14 Quoted in Moshe Gil, *A History of Palestine 634–1099* (Cambridge, 1992), p. 821.

CHAPTER 6

1 RA 331–2 (297); AA 98, 134; PT 50; AA 322, 356.
2 RA 331–2 (297), RC 692.
3 GN 310.
4 AA 426; WT 8.6.
5 RA 289 (290); RA 325–6 (296).
6 RA 214–15 (278).
7 RA 325–32 (296–7); GF 90; AA 412–14.
8 PT 106; RA 332 (297); AA 414.
9 GF 91.
10 BD 100.

CHAPTER 7

1 RA 287–91 (289–90); RC 683; AA 422.
2 AA 422, 428; FC 1.xvii.12.
3 AA 416.
4 RF 645–6.
5 AA 416–18.
6 GN 7.3.
7 RA 337–9 (298–9); AA 422.
8 RF 647–8; BD 100–1.
9 RA 299.

CHAPTER 8

1 RF 644–5.
2 RF 645.
3 RA 342 (299).
4 AA 422–4; RM 868.
5 AA 424.

6   AA 426; RC 692.
7   RC 693.
8   RA 343 (300).
9   AA 428; GF 90–1; RC 693.
10 RC 693.
11 AA 428–30.
12 RA 344 (300).
13 GF 91; WT 8. 19.
14 GF 91, 92; AA 438; WT 8.19, 8.24; Ibn al-Athīr, *al-Kamil fi'l-ta'rikh*, trans. D. S. Richards, 2 (Aldershot, 2006), 1. 21; Ibn al-Qalānisī, *The Damascus Chronicle of the Crusades*, trans. H. A. R. Gibb (New York, 2002), p. 48.
15 AA 430.
16 RC 701.
17 AA 442; RA 345 (300).
18 FC I.xxix.I (304); AA 432; WT 8.20; BD 103.
19 S. D. Goitein, 'Contemporary letters on the capture of Jerusalem by the Crusaders', *The Journal Of Jewish Studies* 3, 4 (1952), pp. 162–77; M. Gil, *A History of Palestine, 634–1099* (Cambridge, 1992) pp. 831–7.
20 Al-'Azimi in Carole Hillenbrand, *The Crusades – Islamic Perspectives* (Edinburgh, 1999), p. 64; Ibn al-Qalānisī, *The Damascus Chronicle*, p. 48.
21 AA 432–4, RC 695–6, Ibn al-Athīr, *al-Kamil fi'l-ta'rikh*, 1. 21–2.
22 AA 436.
23 AA 430.
24 RC 697–8.
25 RA 347 (300); FC 1.xxix.4.

CHAPTER 9

1   WT 8.21.
2   RA 348 (300).
3   WT 8.23.
4   AA 438–40; GF 92.
5   S. D. Goitein, 'Contemporary letters on the capture of Jerusalem by the Crusaders', *The Journal Of Jewish Studies* 3, 4 (1952), p. 165; M. Gil, *A History of Palestine, 634–1099* (Cambridge, 1992), p. 831.
6   GF 92; PT 110; BD 103; WT 8. 24.
7   AA 440–2; BD 103; S. D. Goitein, 'Contemporary letters', p. 171.
8   RC 699–702.
9   RC 702.
10 Bernold of St Blaisen (Constance), *Chronicon*, ed. I. S. Robinson, *Die Chroniken Bertholds von Reichenau und Bernolds von Konstanz, MGH Scriptores Rerum Germanicorum nova series* 14 (Hanover, 2003), p. 540.
11 RA 351–2 (301).
12 A. V. Murray, *The Crusader Kingdom of Jerusalem, A Dynastic History 1099-1125* (Oxford, 2000), pp. 38–40; AA 112, 332–4.
13 AA 142–4; GN 7.5.

14   RA 282 (289).
15   RA 352 (301), AA 444–6, WT 9.2.
16   Gregory VII, *Registrum* I.9, pp. 13–15 (6 May 1073).
17   RA 352 (301).
18   RA 354 (301); WT 9.2.
19   GF 92; FC I.xxx.1; AA 446.
20   RA 355 (301).
21   RA 356–7 (301–2).
22   FC I.xxix.4; AA 450–2.
23   C. W. David, *Robert Curthose, Duke of Normandy* (Cambridge, Mass., 1920), pp. 217–20.
24   RA 358 (302).
25   RC 699–700.
26   AA 452–4.
27   AA 464; Y. Lev, 'Army, regime, and society in Fatimid Egypt, 358–487/968–1094', *International Journal of Middle East Studies* 19, 3 (1987), pp. 337–65.
28   PT 111–12.
29   AA 456.
30   RA 364 (303).
31   RA 361–5 (303–4).
32   GF 94–5; RA 368 (304).
33   RA 369 (304); AA 460–2.
34   GF 95–6; AA 464–6.
35   PT 115; AA 468; GF 97.

CHAPTER 10

1   For example, in *La Chanson de Jérusalem*, ed. Nigel R. Thorpe (Tuscaloosa, 1991), *Le Chevalier au Cygne*, ed. G. C. Pukatzki (Tuscaloosa, 1971).
2   OV VI, 162–3.
3   Ivo of Chartres, Letter 135 to Paschal II, *PL*162 col. 144D.
4   J. Prawer, *Crusader Institutions* (Oxford, 1980), pp. 124, 140–1.
5   WT 20.19.
6   FC III.37.4, Fulcher of Chartres, *A History of the Expedition to Jerusalem 1095-1127,* trans. F. R. Ryan, introduction and notes H. S. Fink (Knoxville, 1941), p. 271.
7   FC II.4.4
8   B. Z. Kedar, 'Multidirectional conversion in the Frankish Levant', in *Varieties of Religious Conversion in the Middle Ages*, ed. J. Muldoon (Gainesville, 1997), pp. 190–9.
9   Ibn al-Qalānisī, *The Damascus Chronicle of the Crusades*, trans. H. A. R. Gibb (New York, 2002), p. 284.
10   Conrad III to Abbot Wibald of Korvey, September/November 1148. MGH Diplomatum Regum et Imperatorum Germaniae IX, Conradi III et filii eius Heinrici Diplomata, ed. Friedrich Hausman (1969), pp. 356–7.
11   WT 17.26.
12   WT 20.10, trans. E. A. Babcock and A. C. Krey, 2 (New York, 1943), 2.357–8.
13   Bahā' al-Dīn Ibn Shaddād, *The Rare and Excellent History of Saladin*, trans. D. S. Richards (Aldershot, 2002), pp. 19, 25, 244.
14   Ibn al-Athīr, *al-Kamil fi'l-ta'rikh*, trans. D. S. Richards, 2 (Aldershot, 2006), 2. 395.

15 P. W. Edbury, *The Conquest of Jerusalem and the Third Crusade* (Aldershot, 1998), p. 58.
16 Ibid., p. 62.
17 Al-Athir, *al-Kamil fi'l-ta'rikh*, 1. 333–4.
18 P. W. Edbury, *The Conquest of Jerusalem*. p. 62.
19 Ibid., p. 63.
20 Ibid., p. 64.
21 Ibn Shaddād, *The Rare and Excellent History* p. 78. Al-Athir, *al-Kamil fi'l-ta'rikh*, I. 332–5.
22 Martin Luther, *Works*, 55 (Philadelphia, 1955–86), 46:185.

APPENDIX

1 See J. H. Hill and L. L. Hill, *Raymond IV, Count of Toulouse* (Syracuse, 1962).
2 Editions of the *Gesta Francorum*: J. Bongars, *Gesta Dei per Francos* (Hanover, 1611); *RHC Oc.* 3, 121–63; *Anonymi Gesta Francorum et aliorum Hierosolimitanorum*, ed. H. Hagenmeyer (Heidelberg, 1890); *Anonymi Gesta Francorum*, ed. B. A. Lees (Oxford, 1924); *Histoire Anonyme de la première Croisade* ed. L. Bréhier (Paris, 1924); *Gesta Francorum et aliorum Hierosolimitanorum* ed. R. Hill (Oxford, 1962), hereafter GF.
3 Conor Kostick, 'A further discussion on the authorship of the *Gesta Francorum*', *Reading Medieval Studies* XXXIII (2009), pp. 1–11.
4 Editions of the *Historia de Hierosolymitano itinere*: J. Bongars, *Gesta Dei per Francos* (Hanover, 1611); J. Besly in *Historiae Francorum Scriptores*, IV ed. A. Duchesne (Paris, 1841); *RHC Oc.* 3, 3–117; J. H. Hill and L. L. Hill, *Petrus Tudebodus, Historia de Hierosolymitano Itinere* (Paris, 1977). English translation: J. H. Hill and L. L. Hill, *Peter Tudebode, Historia de Hierosolymitano Itinere* (Philadelphia, 1974).
5 Editions of the *Historia Francorum*: J. Bongars, *Gesta Dei per Francos* (Hanover, 1611); *RHC Oc.* 3, 235–309; J. France, *A Critical Edition of the* Historia Francorum *of Raymond of Aguilers* (unpublished Ph.D. thesis: University of Nottingham, 1967); *Le 'Liber' de Raymond d'Aguilers*, eds J. H. Hill and L. L. Hill (Paris, 1969). I am grateful to J. France for permission to quote from his thesis.
6 Raymond of Aguilers, *Historia Francorum qui ceperunt Jherusalem*, trans. J. H. Hill and L. L. Hill (Philadelphia, 1968).
7 RA 5 (235); RA 11–12, 17 (237, 238); RA 202 (276); RA 100 (255).
8 Fulcher of Chartres, *Historia Hierosolymitana (1095–1127)*, ed. H. Hagenmeyer (Heidelberg, 1913). Earlier editions: J. Bongars, *Gesta Dei per Francos* (Hanover, 1611); *PL* 150, cols. 823–942B; *RHC Oc.* 3, 311–485.
9 Birth year: FC III.xxiv.17 (687); III.xliv.4 (771). Chartres: FC I.v.12 (153); I.xiv.15 (215); I.xxxiii.12 (330). Sets out: FC I.vii.1–viii.9 (163–76). With Baldwin: FC I.xiv.2 (206). Missed the siege: GN 329; FC 16. Journeyed to Jerusalem: FC II.iii.12 (368); FC II.v.12 (383–4).
10 Albert of Aachen, *Historia Ierosolimitana*, ed. S. B. Edgington (Oxford, 2007).
11 P. Knoch, *Studien zu Albert von Aachen* (Stuttgart, 1966), p. 89; AA xxiv–v.
12 AA i.1 (2): *relatione nota fierent ab hiis qui presentes affuissent.* See also AA iii.2 (138).
13 J. France, 'The text of the account of the capture of Jerusalem in the Ripoll Manuscript, Bibliothèque Nationale (Latin) 5132', *The English Historical Review* 103, 408 (July 1988), pp. 640–57.
14 See F. J. E. Raby, *A History of Secular Latin Poetry in the Middle Ages*, 2 (Oxford, 1997), I, 337–48.
15 The 1611 edition in the collection of Jacques Bongars was based upon Paris, B. N. MS Latin 5513. This manuscript has been the subject of a study by N. L. Paul, who concluded that it

was an untypical version of the *Historia Hierosolymitana* 'redacted to suit the political and commemorative imperatives of the seigneurial family of Amboise'. J. P. Migne reproduced Bongar's edition for volume 166 of the *Patrologia Latina* (1854).

16   BD 10.

17   BD xi–xii.

18   An edition of the *Historia Iherosolimitana* appeared as early at 1492 in Cologne; it was printed in Basle in 1533 and Frankfurt-am-Main in 1584. It was included in Jacques Bongars' important 1611 collection of crusading accounts *Gesta Dei per Francos* (Hanover, 1611) and was printed in the *Patrologia Latina* series in 1844 by J. P. Migne, *PL*, 155, 669–758. *RHC Oc.* 3, 717–882.

19   RM 725.

20   RM 723.

21   GP, p. lx; Sweetman, *Robert the Monk's History*, p. 34.

22   GP xviii. For further discussion of Gilo's career see GP xix–xxii and R. Hüls, *Kardinäle, Klerus and Kirchen Roms* (Tübingen, 1977), pp. 142–3.

23   C. W. Grocock and J. E. Siberry (eds), The *Historia Vie Hierosolimitane* of Gilo of Paris and a second anonymous author (Oxford, 1997).

24   J. Bongars, *Gesta Dei per Francos* (Hanover, 1611); Dom. L. D'Achery, *Venerabilis Guiberti abbatis B. Mariae de Novigento opera ominia* (Paris, 1651), pp. 367–453; PL 156 (Paris, 1853), cols. 679B–834A; *RHC Oc.* 4, 117–260; Guibert of Nogent, *Gesta Dei per Francos*, ed. R. B. C. Huygens, *CC* LXXVIIa, (Turnhout, 1996), hereafter GN. For a discussion of these editions see GN 18–23.

25   GN 51–6.

26   RC 604.

27   Ralph of Caen, *Gesta Tancredi, RHC Oc.* 3, 587–716; B. S. Bachrach and D. S. Bachrach, eds., The *Gesta* Tancredi *of Ralph of Caen* (Aldershot 2005).

28   William of Tyre, *Chronicon*, ed. R. B. C. Huygens, CC 63 (Turnhout, 1986).

29   S. Eidelberg ed., *The Jews and the Crusaders: the Hebrew chronicles of the first and second crusaders* (New Jersey, 1996). See also N. Golb, 'New light on the persecution of French Jews at the time of the First Crusade', *Proceedings of the American Academy for Jewish Research* 34 (1966), pp. 1–63. R. Chazan, *European Jewry and the First Crusade*, (Berkeley, 1987); J. Riley-Smith, 'The First Crusade and the persecution of the Jews', *Studies in Church History*, 21 (1984), pp. 51–72; R. Chazan, *In the year 1096: The First Crusade and the Jews* (Philadelphia, 1996); A. Havercamp ed., *Juden und Christen zur Zeit der Krezzüge* (Sigmaringen, 1999); D. Malkiel, 'Destruction and conversion: intention and reaction, Crusaders and Jews in 1096', *Jewish History* 15 (2001), pp. 257–80.

30   S. D. Goitein, 'Contemporary letters on the capture of Jerusalem by the Crusaders', *The Journal Of Jewish Studies* 3, 4 (1952), pp. 162–77; M. Gil, *A History of Palestine, 634–1099* (Cambridge, 1992).

31   In C. Hillenbrand, *The Crusades – Islamic Perspectives* (Edinburgh, 1999), p. 64.

32   Ibn al-Qalānisī, *The Damascus Chronicle of the Crusades*, trans. H. A. R. Gibb (New York, 2002).

33   In C. Hillenbrand, *The Crusades – Islamic Perspectives*, p. 65.

34   Ibn al-Athīr, *al-Kamil fi'l-ta'rikh*, trans. D. S. Richards, 2 (Aldershot, 2006), 1, 21–2.

35   C. Hillenbrand, *The Crusades – Islamic Perspectives*, p. 66.

36   Al-Sulami, 'Book of Holy War' in C. Hillenbrand, *The Crusades – Islamic Perspectives*, p. 73.

37   See C. Hillenbrand, *The Crusades – Islamic Perspectives*, pp. 69–88.

Select Bibliography

PRIMARY SOURCES

Albert of Aachen, *Historia Iherosolimitana.*
    Historia Iherosolimitana, RHC Oc. 4, 265–713.
    Historia Ierosolimitana, ed. S. B. Edgington (Oxford, 2007).
Anonymous, J. France ed., 'The text of the account of the capture of Jerusalem in the Ripoll Manuscript, Bibliothèque Nationale (Latin) 5132', *The English Historical Review* 103, 408 (July 1988), pp. 640–57.
Bahā' al-Dīn Ibn Shaddād, *The Rare and Excellent History of Saladin*, trans. D. S. Richards (Aldershot, 2002).
Baldric of Dol, *Historia Hierosolymitana, RHC Oc.* 4, 1–111.
Bernard A. and A. Bruel, eds, *Recueil des Chartes de l'Abbaye de Cluny* 6 (Paris, 1876–1903).
Bernold of St Blaisen (Constance), *Chronicon*, ed. I. S. Robinson, *Die Chroniken Bertholds von Reichenau und Bernolds von Konstanz, MGH Scriptores Rerum Germanicorum nova series* 14 (Hanover, 2003), pp. 383–540.
Bongars, J., *Gesta Dei per Francos* (Hanover, 1611).
Caffaro, *Annales Ianuenses*, ed. L. T. Belgrano, *Annali Genovesi di Caffaro e de' suoi continuatori* (Rome, 1890).
La Chanson d'Antioche
    P. Paris, ed. 2 (*reprint: Geneva, 1969*).
    Duparc-Quioc, S. ed. 2 (Paris, 1977).
La Chanson de Jérusalem, ed. Nigel R. Thorpe (Tuscaloosa, 1991).
Le Chevalier au Cygne, ed. G. C. Pukatzki (Tuscaloosa, 1971).
Comnena, Anna, *The Alexiad*, trans. E. R. A. Sewter, (Middlesex, 1979).
Conrad III of Germany, Letter to Abbot Wibald of Korvey, September/ November 1148. *MGH Diplomatum Regum et Imperatorum Germaniae IX, Conradi III et filii eius Heinrici Diplomata*, ed. Friedrich Hausman (1969), Vienna, pp. 356–7.

Dudo of Saint-Quentin, *Libri III de moribus et actis primorum Normanniae ducum*, PL 141, Cols. 608B–759A.

Eidelberg, S. ed., *The Jews and the Crusaders: The Hebrew Chronicles of the First and Second Crusaders* (New Jersey, 1996).

Ekkehard of Aura, *Chronicon*.

    Hierosolymita, RHC Oc. 5, 1–40.

    Chronicon Universale, MGH SS 6, 33–231.

    Frutolfs und Ekkehards Chroniken und die Anonyme Kaiserchronik, ed. F-J Schmale and I. Schamle-Ott (Darmstadt, 1972).

Frutolf, *Chronicon, Frutolfs und Ekkehards Chroniken und die Anonyme Kaiserchronik*, ed. F-J Schmale and I. Schmale-Ott (Darmstadt, 1972).

Fulcher of Chartres, *Historia Hierosolymitana*.

    Gesta Francorum Iherusalem Peregrinantium, RHC Oc. 3, 311–485.

    Fulcher of Chartres, *Historia Hierosolymitana (1095–1127)*, ed. H. Hagenmeyer (Heidelberg, 1913).

    Fulcher of Chartres, *A History of the Expedition to Jerusalem 1095–1127*, trans. F. R. Ryan, introduction and notes H. S. Fink (Knoxville, 1941).

    Fulcher of Chartres, *Chronicle of the First Crusade*, trans. M. E. McGinty (Philadelphia, 1941).

Gesta Francorum et aliorum Hierosolimitanorum.

    Anonymi Gesta Francorum et aliorum Hierosolimitanorum, ed. H. Hagenmeyer (Heidelberg, 1890).

    Histoire Anonyme de la première Croisade, ed. L. Bréhier (Paris, 1924).

    Anonymi Gesta Francorum, ed. B. A. Lees (Oxford, 1924).

    Gesta Francorum et aliorum Hierosolimitanorum, ed. and trans. R. Hill (London, 1962).

Gilo of Paris and a second, anonymous author, *Historia Vie Hierosolimitane*, ed. C. W. Grocock and J. E. Siberry (Oxford, 1997).

Gregory VII, *Registrum*, ed. E. Caspar, *MGH Epistolae selectae* 2 (Berlin, 1920, 1923).

Guibert of Nogent, *Gesta Dei per Francos*, ed. R. B. C. Huygens, CC LXXVIIa (Turnhout, 1996).

Guibert of Nogent, *Monodiae*, ed. E.–R. Labande (Paris, 1981).

Hagenmeyer, H. (ed.), *Epistulae et Chartae ad Historiam Primi Belli Sacri Spectantes Quae Supersunt Aevo Aequales ac Genuinae: Die Kreuzzugsbriefe aus den Jahren 1088–1100* (Innsbruck, 1901).

Historia Belli Sacri, RHC Oc. 3, pp. 169–229.

Ibn al-Athīr, *al-Kamil fi'l-ta'rikh*, trans. D. S. Richards, 2 (Aldershot, 2006).

Ibn al-Qalānisī, *The Damascus Chronicle of the Crusades*, trans. H. A. R. Gibb (New York, 2002).

Ivo of Chartres, Letter 135, to Paschal II, *PL* 162 col. 144D.

Josephi historiographi Tractatus de exordio sacrae domus Hospitalis Jerosolimitano, *RHC Oc.* 5, 405–421.

Martin Luther, *Works*, 55 (Philadelphia, 1955–86).

Orderic Vitalis, *The Ecclesiastical History*, ed. and trans. M. Chibnall, 6 (Oxford, 1969–79).

Peter Tudebode, *Historia de Hierosolymitano Itinere*.

> *Historia de Hierosolymitano Itinere* ed. J. H. Hill and L. L. Hill (Paris, 1977).

> Peter Tudebode, *Historia de Hierosolymitana*, trans. J. H. Hill and L. L. Hill (Philadelphia, 1968).

Ralf of Caen, *Gesta Tancredi*, *RHC Oc.* 3, 587–716.

> The *Gesta Tancredi* of Ralph of Caen, trans. B. S. Bachrach and D. S. Bachrach (Aldershot, 2005).

Raymond of Aguilers, *Historia Francorum qui ceperunt Iherusalem*.

> Raymond of Aguilers, *Historia Francorum qui ceperunt Iherusalem*, *RHC Oc.* 3, 235–309.

> *Historia Francorum qui ceperunt Iherusalem*, ed. John France (unpublished Ph.D. thesis: University of Nottingham, 1967).

> *Le 'Liber' de Raymond d'Aguilers*, ed. J. H. Hill and L. L. Hill (Paris,1969).

> *Raymond of Aguilers, Historia Francorum qui ceperunt Jherusalem*, trans. J. H. Hill and L. L. Hill (Philadelphia, 1968).

Robert the Monk, *Historia Iherosolimitana*.

> *Historia Iherosolimitana*, *RHC Oc.* 3, 717–882.

> Robert the Monk, *History of the First Crusade*, trans. C. Sweetenham (Aldershot, 2005).

Snorri Sturlason, *Heimskringla*, ed. E. Monsen, trans. A. H. Smith (New York, 1990).

Usāmah Ibn-Munqidh, *Memoirs of an Arab-Syrian Gentleman*, trans. P. K. Hitti (Beirut, 1964).

William of Malmesbury, *Gesta Regum Anglorum* I, ed. and trans. R. A. B. Mynors (Oxford, 1998).

William of Tyre, *Chronicon*.

> *Historia Rerum in Partibus Transmarinis Gestarum*, *RHC Oc.* 1, 3–702.

> William, Archbishop of Tyre, *A History of Deeds Done beyond the Sea*, trans. E. A. Babcock and A. C. Krey, 2 (New York, 1943).

> *Chronicon*, ed. R. B. C. Huygens CC 63 (Turnhout, 1986).

SECONDARY WORKS

Alphandéry, P., *L'Europe et L'idée de Croisades*, 2 (Paris, 1954).

Alphandéry, P. and A. Dupront, *La Chrétienité et l'idée de croisade*, 2 (Paris 1954-9).

Andressohn, J. C., *The Ancestry and Life of Godfrey of Bouillon* (Bloomington, 1947).

Asbridge, T., *The First Crusade: A New History* (London, 2004).

Blake, E. O. and C. Morris, 'A hermit goes to war: Peter and the origins of the First Crusade', *Studies in Church History* 22 (1984), pp. 79-107.

Brundage, J. A., 'Adhémar of Puy: the Bishop and his critics', *Speculum* 34 (1959), pp. 201-12.

Chazan, R., *European Jewry and the First Crusade* (Berkeley, 1987).

Chazan, R., *In the Year 1096: The First Crusade and the Jews* (Philadelphia, 1996).

Cheney, C. R., *A Handbook of Dates* (Cambridge, 2000).

Chibnall, M., *The World of Orderic Vitalis* (Oxford, 1984).

Clare, L., *La Quintaine, la Course de Bague et le Jue des Têtes* (Paris, 1983).

Cohen, R., 'An introduction to the First Crusade', *Past and Present* 6 (1954), pp. 6-30.

Cohn, N., *The Pursuit of the Millennium* (fifth edition: London, 1970).

Coupe, M. D., 'Peter the Hermit – a reassessment', *Nottingham Medieval Studies 31* (1987), pp. 37-45.

Daniel, N., *The Arabs and Mediaeval Europe* (London, 1979).

David, C. W., *Robert Curthose Duke of Normandy* (Cambridge, Mass., 1920).

Davis, R. H. C., *The Medieval Warhorse* (London, 1989).

Dugdale, W., *Monasticon Anglicanum*, 3 (London, 1718).

Duncalf, F. 'The peasants' crusade', *American Historical Review* 26 (1920/1), pp. 440-53.

Edbury, P. W., *The Conquest of Jerusalem and the Third Crusade* (Aldershot, 1998).

Edbury, P. W. and J. G. Rowe, ed., *William of Tyre, Historian of the Latin East* (Cambridge, 1988).

Edgington, S. B., 'Albert of Aachen reappraised', in *From Clermont to Jerusalem*, ed. A. V. Murray (Turnhout, 1998), pp. 55-68.

Edgington, S. B., 'The First Crusade: reviewing the evidence', in *The First Crusade, Origins and Impact*, ed. J. Phillips (Manchester, 1997), pp. 55-77.

Edgington, S. B. and S. Lambert, ed., *Gendering the Crusades* (Cardiff, 2001).

Ellenblum, R., 'Frankish castles, Muslim castles, and the medieval citadel of Jerusalem', in *In Laudem Hierosolymitani*, ed. I. Shabrir, R. Ellenblum and J. Riley-Smith (Aldershot, 2007), pp. 93–110.

Ellenblum, R., *Frankish Rural Settlement in the Latin Kingdom of Jerusalem* (Cambridge, 1998).

Epp, V., *Fulcher von Chartres* (Dusseldorf, 1990).

Flori, J., *Pierre l'Ermite et la Première Croisade* (Paris, 1999).

Foreville, R., 'Un chef de la première croisade: Arnulf Malecouronne', *Bulletin Philologique et Historique du Comité des Travaux Historiques et Scientifiques* (1953–4), pp. 377–90.

France, J. 'The crisis of the First Crusade: from the defeat of Kerbogha to the departure from Arqa', *Byzantion* 40 (1970), pp. 276–308.

France, J., 'An unknown account of the capture of Jerusalem', *English Historical Review* 87 (1972), pp. 771–83.

France, J., 'The election and title of Godfrey de Bouillon', *Canadian Journal of History* 18 (1983).

France, J., Victory in the East. A Military History of the First Crusade (Cambridge, 1994).

France, J., 'The use of the Anonymous *Gesta Francorum* in the early twelfth-century sources for the First Crusade', in *From Clermont to Jerusalem. The Crusades and Crusader Societies 1095–1500*, ed. A. V. Murray (Turnhout,1998), pp. 29–42.

France, J., *Western Warfare in the Age of the Crusades, 1100–1300* (London, 1999).

France, J., and W. G. Zajac, ed., *The Crusades and Their Sources: Essays Presented to Bernard Hamilton* (Aldershot, 1998).

Gabrieli, F. *Arab Historians of the Crusades* (London, 1969).

Gil, M., *A History of Palestine, 634–1099* (Cambridge, 1992).

Goitein, S. D., 'Contemporary letters on the capture of Jerusalem by the Crusaders', *The Journal Of Jewish Studies* 3, No. 4 (1952), pp. 162–77.

Golb, N., 'New light on the persecution of French Jews at the time of the First Crusade', *Proceedings of the American Academy for Jewish Research* 34 (1966), pp. 1–63.

Hagenmeyer, H., *Peter der Eremite* (Leipzig, 1879).

Hagenmeyer, H., *Chronologie de la Première Croisade 1094–1100*, (Hildesheim, 1973).

Havercamp, A., ed., *Juden und Christen zur Zeit der Krezzüge* (Sigmaringen, 1999).

Hill, J. H. and L. L. Hill, *Raymond IV, Count of Toulouse* (Syracuse, 1962).

Hillenbrand, C., *The Crusades – Islamic Perspectives* (Edinburgh, 1999).

Hodgson, N., 'Ralph of Caen', in *Anglo-Norman Studies* 30. 117–132.

Huygens, R. B. C., 'Guillaume de Tyre étudiant. Un chapitre (xix.12) de son *Histoire* retrouvé', *Latomus* xxi (1962), pp. 811–29.

Huygens, R. B. C., 'Editing William of Tyre', *Sacris Erudiri* 27 (1984), pp. 461–73.

Jacobsen, P. Ch., *Albert von Aachen, Lexicon des Mittelalters 1* (Munich, 1977), pp. 286–7.

Jewett, J. R., 'Arabic proverbs and proverbial phrases', *Journal of the American Oriental Society* 15 (1893), pp. 28–120.

Kangas, S., 'Non ego sed dominus. Clerical participation in the acts of violence during the First Crusade', in *Church and War in the Middle Ages* ed. Kurt Villads Jensen, Torben K. Nielsen and Carsten Selch Jensen (Brepols, 2009).

Kangas, S., *Deus vult: Images of Crusader Violence c.1095–1100* (Leiden, 2010).

Kedar, B. Z., 'Multidirectional conversion in the Frankish Levant', in *Varieties of Religious Conversion in the Middle Ages*, ed. J. Muldoon (Gainesville, 1997), pp. 190–9.

Knappen, M. M., 'Robert II of Flanders in the First Crusade', in *The Crusades and Other Historical Essays Presented to Dana C. Munro*, ed. L. J. Paetow (New York, 1928), pp. 79–100.

Knoch, P., *Studien zu Albert von Aachen* (Stuttgart, 1966).

Kostick, C., 'William of Tyre, Livy, and the Vocabulary of Class', *Journal of History of Ideas* 65, 3 (2004), pp. 353–68.

Kostick, C. 'Women and the First Crusade: prostitutes or pilgrims?' in *Studies on Medieval and Early Modern Women 4: Victims or Viragos?* ed. C. Meek and C. Lawless (Dublin, 2005), pp. 57–68.

Kostick, C. 'The terms *milites*, *equites* and *equestres* in the early crusading histories', M. Jones (ed.), *Nottingham Medieval Studies*, 50 (2006), pp. 1–21.

Kostick, C., *The Social Structure of the First Crusade* (Leiden, 2008).

Kostick, C., 'The afterlife of Bishop Adhémar of Le Puy', in *Studies in Church History*, 45 (2009). pp. 120–9.

La Monte, J. L., 'The Lords of Le Puiset on the Crusades', *Speculum* 17, I (1942), pp. 100–18.

Lev, Y., 'Army, regime, and society in Fatimid Egypt, 358–487/968–1094', *International Journal of Middle East Studies* 19, 3 (1987), pp. 337–65.

Maalouf, A., *The Crusades through Arab Eyes* (London, 1984).

Malkiel, D., 'Destruction and conversion: intention and reaction, Crusaders and Jews in 1096', *Jewish History* 15 (2001), pp. 257–80.

Morris, C., 'Policy and visions – The case of the Holy Lance at Antioch', in *War and Government in the Middle Ages: Essays in Honour of J. O. Prestwich*, ed. J. Gillingham and J. C. Holt (Woodbridge, 1984), pp. 33–45.

Morris, C., 'The aims and spirituality of the crusade as seen through the eyes of Albert of Aix', *Reading Medieval Studies* 16 (1990), pp. 99–117.

Morris, C., 'The *Gesta Francorum* as narrative history', *Reading Medieval Studies* 19 (1993), pp. 55–71.

Muldoon, J., ed., *Varieties of Religious Conversion in the Middle Ages* (Gainesville, 1997).

Munro, D. C., 'The speech of Pope Urban II at Clermont, 1095', *American Historical Review* 11 (1905–6), pp. 231–42.

Munro, D. C., 'A Crusader', *Speculum* 7 (1932), pp. 321–35.

Murray, A. V., 'The title of Godfrey of Bouillon as ruler of Jerusalem', *Collegium Medievale* 3 (1990).

Murray, A. V., 'The army of Godfrey of Bouillon', *Revue Belge de Philologie et d'Histoire* 70 (1992), pp. 301–29.

Murray, A. V., 'Bibliography of the First Crusade', *From Clermont to Jerusalem. The Crusades and Crusader Societies 1095–1500*, ed. A. V. Murray (Turnhout, 1998), pp. 267–310.

Murray, A. V., ed., *From Clermont to Jerusalem. The Crusades and Crusader Societies 1095–1500* (Turnhout,1998).

Murray, A. V., *The Crusader Kingdom of Jerusalem, A Dynastic History 1099–1125* (Oxford, 2000).

Nader, M., *Burgesses and the Burgess Law in the Latin Kingdom of Jerusalem and Cyprus (1099–1325)* (Aldershot, 2006).

Nicholson, R. L., *Tancred: A Study of His Career and Work in Their Relation to the First Crusade and the Establishment of the Latin States in Syria and Palestine* (Chicago, 1940).

Oehler, H., 'Studien zu den *Gesta Francorum*', *Mittellateinisches Jahrbuch* 6 (1970), 58–97.

Paterson, L. M. and C. E. Sweetenham, *The Canso d'Antioca. An Occitan Epic of the First Crusade* (Aldershot, 2003).

N. L. Paul, 'Crusade, memory and regional politics in twelfth-century Amboise', *Journal of Medieval History,* 31.2 (June 2005), pp. 127–41.

Phillips, J., ed., *The First Crusade: Origins and impact* (Manchester, 1997).

Porges, W., 'The clergy, the poor and the non-Combatants on the First Crusade', *Speculum* 21 (1946), pp. 1–21.

Prawer, J., *Crusader Institutions* (Oxford, 1980).

Prawer, J., *The Latin Kingdom of Jerusalem: European Colonisation in the Middle Ages* (London, 1972).

Regnier, J., *Bulletin du Bibliophile et du Bibliothecaire* (Paris, 1862).

Richard, J., 'La confrérie de la première croisade', in *Etudes de Civilisation Médiéval: Mélanges Offerts à E. R. Labande*, ed. B. Jeannau (Poitiers, 1974), pp. 617–22.

Riley-Smith, J., 'The title of Godfrey of Bouillon', *Bulletin of the Institute of Historical Research* 52 (1979).

Riley-Smith, J., 'The First Crusade and the persecution of the Jews', *Studies in Church History* 21 (1984), pp. 51–72.

Riley-Smith, J., *The First Crusaders 1095–1131* (Cambridge, 1997).

Rouche, M., 'Cannibalisme sacré chez les croisés populaires', in *la Réligion Populaire*, ed. Y. M. Hilaire (Paris, 1981), pp. 56–69.

Rousset, P., *Les Origines et Les Caractéres de la Première Croisade* (Geneva, 1945).

Rubenstein, J., *Guibert of Nogent: Portrait of a Medieval Mind* (New York, 2002).

Rubenstein, J., 'How, or how much, to re-evaluate Peter the Hermit', in *The Medieval Crusade*, ed. S. J. Ridyard (Woodbridge, 2004), pp. 53–70.

Rubenstein, J., 'Putting history to use: three crusading chronicles in context', *Viator* 35 (2004), pp. 131–68.

Rubenstein, J., '*What is the Gesta Francorum*, and who was Peter Tudebode?' *Revue Mabillon* 16 (2005), pp. 179–204.

Runciman, S., 'The Holy Lance found at Antioch', *Analecta Bollandiana* 68 (1950), pp. 197–205.

Runciman, S., *A History of the Crusades*, 3 (fifth edition: London, 1991).

Shabrir, I., R. Ellenblum and J. Riley-Smith, eds., *In Laudem Hierosolymitani* (Aldershot, 2007).

Somerville, R., *The Councils of Urban II, 1, Decreta Claromontensia* (Amsterdam, 1972).

Somerville, R., 'The council of Clermont and the First Crusade', *Studia Gratiana* 20 (1976), pp. 323–37.

Somerville, R., *Pope Alexander III and the Council of Tours* (Los Angeles, 1977).

Sumberg, L. A. M., 'The "Tafurs" and the First Crusade', *Mediaeval Studies* 21 (1951), pp. 224–46.

Thomson, R., 'William of Malmesbury, historian of Crusade', *Reading Medieval Studies* 23 (1997), pp 121–34.

Wolf, K. B., 'Crusade and narrative: Bohemond and the *Gesta Francorum*', *Journal of Medieval History* 17, II (1991), pp. 207–16.

Yewdale, R. B., *Bohemond I, Prince of Antioch* (New York, 1924).

Zajac, W. G. 'Captured property on the First Crusade', in *The First Crusade, Origins and Impact*, ed. J. Phillips (Manchester 1997), pp. 153–180.

Index

Abbasid dynasty 51
Abu Shama 165
Achard of Montmerle 74, 76
Acre 52, 156
Adelolf 128
Adhémar, bishop of Le Puy 2, 6, 8, 17,
      20, 21, 26, 31, 41, 42, 44, 45, 47, 49,
      61, 93, 96, 97, 104, 133, 138, 139,
      142, 175, 177
al-Adid 168
Adrianople 16
al-Afdal, vizier of Egypt 52, 53–4, 56, 64,
      72, 73, 79, 83, 88–9, 91, 92, 102,
      112–13, 147–8, 151–3, 154, 155,
      176, 183
Agamemnon 85
Agrippa 1
Akhzib 160
Alamūt 162
Albara 35, 84
   bishop of *see* Peter of Narbonne
Albert III, count of Namur 80
Albert of Aachen 178–9
Aleppo 35, 158, 162, 164, 166, 168, 169
Alexander, papal legate, 6
Alexius I Comnenus, Byzantine
      emperor 9, 10, 12, 14, 15–18, 21,
      23, 24, 25, 26–7, 34, 43, 44, 45, 46,
      47, 53, 85, 123, 137, 157–8
Alfonso I, king of Aragon 164
Alfonso VI, king of Leon and
      Castille 141

Amalfi 7
Amalric, king of Jerusalem 167
Amiens 75
Antioch 34, 45, 46, 47, 53, 54, 55, 57,
      60, 70, 71, 78, 81, 87, 89, 96, 140,
      142, 155, 157, 158, 159, 161, 162,
      176, 181
   siege 34–40, 58, 63, 75, 79, 80, 93, 123,
      140, 142, 176
al-Aqsā Mosque 54, 55, 126–7, 129–30,
      134–5, 164, 184
Arnulf, bishop of Matera 136–8, 149
Arnulf of Choques, later Patriarch of
      Jerusalem 6, 48–9, 97–8, 104, 123,
      136–8, 146–7, 149, 151, 159, 182
'Arqā 48, 49, 50, 56, 58, 67, 97, 104, 147
Artuq 55, 81
Ascalon 73, 76, 78, 88, 122, 134, 148,
      149, 151–3, 166, 176, 177, 184
   Jaffa Gate 152
   Jerusalem Gate 152
Assassins *see* Bātinīds
Atsiz b. Uwaq 81
Aubrey of Grandmesnil 40
Avignon 141
al-'Azimi 183

Bachrach, B. S. 182
Bachrach, D. S. 182
Badr al-Jamāli 52
Baisy 140
Baldric, archbishop of Dol 179–80, 182

Baldric, chamberlain 128

Baldwin IV, king of Jerusalem 170

Baldwin V, king of Jerusalem 170

Baldwin of Boulogne (Baldwin I of
    Jerusalem) 6, 17, 20, 32–4, 44, 57,
    74–5, 78, 93, 156, 157, 159, 162

Baldwin of Bourcq (Baldwin II of
    Jerusalem) 74–7, 159, 162

Baldwin of Ibelin 170

Balian of Ibelin 171

Bari 80

Bāṭinīds 52, 53, 162–3, 168

Beirut 156

Beit-Jibrin 160

Bernard, advocate of the monastery of
    Saint Valery-sur-Somme 120

Bernard of Clairvaux 163

Bernard the Stranger 158–9

Bertrade of Montfort 1

Bertrand I, count of Toulouse 2, 141

Bethlehem 61, 67, 71, 73, 83, 87, 89, 94,
    137, 144

Bohemond I of Taranto 7, 15, 16, 17,
    19, 26–7, 28–31, 34–5, 36–7, 38–9,
    40, 41, 44, 45, 46, 57, 63, 71, 78, 87,
    142, 144, 146, 149, 156, 157–8, 162,
    176, 181

Bohemond III, prince of Antioch 170

Bonneval abbey 64, 160

Book of Holy War 163

Bosphorus 18, 19, 27

Bouillon Castle 80, 140

Boutoumites 21, 23–4

Bull, Marcus 176, 180

Caen 181

Caesarea 148

Cairo 51–2, 53, 54, 55, 56, 64, 66, 72,
    79, 88, 109, 147, 155, 162, 167,
    169, 183

Cambrai 3

Castle Imbert see Akhzib

Cecilia, daughter of Philip I of
    France 157

Cecilia, daughter of William the
    Conqueror 157

Charles III, 'the simple', king of Western
    Francia 17

Chartres 160, 161, 178

Chastel-Rouge 47, 142

Chronicon of William of Tyre 182

Church of the Holy Sepulchre see Holy
    Sepulchre

Church of the Lord's Nativity,
    Bethlehem 61

Church of the Virgin, Jerusalem 59,
    113, 121

Civitot 10, 12, 19, 20
    battle 21 October 1096 13–15, 26,
        133

Clarembald of Vendeuil 5, 15–16, 30, 39

Clermont 1
    council, 18–28 November 1095 1–2,
        180

Cluny, monastery 74

Cologne 4, 5, 50

Coloman I, king of Hungary 9–10, 15

The Complete History 184

Conan of Montague 33

Conrad III, king of Germany 164, 165–6

Constance, daughter of Philip I of
    France 157

Constantinople 7–9, 12, 14, 17, 18,
    158, 165

Continuation of the Chronicle of
    Damascus 183

Cyprus 70, 72, 145

Daimbert of Pisa, Patriarch of
    Jerusalem 155, 159

Damascus 35, 72, 83, 162, 163, 164–5,
    168, 169
    siege 1148 165–6

Daron 161

David's Tomb, Jerusalem 59
David's Tower, citadel of Jerusalem 58–9,
   77, 81, 98, 109, 121–2, 125, 128, 132,
   133, 144, 149, 156, 158–9, 175, 184
Digne 141
al-Dimashqī 91
Dome of the Rock 54, 55, 126–7, 128–9,
   133, 136, 146, 149, 183–4
Dorylaeum 27
   battle 1 July 1097 28–31, 43, 69, 75,
   85, 93, 95, 146
Drogo of Nesle 15–16, 30, 39, 40, 44, 60,
   93, 129
Duquq of Damascus 35, 43, 86
Durazzo 17, 18
Dyrrhachium 158

Edessa 33, 44, 57, 74, 75, 78, 155,
   162, 178
   capture by Zankī, 1144 163, 164, 166
Edgington, S. B. 178
Elvira, wife of Count Raymond of
   Toulouse 141
Emicho, count of Flonheim 5, 15
Emir of Tripoli see Jalāl al-Mulk
Emma of Hereford 277
Engelbert of Tournai 120–1
Eugenius III, pope 164
Eustace III, count of Boulogne 6, 45, 60,
   101–2, 121, 144, 148, 159
Everard III, lord of Le Puiset 37, 60,
   129–30

Fatimid dynasty 51–2, 53, 54, 55
Field of Blood 162
Firouz 38–40, 89
France, John 176, 177, 179
Frederick I, duke of Swabia 138
Fulcher of Chartres, chronicler 161–2,
   178
Fulcher of Chartres, knight 39, 44, 93
Fulk IV, count of Anjou 1

Galilee 197
Gaston IV, viscount of Béarn ix–xi, 39,
   44, 60, 80, 92–4, 104, 118, 126–7,
   129, 133, 140
Gaudry, bishop of Laon 85
Gaza 53
Geldmar Carpinel 74–6
Gembloux, monastery 182
Genappe 140
Genoa 45
Genzia documents 183
Gerard, founder of the Hospitallers 90
Gerard of Quierzy 85–6
Gerard of Ridefort 171
Gesta Dei Per Francos 181
Gesta Francorum 176–7, 180, 181
Gesta Tancredi 181
Gibb, H. A. R. 183
Gihon, spring 67–9, 72
Gil, Moshe 183
Gilbert of Traves 74, 76
Gilo, cardinal-bishop of
   Tusculum 180–1
Godfrey IV, duke of Lower Lotharingia,
   6–7, 15–16, 17, 19, 20, 22, 26, 30, 33,
   36, 37–8, 43, 44, 53, 60, 63, 64, 74,
   80, 93–4, 99, 104, 108, 110, 118, 119,
   121, 123, 127–8, 137–8, 139–41,
   142, 143–4, 145, 147, 148, 150,
   151–4, 155–6, 178, 183
Goitein, S. D. 183
Goliath Citadel, Jerusalem 81
Gottschalk, priest 5, 9–10
Gregory VII, pope 59, 138, 143
Grocock, C. W. 181
Guibert, abbot of Nogent 181
Guy of Brisebarre 165
Guy of Lusignan 170
Guy Trousseau of Montlhéry 40

Hadrumetum 17
Hagenmeyer, Heinrich 178

Hamdan b. 'Abd al-Rahim 183
Haram es-Sharif 55, 56, 71, 126–7, 128–9
Harem 36
Harran, battle 1104 162
Hartmann, count of Dillingen and
    Kyburg 21, 23, 140
Hasan Ibn Sabbăh 52, 162–3
Hastings, battle 1066 135
Helen of Burgundy 141
Henry I, king of England 156–7
Henry II, king of England 170
Henry IV, king of Germany 3, 138
Henry of Esch 21, 23, 26, 140
Heraclea 32
Heraclius, patriarch of Jerusalem 171
Hezekiah, king of Judea 68
Hezekiah's Pool, Jerusalem 71
Hill, J. H. 177
Hill, L. L. 177
Hill, Rosalind 176
Hillenbrand, Carole 184
Hims 168
*Historia de Hierosolymitano
    Itinere* 176–7
Historia Ecclesiastica 182
*Historia Francorum qui Ceperunt
    Iherusalem* 177–8
Historia Hierosolymitana of Baldric
    of Dol 179–80, 182
Historia Hierosolymitana of Fulcher
    of Chartres 178
Historia Iherosolimitana of Albert
    of Aachen 178–9
Historia Iherosolimitana of Robert the
    Monk 180
Historia Vie Hierosolimitane 180–1
*History of the Franks who Invaded the
    Islamic Lands* 183
Holy Sepulchre 57, 70, 112, 113, 128,
    130–1, 132, 136, 149, 154, 164, 171
Horns of Hamah, battle 1175 168
Horns of Hattin, battle 1187 171

Hosn al-Akrad 47
Hospitallers 164, 167, 171
Hugh 'the Great', count of Vermandois 6,
    15–16, 26, 30, 31, 39, 44, 60, 85,
    93, 129
Husechin, knight 141
Huygens, R. C. 181, 182

Ibn al-Athīr 53, 184
Ibn al-Jawzī 183, 184
Ibn Shaddād 169
Iconium 32
Iftikhar al-Dawla 56, 67, 70, 83, 87,
    88–9, 90, 91, 99, 100, 101, 102, 106,
    109, 111, 114, 115, 118, 119, 121–2,
    125, 126, 133–4, 136, 145, 148
Īlghāzī 55, 81, 162
Isoard I, count of Die 96, 97, 122
Ivo, bishop of Chartres 160
Ivo of Grandmesnil 40

Jabala 48
Jaffa 72, 74, 75, 76, 77–8, 84
Jalāl al-Mulk, ruler of Tripoli 48, 56, 101,
    109, 122, 142, 159
Janāh al-Dawla, atabeg of Homs 35
Jerusalem
    assault 13 June 1099 62–3, 79
    cisterns 70–1
    Jaffa Gate 58
    Nablus Gate 57
    Pool of Israel 70
    Sheep's Pool 71
    siege 63BC 56–7
    siege 70AD 82
    siege 636–7AD 54, 64
    siege 1098AD 55, 83, 88–9
    siege 1187AD 171–2
    Siloam Pool 68–9, 71, 81
    topography 56–7, 68, 72, 73, 81
John II Comnenus 16
Jokermish, governor of Mosul 162

Joppa 47, 166
Jordan, river 78, 145
Joscelin II of Courtenay, count of
    Edessa 163
Joscelin III of Courtenay 170
Josephus 83
Judas Maccabeus 59–60
Julius Caesar 130

Kerbogha, atabeg of Mosul 39, 40, 41,
    42, 43, 44, 54, 55, 60, 74, 75, 85, 123,
    140, 155
Kidron Valley, Jerusalem 62, 67, 68, 81,
    88, 98, 123
Knoch, Peter 178

Lambert the Poor 40
Laon 75
Latakia 36, 78, 158
Lethold of Tournai 120–1
Louis VI, king of France 64, 156, 159
Louis VI, king of France 164, 165
Lyon 1

Ma'arra (Ma'rrat-an-Nu'man) 45, 46, 47,
    70, 74, 80, 84, 90, 123, 139, 142
Mainz 5
Malik as-Salih 168
Malik Ghāzi Gumushtekin 14, 27, 157,
    158
Mamistra 33
Marius 130
Martin Luther 173
Mecca 54
Medina 54
Mei Nefto'ah, spring 72
Melisende, queen of Jerusalem 164, 165
Melitene 14, 157
Montfaucon, castle 140
Montmorency 64
Mosony 9
Mosul 162, 164, 165, 166, 168, 169, 184

Mount of Olives, Jerusalem 61, 62, 88,
    98–9, 104, 122, 128
Mount Pilgrim, castle 159
Mount Zion, Jerusalem 57, 59–60, 61,
    81, 85, 90, 91, 92, 93, 98, 105, 109,
    113, 115, 184
Mouzay 140
Mu'in al-Dīn Unur 166
al-Musta'li 52
al-Mustansir 51–2

Nablus 83, 86, 102, 144–5, 148
Neufmoutier 159
New Forest 156
Nicea 10–12, 18, 19, 27, 51, 53, 55, 57,
    81, 96
  siege of 18–24, 25, 80, 82, 92, 105,
    123, 140, 146
Nicetas, governor of Bulgaria 9
Nîmes 2
Nish 9, 10
Nizār 52
Notre-Dame Cathedral 86
Nur ad-Dīn 165, 166, 167, 168, 169

Odo of Bayeux 146
Orderic Vitalis 182
Otbert, bishop of Liége 140
Otto, bishop of Strasbourg 138–9, 146

Paris 7
Paschal II, pope 64, 159
Peter Bartholomew xi, 41–2, 44, 45, 48,
    60, 95, 96–7, 104, 137, 145, 146
Peter Desiderius 49, 60, 96–8
Peter of Narbonne, bishop of Albara 47,
    84, 122, 139, 144
Peter Raymond of Hautpoul 42
Peter the Hermit 3–5, 6, 8–9, 10, 12, 14,
    15, 19, 25, 26, 42–3, 50, 97–8, 133,
    149, 151, 159, 174
Peter Tudebode 176–7

Philip I, king of France 1, 6, 15, 157
Philippopolis 16
Pompey, Roman General 56, 70
Portsmouth 156
Prawer, Joshua 176
Puy-de-Dôme 1

al-Qalānisī 183
Qilij Arslān I, sultan of Rūm 10, 11–14,
    18, 19, 20, 23, 26, 27, 30–1, 32, 69,
    85, 158
Quantum Praedecessores 164

Raimbold Croton 60, 63–4, 79, 129, 160
Rainald III, count of Toul 39, 44
Rainald of Beauvais 202–3, 211
Ralph of Caen 181–2
Ramla 66, 70, 71, 75, 148–9
    battle 17 May 1102 162
Raoul, count of Vermandois 159
Raymond, vicomte of Turenne 74–5
Raymond III, count of Tripoli 168, 170–2
Raymond IV, count of Toulouse xi, 2, 6,
    8, 17, 18, 19–20, 21, 26, 30, 31–2,
    37, 42, 43, 45, 46, 47–8, 49, 56, 58,
    59–60, 61, 63, 69, 72, 74, 78, 80,
    84–5, 92, 93, 94, 96–7, 98, 101, 104,
    109–10, 111, 115, 118, 121–2, 127,
    132, 133, 139, 141–3, 144, 145, 149,
    150, 152, 153, 158–9, 175, 177
Raymond of Aguilers 177–8
Raymond Pilet 45, 74, 76, 77–8, 84, 122
Reims 75, 159, 161, 180
Reynald of Châtillon 170
Richard I, king of England 72
Richard of the Principate, count of
    Salerno 18, 33
Richards, D. S. 184
Richer, bishop of Verdun 140
Ridwan, emir of Aleppo 35–7, 43, 45,
    150, 158
Robert I, count of Flanders 6

Robert II, count of Flanders 6, 26, 30,
    34–5, 43, 45, 46, 60, 63, 85, 86, 93,
    102, 104, 111, 118, 121, 123, 127,
    139–40, 142, 144, 149, 152, 153, 156
Robert II, duke of Normandy 6, 22, 26,
    29, 36, 45, 48, 60, 63, 80, 85, 93, 102,
    104, 111, 118, 119, 123, 127, 136,
    139–40, 142, 144, 147, 149, 150, 152,
    153–4, 156–7, 178, 182
Robert Guiscard, duke of Apulia and
    Calabria x, 7, 62
Robert the Monk 180–1
Roger I, king of Sicily 7
Roger I, prince of Antioch 162
Roger Borsa 7
Rollo of Normandy 17
Rothard, steward 128
Rouergue 141
Ruthard, bishop of Mainz 5

Saif al-Dīn Ghazi 166, 171
St Andrew 42, 45, 49, 96
St Cyprian 104
St George 96, 104
St Gertrude at Nivelles, abbey 140
St Jean of Laon, convent 85
St John Chrysostom 104
St Leontius 104
St Martin of Pannonhalma, abbey 9
St Mary of Le Puy, church 177
St Mary of Trier, convent 26, 30
St Mary's Church, Antioch 41
St Peter's Church, Antioch 42, 46
St Symeon's Port 37
Saints 1
Saladin 154, 167–9, 170–2
Savanj 55
Seleucid Empire 59
Semois, river 80
Shaizar, emir of 142
Shams-ad-Daulah 35, 43
Shawar, vizier of Cairo 167

Shirkuh 167, 168
Siberry, J. E. 181
Siloam Pool *see* Jerusalem
Simeon II, patriarch of Jerusalem 70, 133, 145–6
Speyer 5, 164
Stabelo the Chamberlain 128
Stenay 140
Stephen II, count of Blois 6, 26, 36, 40, 44, 178
Stephen of Valence 41, 44
al-Sulami 163, 184
Sulla 130
Suqmān ibn Ortuq 55, 81, 162
Swan Knight 155
Sybil, queen of Jerusalem 170–1
Sybille, countess of Coucy 85

tafurs 34, 46
Tancred ix–xi, 7, 17–18, 20, 26–7, 29, 32–3, 40, 44, 48, 60, 61, 62, 75, 80, 84, 87, 88, 93–4, 98, 101–2, 104, 118, 119, 126–7, 128–9, 133, 134, 136–8, 142, 144, 148, 152, 153, 155, 157–9, 181–2
Tarsus 32, 75, 158, 178
Taticius 21, 23, 36, 40
Tekoah 73
Templars 163–4, 165, 171
Temple of Solomon *see* Dome of the Rock
Thierry, count of Flanders 165
Thomas of Marle 5, 30, 60, 74–7, 93, 129, 159–60
Thoros, lord of Edessa 33
Tiberias 170
Tinchebray, battle 1106 157
Titus Flavius Sabinus Vespasianus 82, 83
Tortosa 74, 159
Toucy 181
Tower of David *see* David's Tower
Treaty of Devol 158

Tripoli 49, 56, 96, 156, 159
True Cross, relic 64, 145, 149, 151
Tughtagīn 168
Tughtigin, atabeg of Damascus 35
Turtush 81
Tyre 54, 161

'Umar I, caliphe 54, 64
Urban II, pope 1–3, 8, 15, 59, 133, 141, 145, 174
Uwaq 81

Vardar, river 17
Verdun 140
Viviers 141

Walter Sanzavohir 4–5, 8–9, 12–14, 19
Warner, count of Grez 37
William, bishop of Orange 31, 139
William, brother of Tancred 29
William I, duke of Normandy, king of England, 'the Conqueror' 6, 80
William II, king of England 156
William VI of Montpellier 46, 61, 97
William Embracio 77–8, 84, 92
William Hugh of Monteil 49, 61, 97
William Sabran 74, 122
William of Grandmesnil 40
William of Tyre 160, 165, 166, 167–8, 172, 182
William Peyre of Cunhlat 41
William 'the Carpenter' of Melun 16, 40
Worms 5

Yaghī-Siyān, governor of Antioch 34, 35, 37, 38–9, 43
Yāqūtī 55

Zankī, atabeg of Mosul 163, 164, 166, 168, 169
Zemun 12